Labour Relatio

Labour Relations

Third Edition

Frank Burchill

First published 2008 by
PALGRAVE MACMILLAN

Palgrave Macmillan in the UK is an imprint of Macmillan Publishers Limited,
registered in England, company number 785998, of Houndmills, Basingstoke,
Hampshire RG21 6XS.

Palgrave Macmillan in the US is a division of St Martin's Press LLC,
175 Fifth Avenue, New York, NY 10010.

Palgrave Macmillan is the global academic imprint of the above companies
and has companies and representatives throughout the world.

Palgrave® and Macmillan® are registered trademarks in the United States,
the United Kingdom, Europe and other countries.

ISBN 978-1-4039-0384-6 paperback

This book is printed on paper suitable for recycling and made from fully
managed and sustained forest sources. Logging, pulping and manufacturing
processes are expected to conform to the environmental regulations of the
country of origin.

A catalogue record for this book is available from the British Library.

A catalog record for this book is available from the Library of Congress.

Printed in Great Britain by the MPG Books Group, Bodmin and King's Lynn

To Alice

Contents

List of Tables

List of Figures

List of Abbreviations

ACAS	Advisory, Conciliation and Arbitration Service
AEEU	Amalgamated Engineering and Electrical Union (merger of AEU and EETPU)
AEU	Amalgamated Engineering Union
AFL-CIO	Amalgamated Federation of Labor – Congress of Industrial Organisations
APEX	Association of Professional, Executive, Clerical and Computer Staff (now part of GMB)
Amicus	The union
ASE	Amalgamated Society of Engineers
ASTMS	Association of Scientific, Technical and Managerial Staffs (now MSF)
AUCCTU	All-Union Central Council of Trade Unions
BALPA	British Airline Pilots' Association
BAOT	British Association of Occupational Therapists
BIFU	Banking, Insurance and Finance Union
BMA	British Medical Association
CAC	Central Arbitration Committee
CATU	Ceramic and Allied Trades Union
CBI	Confederation of British Industry
CDNA	Community and District Nursing Association
CEEP	European Centre of Public Enterprises
CGT	Confédération Générale du Travail
CIPD	Chartered Institute of Personnel and Development
CISL	Confederazione Italiana Sindacati Lavoratori
COHSE	Confederation of Health Service Employees (see UNISON)
CPSA	Civil and Public Services Association
CSP	Chartered Society of Physiotherapy
CWU	Communication Workers Union (formed from UCW and NCU)
EAT	Employment Appeal Tribunal
ECOSOC	Economic and Social Committee
EEF	Engineering Employers' Association
EETPU	Electrical, Electronic, Telecommunications and Plumbing Union (see AEEU)

EIS	Educational Institute of Scotland
EMF	European Metalworkers' Federation
ETUC	European Trade Union Confederation
ETUF	European Trade Union Forum
EWCs	European Works Councils
FBU	Fire Brigades Union
FOA	Final Offer Arbitration
GATT	General Agreement on Tariffs and Trade
GCHQ	Government Communications Headquarters
GCTU	General Confederation of Trade Unions
GDR	German Democratic Republic
GMB	GMB Union (formerly GMBATU)
GMBATU	General, Municipal, Boilermakers and Allied Trades Union (see GMB)
GPMU	Graphical, Paper and Media Union (formed from NGA 82 and SOGAT 82)
HRM	Human Resource Management
HVA	Health Visitors Association
IBB	Interest-Based Bargaining
ICC	International Chamber of Commerce
ICF	International Chemical Workers' Federation
ICFTU	International Confederation of Free Trade Unions
ILO	International Labour Organisation
IOE	International Organisation of Employers
IPCS	Institution of Professional Civil Servants (now IPMS)
IPD	Institute of Personnel and Development
IPM	Institute of Personnel Management (now IPD)
IPMS	Institution of Professionals, Managers and Specialists
IRSF	Inland Revenue Staff Federation (see PTC)
ITS	International Trade Secretariats
ITUC	International Trade Union Confederation
JIT	just in time
MSF	Manufacturing, Science and Finance Union
NALGO	National and Local Government Officers' Association (see UNISON)
NCB	National Coal Board
NCU	National Communications Union (formerly POEU, see CWU)
NEDO	National Economic Development Office
NGA 82	National Graphical Association (see GPMU)
NHS	National Health Service
NHSE	National Health Service Executive

NICER	National Information and Consultation of Employees Regulations
NJC	National Joint Council
NUCPS	National Union of Civil and Public Servants (see PTC)
NUET	National Union of Elementary Teachers
NUJ	National Union of Journalists
NUM	National Union of Mineworkers
NUPE	National Union of Public Employees (see UNISON)
NUR	National Union of Railwaymen (now part of RMT)
NUT	National Union of Teachers
NVQ	National Vocational Qualification
OECD	Organisation for Economic Co-operation and Development
PFI	Private Finance Initiative
POEU	Post Office Engineering Union
PPP	Public Private Partnerships
PRB	Pay Review Bodies
PRP	Performance Related Pay
PTC	Public Services, Tax and Commerce (Union) (formed from IRSF and NUCPS)
RCM	Royal College of Midwives
RCN	Royal College of Nursing
RMT	National Union of Rail, Maritime and Transport Workers
RTUI	Red Trade Union International
SOGAT 82	Society of Graphical and Allied Trades (see GPMU)
SoR	Society of Radiographers
TGWU	Transport and General Workers' Union
TICER	Transnational Information and Consultation of Employees Regulations
TQM	Total Quality Management
TUC	Trades Union Congress
TURERA	Trade Union Reform and Employment Rights Act
TWU	Tobacco Workers' Union
UCW	Union of Communication Workers (see CWU)
UNICE	Union des Confedérations de l'Industrie et des Employeurs d'Europe
UNISON	The Public Service Union (formed from COHSE, NALGO and NUPE)
Unite	The union, derived from 2007 merger of Amicus and the TGWU
WCL	World Confederation of Labour
WFTU	World Federation of Trade Unions

Introduction to the Third Edition

The first edition of this text was written as part of a series designed very much for the general reader. This still remained the case with the second edition which differed from the first mainly to the extent that it included some references in the text and engaged with some of the literature in a more direct fashion, while including recommended reading. These additions reflected the fact that the first edition appears to have been more widely recommended in universities as an introductory text for undergraduates than was intended or anticipated. Nevertheless, these additions were highly selective, and this remains the case for this third edition. This has been intentional. This is because a general reaction has been that the original text was very readable, and it is hoped that the third edition remains so. Equally, a choice of, rather than exhaustive, referencing is designed to encourage the reader. The objective is to persuade the reader that labour relations is an interesting, important and relevant subject. As explained in the original text, the choice of the title '*Labour Relations*' was designed to emphasise the concept of labour as a 'factor of production' and the importance of economic forces in determining its behaviour.

This edition has been brought up to date and includes an additional chapter. The additional chapter reflects some of the author's experience of labour relations in recent years.

FRANK BURCHILL

1

Harmony and Conflict

Trade unions have existed in the United Kingdom longer than in any other country, and currently millions of people are members of these unions. The trade unions have been through a period of existence during which they were presented as a problem by a hostile government and media and have faced the ravages of large-scale unemployment. From this they have emerged weakened in terms of membership and influence but, in early 2007, are popular in opinion polls.

Throughout their existence trade unions have been subjected to a cycle of criticism and accommodation. The recent phase of the critique has presented them as organisers of disruptive and violent strikes; creators of inflation and balance-of-payments problems through their enforcement of excessive pay demands; as engaging in restrictive practices, thus preventing the introduction of new technology and inhibiting productivity as a consequence. It is not just the media and government who have been critical. Academics generally assert that unions have a '*significant negative* impact on profitability' (Booth, 1995: 215). Such comment fits very well with neoclassical models of the economy, which predict that individuals competing freely in the marketplace without hindrance of any kind of combination – be it of labour or of capital – will promote the maximum efficiency within a society and as a result will produce exactly those goods and services which people want. This kind of analysis challenges the contribution of the institutions central to our study of labour relations – trade unions, employers' associations and collective bargaining.

For the past two decades the free market model has provided a popular source of the type of criticism referred to. This model is not, and never has been, the only perception of society on which such criticism is based. A combination of antagonistic populist and academic views of collective labour relations is a recurrent phenomenon. It seems to become more clamorous and more acceptable on a cyclical basis, drowning out periodically the sound of different approaches to our subject matter. At the time of writing, the collapse of the so-called 'monetarist experiment' (usually linked to free market precepts) had subdued the tone of academics and, as suggested above, had created a more favourable view of unions amongst the population at large. The period referred to contrasts with other phases of history where governments have taken measures to accommodate trade unions and reinforce collective bargaining, and alternative academic views have been in the ascendancy. In Autumn 2004 the hourly rate of pay for trade unionists in the United Kingdom was 17 per cent higher than for non-trade unionists. Does this suggest that trade unions are good for the nation or bad for the nation?

Each approach generates its own rationalisations. That approach of the two decades referred to relied on a model with antecedents spanning 200 years and a declaration that the then Conservative Government was doing what everybody knew should have been done a long time ago but which no previous government had the courage to undertake. After a secondary boost to the certainties of industrial capitalism, following from the collapse of the so-called communist bloc states, we entered a new period of uncertainty and awaited a revival of some other set of rationalisations. In developed Western economies, and in the United Kingdom especially, the future did not look quite as good as it used to. However, in terms of levels of employment in the United Kingdom the present looks more secure than was anticipated in the mid-1990s.

What is being suggested above is that in the field of labour relations, as elsewhere, the facts do not always speak for themselves. There are different approaches to these facts. Texts on the subject usually contain some analysis of how different perspectives affect what is going on in this area of study. What follows summarises some of the different sets of conclusions which might arise from the facts when alternative perspectives are brought to bear upon them. This approach is then used throughout the text. Hopefully it will help us to a better understanding of management, trade union and government attitudes and behaviour. Equally important, it might persuade us to examine our own reactions to various phenomena in the field of labour relations.

Perspectives

The perspectives discussed below represent views of the world. They are not simply brought to bear on aspects of labour relations where they are held. Any attempt at classification is bound to oversimplify the views expressed and distort points of overlap and difference between them.

These descriptions of perspectives are best seen as caricatures of extreme positions.

A Unitary Perspective: 'Where there is discord, let there be harmony'

This view of the world places emphasis on common objectives and the possibility of harmony. Where conflict arises, it is variously seen as the result of the activities of deviants and troublemakers or as arising from ignorance. In this model the productive enterprise has objectives which are in the interests of all associated with it. Managerial style often emphasises team spirit, working together and notions of leadership rather than of power. Sanctions are needed to deal with troublemakers and deviants and there is an emphasis on discipline at the place of work, and there are stronger laws to deal with such people. Ignorance is overcome by training and 'good' communications.

From a unitary perspective, strikes are always pathological – in either the criminal or the medical sense of the word. They are destructive of the organisation's objectives and, consequently, do not even serve the interests of those who participate in them. Instigators and participants need to be punished by dismissals and fines, for example, or to be cured by education and training. With 'proper' management, all problems can be eliminated. Where trade unions exist, they may be seen as deliberately obstructive where they are oppositional and therefore to be curbed and controlled; they may be seen as anachronistic and pointless and, if left alone, likely to disappear.

An alternative view within this perspective is to see trade unions as an extension of the management bureaucracy, acting as channels of communication with workers and as instruments of unity and control, able to explain and pass on the company message. Recent commentary (see in particular House of Commons 1993–4) has identified a lesser oppositional role for trade unions in a 'modern economy'. In exchange for recognition they would give up the 'strike weapon', provide skills training for members, make service agreements with individuals, abandon political objectives and associations, and offer members traditional, friendly society benefits such as cheap loans, stock exchange advice and so on. If we were to add funeral society benefits, unemployment pay and sickness benefits, they would be perfectly in keeping with Victorian and Thatcherite notions of self-help, and compatible with free market economics and 'rolling back' the state. In this view, collective bargaining (see Chapter 6) is not part of the role of trade unions because it distorts the market and crystallises the notion of opposition and conflict; such things have no place in the unitary view of the world.

It is possible to argue, of course, that those who give vent to it do not necessarily believe the rhetoric of unitarism. Such rhetoric may simply be a device used to manipulate and control the workforce. Where this is the case, the expression of unitarist sentiment would be best regarded as a management tool or technique rather than as a perspective. Where the perspective is genuinely held, it must give some reassurance to more authoritarian managers that their actions have legitimacy.

Pluralism: 'Beer and sandwiches at Number Ten'

This view acknowledges divergent interests within society and the organisation, and accepts that there will inevitably be some conflict. The productive enterprise is a coalition, and not all parties are committed to all of its formal objectives. Conflict is built into organisations and society, because individuals, and groups, have interests which clash. In the employment relationship, employees and managers often have objectives which differ; hours of work impinge on social life; change can necessitate redundancy; higher pay may compete with investment demands and so on. Given these divisions, it is not surprising that organisations emerge to represent the interested parties.

Within this perspective employers might see trade unions as a nuisance, but they do have legitimacy. Some would go further and argue that, given the inevitability of conflict, trade unions are necessary as channels of discontent. Conflict may also play a positive role in promoting change and efficiency. However, it should not be allowed to become destructive. Not surprisingly, collective bargaining is the pluralist concept *par excellence*. It acknowledges conflict but suggests compromise.

These are not abstract economic concepts. The case for a pluralist view of the world was put to and by the Donovan Commission (1968) when it investigated and reported on industrial relations in the 1960s. This was one of the periods referred to earlier when trade unions seem to have been seen in a more positive light. It produced an emphasis on collective bargaining reforms rather than penal use of the law as a way of 'improving' industrial relations. It may be argued, of course, that with a Labour Government in office it was inevitable that a rationalisation compatible with that government's relations with trade unions would be given prominence. Since then we have seen a period with an emphasis on a more unitary approach, with both collective bargaining and trade unions under attack.

One effect of the Donovan Report was that pluralism emerged as an apparently enlightened philosophy. It had an appeal. The recognition of conflict seemed almost 'hard headed'. Academics could absorb it and feel closely in touch with the real world. Managers could understand it and feel sophisticated. The world was more complicated than the unitarist vision suggested, but not too complicated to understand. Personnel management got a boost, being seen as a source of insight into, and understanding of, labour relations. Trade union leaders became recognised as people who could contribute to government.

The interesting aspect of both sets of rationalisation is that they do not challenge the *status quo*. Capitalism is essentially a benevolent phenomenon that only requires proper management. In fact, both are managerial ideologies designed to reassure management. Unitarism excuses authoritarianism when unions are weak; pluralism excuses compromise when management is weak. Shifts in the balance of power might explain the shifts in the types of rationalisation used to explain the so-called facts.

Conflict: 'The workers united will never be defeated'

The conflict perspective, as described here, is rooted in Marxist analyses. As with the above perspectives, there are variants. A crucial component of such analyses is the notion that society is essentially divided into two classes – those who own the means of production and those who do not. Those who own are concerned with maximising their profits by whatever means are available and regard labour as simply one factor of production to be exploited in a similar fashion to any other factor in pursuit of this objective. The owners of capital deal with labour only to the extent that they need it. Manipulation of labour might require concession and compromise, but these represent temporary devices used in the pursuit of absolute control. Labour relations are essentially about refining the techniques of control and devising methods of dealing with opposition. In this model, managers are part of the labour force to which owners devolve some authority, but only as an expedient. They are equally disposable when the circumstances allow for it.

Competition among owners also creates problems for them. Economic growth and full employment shift the balance of power towards labour and lead to demands on the redistribution of income from capital to labour. Attempts to control this may lead to recession and create strains on the system of government. Within the model there are trade cycles. These are explained in a variety of ways, but they are a common feature of the conflict model and always have been. It is thought that unitarist and pluralist models had found technical solutions to the long-term trade cycle. In the light of the past 20 years, this position has been adjusted, and there has been some reversal, in these models, to explanation of depression and recession as essentially benign phenomena which help to prune and revitalise industrial capitalism – to which there is now no alternative (see Chapter 2).

From a conflict point of view an emphasis on pluralist approaches can be seen to reflect the need to incorporate labour, often through its leaders, as a way of mitigating the power of labour in a boom period. Unitarism and authoritarianism reflect approaches used when labour is weak – thus the debate on whether labour laws would be effective if employment grew and the demand for labour followed. The role of government is to support the interests of the owning, or ruling, class with appropriate policies and rationalisations according to circumstances.

The enterprise also lacks legitimacy in this view of the world. As suggested above, its role is to exploit labour. This relationship is an inevitable and fundamental source of conflict. Conflict permeates the whole system and is a feature of it, not an irrational symptom, and the only questions revolve around how exactly it will manifest itself in different circumstances, and why it takes particular forms. An understanding of labour relations cannot be achieved if it is divorced from the economy as a whole. Labour relations simply constitute an examination of the manifestation of the power struggle in somewhat artificially selected institutions which operate within a much broader system. The subject cannot properly be separated out from the total system.

Trade unions emerge as a form of protection against uninhibited exploitation. Workers join together to secure a stronger defence against the employer. However, trade unions and their leaders are often incorporated into the management of capitalism and also develop sectional and local workplace interests, perhaps ending up competing with each other. Effective opposition to capitalism requires workers to organise on a wider base than sectional trade union interest.

Conclusion and Further Reading

The above (summarised in Table 1.1) represents a somewhat abbreviated presentation of what are variously called perspectives, views, ideologies, even theories of labour relations. There is no need to get involved in the methodological implications of the choices of terminology in a text of this type. Interestingly enough they began to be incorporated as an element in introductory texts on labour relations after the Donovan Report. They had already been incorporated in social theory for a long time before this, but not quite so explicitly. It is feasible, for example, to classify Adam Smith as a unitarist, John Maynard Keynes as a pluralist and Karl Marx as a conflict theorist. Biskind (2001) uses this approach to analyse American films of the 1950s but uses the terms 'conservative', 'liberal' and 'radical' to label the perspectives.

The key point about the inclusion of the above perspectives here is that it should encourage the reader to recognise, as mentioned earlier, that the facts do not always speak for themselves. Throughout the text the perspectives will be used to suggest different interpretations of elements of our subject matter.

Recent texts have tended to include sections on 'management styles'. These generally focus on versions of unitarism and pluralism and classifications adapted from these concepts. Kessler and Bayliss (1995: 102–7) provide a useful summary of the literature associated with this approach. See also Williams and Adam Smith (2006). The interested reader will find this a useful way into the discussion and a source of appropriate references. For a comprehensive presentation of the conflict approach see Braverman (1974).

TABLE 1.1   *Summary of perspectives of labour relations*

UNITARY FRAME OF REFERENCE

ASSUMED SOURCES OF CONFLICT	PROPOSED SOLUTIONS
AGITATORS	
– troublemakers	– dismissals
– alien ideas	– laws to control trade unions
– Marxists	
MISUNDERSTANDINGS	
– bad communications	– training for managers and employees – faulty structures – joint consultation
– limited intelligence of employees	– quality circles
	– team briefing
PERSONALITY CLASH	
– 'wrong people in the wrong jobs'	– recruitment policy
	– promotion policy
	– psychological testing

'WORK TOGETHER AS A TEAM'

PLURALIST FRAME OF REFERENCE

ASSUMED SOURCES OF CONFLICT	PROPOSED SOLUTIONS
TECHNOLOGICAL CHANGE	
– lack of consultation	– joint consultation
– deskilling	– job enrichment enlargement
– redundancy	– redeployment

TABLE 1.1   *Continued*

COLLECTIVE BARGAINING ARRANGEMENTS
– too centralised	– collective bargaining
– overlong procedures	reform
– partnership	

WORKERS' LOCATION
– social hierarchy	– diversification of
	industry
– type of industry	– share ownership
– geographical	– single status
isolation	

THE WIDER ECONOMY
– business cycles	– incomes policy
– inflation	– money supply
– unemployment	– fiscal policy

CONFLICT ALTERNATIVE

ASSUMED SOURCES OF	PROPOSED SOLUTIONS
CONFLICT	
– production for profit,	– nationalisation
not for need	– planning
– exploitation of the worker	– minimum wage
– boom–slump cycle	– progessive tax
– unequal distribution	
of wealth	

POLITICAL/LEGAL
– parliament unrepresentative	– more democracy
– 'one law for the rich'	– workers' state
– police not neutral	– workers' rights
– 'the right to manage'	– free trade unions

SOCIAL/CULTURAL
– elitist education system	– democratic control
– politically biased media	of society
– sexism and racism	

SOCIALISM/COMMUNISM

2

The Market for Labour

Chapter 1 indicated that the study of labour relations requires a context. Where labour is bought and sold it follows that this fact, and the circumstances under which such transactions take place, will affect the substance of labour relations. For the purpose of this text, labour relations are seen as a study of rules at the place of work, and how such rules come into being. The process of making such rules is influenced more or less closely by institutions such as trade unions, employers' associations and the government. It is also influenced by managers and workers. The text takes for granted that labour relations are intricately bound up, one way or another, with most aspects of life – given the significance of work. However, in examining the processes and institutions influencing such rule-making, there are advantages in being selective and studying in depth the workplace and closely associated institutions.

Regardless of the above comments, we must examine some of the general theories which attempt to explain the workings of industrial capitalism, the system which provides the environment for the labour relations we are interested in. Furthermore, if we are to account for changes in behaviour at the place of work it is instructive to examine how that system of industrial capitalism has been performing in recent years, particularly in respect of the labour market. For the purpose of this text industrial capitalism is a system which requires vast quantities of capital – that is, machinery and equipment – in order to function, and in which these means of production, along with land, are concentrated in private ownership. The products of this system are sold for profit. Capitalism is not simply a social arrangement describing a means of ownership and distribution. It incorporates the need for vast quantities of physical capital; capitalism is an offspring of technology.

The Neoclassical Model

In the neoclassical model, competition is paramount. Combinations, whether of labour or of capital, are detrimental. Here we concentrate on the market for labour. The capacity of labour to combine – in trade unions, for example – is very dependent upon the demand for and supply of labour.

The Demand for Labour

According to the neoclassical model, the demand for labour is determined by its product. It is not demanded for itself but for the value of what it produces. The demand for labour is thus said to be a derived demand. An employer will demand labour up to the point where the price (wage) that has to be paid for additional labour will equal the value of the additional output produced. Up to that point, units of labour employed will generate a surplus of value above their cost. If the demand for labour increases, as a result, for example, of increased demand for its product, and therefore increased prices for the product, then wages will rise. The higher wage will have to be paid to attract labour from alternative employment or to attract those who have chosen not to work because they valued their leisure more than they valued the previously lower wages.

The model acknowledges that some types of labour will be more productive than other types, possibly because the former are better trained or better educated. (See the section below on pay differentials.) There will, therefore, be different levels of demand for different types of labour, depending upon the relative productivity of each type. This concept of relative productivity can be extended to the other factors of production. If new technology improves the productivity of capital while that of labour remains the same, capital may be used to replace labour. Capital and labour are seen to be in competition with each other.

Not surprisingly new developments in technology, the microchip being a good example, are often seen as permanently reducing the demand for labour. There is no absolute reason why this should be the case. One effect of new technology is to widen the range of goods and services available. If demand for such goods arises, this could affect the level of employment.

The Supply of Labour

Individuals who make themselves available for work provide labour. Demographic factors, such as population size, age and sex distribution affect this process. So also do pay, terms and conditions of employment, people's attitudes to work and status, attitudes to leisure and so on. Economists talk about net advantages from work – such being determined by the types of things just listed. Individuals are believed to weigh up the advantages of being in work, as opposed to the disadvantages, and to act accordingly. Consequently, if pay is increased, other things being equal, then the net advantages of being in work increase and more people are willing to make themselves available for work.

If the demand for products grows, other things being equal, employers will demand more of the factors of production. To the extent that capital cannot be substituted or is relatively more expensive, employers will want more labour and will offer to pay more for it. Thus, more labour will make itself available and more labour will be employed. If the demand for a particular product grows – for example, computer games – there will be an increase in the demand for those who are capable of programming such games, the pay offered to them will rise and such people will be attracted both from preferring leisure at lower wages and from other occupations. As such when people leave other occupations the pay in those occupations they have left will also rise. As pay levels between occupations are equalised, mobility ceases, having ensured a shift of labour towards the production of computer games. Wages are thus determined by the demand for, and supply of, labour.

In this model anyone who wishes to work can approach an employer who uses the type of labour the person can supply and secure work at the current rate or at a rate slightly lower. If the employer has all the workers required at the current rate then an offer to work at a slightly lower rate enables the employer to reduce pay for everybody to that rate and use the savings to employ additional labour. (This result is achieved by the process of offering dismissal to the nearest employee, pointing out that the new one is prepared to work at a lower rate. This employee will probably accept the slight reduction rather than volunteer to leave. If all employees behave in the same way, savings can be made, and labour will become cheaper relative to capital.) It follows that the lower the rate labour is willing to accept, the greater the quantity of labour employed. There will be a rate which would result in everybody being in work. If the rate is higher than this it is because some people prefer leisure to work. They have volunteered to be unemployed.

If the model works as described, then nobody who wishes to work needs to be unemployed. Where people are offering to work but it would be detrimental to profits to employ people at the existing rate of pay, this rate will fall, allowing greater employment and protection of profits. If employers want more labour than they currently employ, then it can be attracted by pay increases. Where labour is scarce and the pay needed to attract it would be too high for firms to remain profitable, employers substitute capital or try to develop cheaper (more productive) forms of it.

In all of this, consumers are the driving force. Moved by the inner cravings for more or different products, they adjust their demands accordingly. Producers respond to these cravings (so far as they are backed by purchasing power) and the rewards to capital and labour are adjusted to match the new or additional demands (see the computer games example above). If producers come up against the limits of resources, then pressure grows to invent or develop new and cheaper technology which allows for increased production. It is a wonderful world in which the yearnings of people (called 'consumers') are responded to by producers to provide them with exactly the goods and services they desire; all those people who make themselves available for work get it; resources are fully utilised.

People who write about this world know it does not exist, but appear confident that it could if certain things were done – or, for that matter, not done. Before looking at such things, it is worth examining at least one other feature of this world, which is being denied us.

Pay Differentials

In the model the net advantages of jobs are equal – this allows for differences in pay between jobs. There may be advantages other than pay in some jobs which other jobs do not have. People might prefer lower pay in the comfort of an office than higher pay down a coalmine. Nurses work out of a sense of a vocation and accept low pay because of the high level of job satisfaction. Observation would seem to suggest that many high-paid jobs not only have better fringe benefits than low-paid jobs, but are often more comfortable, interesting and exciting. How can this be explained?

According to human capital theory, people have the choice of investing in themselves by securing appropriate education, training and work experience. People impose costs on themselves to secure advantages in the future. They will identify the kinds of education, training and experience which will bring greater returns in terms of job advantages and invest accordingly. Not all people are willing to do this. Many go for short-term returns and thus there is a relatively low supply of people with the qualities this investment bestows, and therefore such people, who invest in themselves, can secure higher net advantages, including pay, once they are in work because of the relatively low rate of competition for the relevant jobs. Such theory has been used to explain the generally higher rates of pay received by men compared with women – because women have been seen to expect to spend a lower proportion of their lives in work, they invest less in themselves.

If people have full knowledge of the choices they make and the consequences of such choices, then net advantages over time are equal. Short-term decisions and gains equal the cost of investment plus the gains from it. One difficulty with this approach is that people born with innate abilities or characteristics in short supply might secure higher net advantages simply for possessing these rather than for any costs incurred. The best the model can do to rationalise high rewards in these circumstances is to argue that everybody benefits if these abilities or characteristics are brought into use. This is a variation of trickle down theory. If entrepreneurial ability is highly rewarded, then jobs and opportunities will be created for others.

Critics of the model suggest that neither net advantage nor human capital theory explain the pay differentials which actually exist. Many seem to persist over time regardless of market conditions. Actual changes in supply and demand factors do not appear to create the redistribution that the model would predict. Similar jobs in different industries attract widely different rates of pay, and these differences are not explained by the location of jobs. Education and training are often used to ration jobs rather than to attract appropriately qualified labour.

A difficulty with criticism of the model is that much of what is predicted by it depends upon circumstances which have never existed. Exponents of it believe that the circumstances could be created. If the model was meant to describe the world as it is, rather than as it could be, then its unreality is obvious. The key question is whether or not attempts to create the required circumstances make any sense. If we were to accept the proposition that unemployment was voluntary, how do free market economists explain the fact that more people seem to have volunteered to be unemployed in recent years and why do people seem to volunteer in such numbers on a cyclical basis?

Supply-side Economics

As one might predict, the answer is a simple one. People and governments have built imperfections into the system to secure short-term gains: people for short-term monetary gains and governments for short-term electoral advantage. The term 'supply-side economics' is used by neoclassical economists to describe the process of removing imperfections from the supply side of the economy – to achieve the circumstances required to enable the market to work efficiently. In the labour market, this would mean making the supply of labour more flexible.

For example, trade unions, by use of such things as the closed shop and strike action, can force employers to pay higher wages than they would in a free market. An effect of this is that the employer is equally forced to employ less labour. Trade unions also prevent the use of additional capital to adjust the wage rate by opposing the introduction of new technology. Thus, unemployment occurs and output is less than it could be, with higher prices, and ultimately to everybody's detriment.

Collective bargaining equalises wages across groups and industries regardless of skills, qualifications and the state of the labour market. Like the closed shop, it inhibits the mobility of labour and the efficient adjustment of wage rates. Employers are prevented from using labour flexibly because unions impose demarcation lines to secure short-term membership gains and employment gains at the expense of the long term. Individuals are prevented from using their skills and abilities because employers are not allowed to develop individual payment packages which reward merit and performance.

If all of the above create imperfections which lead to pay exceeding productivity and generating both unemployment and inflation then all of the above should be removed – hence the emphasis on employment laws which restrict trade union organisation and activity. There is also an emphasis on the decentralisation of pay determination to the place of work, or even to the individual, to allow local labour market conditions to exert their influence. If there is a surplus of labour in the northeast and a shortage in the south-west, why should nurses, railwaymen, teachers and so on have centrally negotiated rates of pay when in an efficient labour market such rates should vary from area to area to allow the forces of supply and demand to operate?

It is not only trade unions and collective bargaining which undermine the proper utilisation of the labour force. Unemployment benefits have been so lavishly developed in the past that many people would find the net advantage of going to work to be negative; they find it more profitable to stay at home or sleep on the street. Like trade unions, unemployment benefit forces employers to pay artificially higher rates of pay to retain and recruit labour, thus making British industry less competitive and reducing output. What is more, unemployment benefits are financed by taxation on those at work, who work less hard, and on investors who therefore invest less. Consequently there is a need to remove unemployment benefits and reduce taxation.

Investment in human capital is also distorted by the above factors. There are other problems with regard to the proper accumulation and deployment of human capital. Because education and training are subsidised, and because finance to relevant institutions has been centrally provided, people's choices of investment in this capital have not been properly based. If they bore the full cost, they would have to train in those areas which promised the best returns to enable these costs to be repaid – hence the idea of student loans. Similarly, colleges required to secure their finance from a student market rather than from the government would have to provide relevant education and training. Also, employers would play a greater part in their financing by paying the full cost of such where they felt their employees needed it.

Within the market model there is nothing which is better provided than through market forces – hence the emphasis in recent years on deregulation. Individual rights at work are best determined through individually negotiated contracts of employment rather than through such things as unfair dismissal or equal pay laws. Employers and employees can best deal with the terms of hiring and firing – hence the weakening of minimum standards legislation and opposition to a minimum wage. Even health and safety can be dealt with by reference to the market; killing employees or customers is bad business. It follows that it is in the employer's interest to ensure proper standards.

Implicit in the above is the belief that total labour costs matter on the demand side and not just pay. Health and safety provision affect labour costs, and so do such things as recruitment policy, training provision, labour search programmes and so on. To the extent that these affect the employee they also influence the supply side. In the model it is essentially up to the individual parties – the employer and the worker – to agree on a package, and if health and safety are traded against pay or vice versa, then so be it. The only additional requirement of this model is that all parties have full knowledge of the information required to enable rational decisions to be made.

In terms of the concepts presented in Chapter 1, the belief in the market model is clearly unitarist in character. If left to work it would do so in everybody's interest. Belief in this model has had a considerable impact on our subject in recent years, as references to the law and deregulation have implied. Attempts to reform the economy in accordance with this model have thus affected substantially the present state of labour relations in the United Kingdom. Understanding the model gives additional insight into this. It also explains long-standing antagonism towards trade unions by most economists. There are critics of the model.

Segmented Labour Markets

The concept of 'non-competing groups' is an old one in economics. Early economists warned about treating the labour market as competitive (Cairnes, 1874). Modern economists talk about segmented labour markets with recent emphasis on a 'dual market'. In this model there is a competitive labour market, known as the secondary labour market, and there is a sector where mobility is systematically limited, known as the primary market. These are not two distinct labour markets but represent extremes between which industries, firms and jobs can be classified. For example, secondary jobs are low paid, have poor conditions of employment and little or no security. Primary jobs are better paid, have greater job security and better conditions of employment. Primary industries and firms would consist of those where primary jobs predominate and similarly for secondary industries and firms. Both these general type of markets might be segmented within them on a geographical or industrial basis.

Jobs in the primary market are protected from competition for a variety of reasons. Training and retraining is expensive and is often specific to firms. Firms may be creating a labour force which is immune to competition from outside and which is expensive to shed and recruit in response to market fluctuations. Many firms have internal promotion procedures to retain loyalty, incremental pay schemes based on tenure and length of service, and so on. Given that circumstances might arise which allow both employers and workers to exploit variations in the labour market, they come to long-term 'fair' agreements about the employment relationship, and current wages may simply reflect an averaging-out over time of this relationship rather than immediate market conditions.

Trade unions can play a constructive part in administering such arrangements, and also by providing a mechanism for an orderly adjustment to longer-term market forces. They can also help administer pay for jobs. Neoclassical theory places the emphasis on the good worker attracting good pay rather than the good job attracting good pay regardless of who performs it. Many jobs are so determined by the technological input they require that the abilities of the actual job-holder are not of great significance. Given the immobilities associated with all of this, employers adjust the quantity of labour rather than the wage to deal with market fluctuations. This suggests discontinuities in adjustment, and neoclassicism abhors discontinuities.

Quantity adjustments can be secured by incorporating the secondary labour market. Employers may subcontract part of their work. Subcontracted labour and part-time labour constitute a large part of the secondary labour market, and such employment relationships can be expanded or reduced to meet product demand variations. Similarly, the primary labour force might be recruited to below known optimum levels and used to work overtime. Labour in the secondary labour market is often non-unionised, low paid, and without holiday or pension entitlements. Economists talk about a core and peripheral labour force, with enterprises in the current high unemployment situation trying to maximise the peripheral labour force which does not have access to the core jobs. This strategy is often referred to as achieving numerical flexibility. At the same time the core labour force is expected to become more flexible within the internal requirements of the enterprise – that is, to drop traditional demarcation lines, accept training in additional skills, and to perform any tasks within its abilities as and when demanded. This has become known as functional flexibility.

As we add such considerations, the perceptive reader will no doubt be wondering how different this model is from the neoclassical model, which recognises that imperfections might exist, but seeks ways of removing them. This is a good question. Long-term 'fair' arrangements suggest a net advantages approach. Discontinuities between the core and peripheral labour force can be explained by barriers to entry and by continued degrading of the peripheral labour force that has been denied access to training and development. Distinguishing between the two approaches is a little like trying to find the dividing line between unitarism and pluralism. The emphasis on discontinuities in the segmented-labour-market approach can lead to different policy stances from the purer neoclassicists, in the same way that similar differences might be found between unitarist and pluralist orientations.

'In the long run we are all dead'

The above quotation is attributed to Keynes. Implicit within it is the clearest criticism of the neoclassical model. In the model all adjustments take place automatically, but within the vaguest time specifications – sometimes the short run, sometimes the medium term, but most especially in the long run. These time periods are specified according to technically determined parameters but are never quantified in terms of days, months or years. The cost of removing imperfections is never estimated, and it is always stated that future benefits will outweigh these. History has never taken place.

It is rational for workers to organise and seek immediate and tangible benefits. The long run might never come, and there is no guarantee if it did that the benefits of restraint might accrue to them, unquantifiable as they are. Without organisation by workers it is possible for employers to suppress wages to the benefit of dividends and other claims on their income. Where employers have monopoly positions, and many do, it is possible for workers to force up both employment and wages. Whatever the causes, there have been periods when unemployment has been substantially high without wages acting as a self-correcting mechanism. Government expenditure can be used to generate demand which creates jobs.

There is also no clear evidence to support the relationship between effort, competitiveness and taxation that the neoclassical model asserts. Employers left to themselves also seek short-term gains. They take risks with health and safety, for example. Does it help the victims of the Bhopal disaster to know that owners have learned a lesson about markets and costs that no doubt will soon be forgotten? Why should a company train staff when it could use a fraction of the money needed to buy staff trained by somebody else? Education and training are both vital to an economy, but are both areas where short-term considerations based on immediate costs are likely to lead to detrimental decisions.

Neoclassical economists see full employment as inevitable. Keynesians see it as possible. Each views the other approach as leading to unemployment. The Keynesian model acknowledges the existence of conflict within the system. Post-Keynesians see the need to deal with the inflationary consequences of the conflict between capital and labour by the use of incomes policies. This approach needs the recognition and participation of trade unions and an interventionist role for the state. Segmentation theorists identify similar needs. Poverty and lack of training arising from the secondary labour markets, and the inevitability of at least frictional unemployment, need to be offset by state welfare expenditure, redundancy payments and spending on training and education. Health and safety need regulation. Sex and race discrimination, explained in the neoclassical model by the prejudices of employers or the protectionism of employees, need positive legislation.

A way perhaps of distinguishing these more pluralist approaches from neoclassicism is in terms of an emphasis on the importance of institutions rather than on the timeless self-regulating processes of competition. If unregulated labour markets do not adjust to unemployment because of the weak wage relationship, then regulation may not incur the costs predicted in the neoclassical model. Emphases on free market approaches, and alternatives, seem to have little to do with accumulations of empirical evidence. The more authoritarian, unitarist, free market approach, as suggested in Chapter 1, seems to achieve dominance in downswings of the trade cycle. In the 1950s heyday of Keynesianism, large-scale unemployment was declared dead, along with its concomitant, the longer-term trade cycle. Samuelson (1958: 588) tells us that today one can give a confident reply along the following lines: 'By proper use of monetary and fiscal policies, nations can successfully fight off the plague of mass unemployment and the plague of inflation' (my emphasis).

Conflict

In terms of our perspectives it is possible to argue that we have simply identified essentially unitarist and pluralist views of the labour market. Both approaches represent either wishful thinking or ideological devices rather than science. Both are seeking ways of managing and preserving capitalism rather than challenging it. Neither is willing to acknowledge the fundamental and irreversible nature of conflict within capitalism and the inevitability of recurring crises.

In the conflict model the demand for products is not autonomous; it does not emanate from within the consumer. Owners manipulate tastes, create dependencies and thus generate a supply of labour which can be controlled by the imperatives of the marketplace. Wages and prices are not devices which determine production, the allocation of goods and services and relative employment levels. They are control mechanisms used by the owners of capital. Trade unions may be able to create a consciousness of class but their tendency is towards representing sectional interests, creating and reinforcing divisions and becoming incorporated by the owning class. Strikes can teach participants something about the nature of capitalism, but ultimately relationships with employers cannot be divorced from the need to organise politically and challenge the wider system.

The above is a very brief summary of what passes for labour market theory. There are many omissions. What can be said with some confidence is that however complete the exposition could be the word 'theory' is far too strong to describe what has been produced in this area. What we have is a series of hypotheses which are not generally amenable to any serious testing. No amount of manipulation of data within computers can produce evidence to test the effects in general, for example, of trade unions on wages or employment, or anything else for that matter. The literature is replete with case study findings which are contradictory and generalisations which refute each other. This reflects two major, but connected, problems. The number of variables at play at any particular time is so enormous that it is impossible to isolate the impact of any one of them. Researchers bring to their studies a variety of perspectives.

The predictions which are available often seem to derive from common sense rather than from elaborate reasoning or theory. If the demand for coal falls then the average citizen would probably be able to predict a fall in the demand for coal miners. Pressed further, such a citizen would no doubt suggest that this would affect the bargaining power of coal miners, the number of mining union members and so on. This is not to say that such forces act in precisely predictable ways. Organisations react to and mould events. Some powerful organisations do not assert the power they have all the time. Weak organisations often find ways of surviving. Nevertheless, industries and institutions come and go, and there does appear to be a long-term trade cycle, however imperfectly it is understood. Each phase of the cycle reacts to and produces changes in the nature of capital and its institutional forms, and in the labour force and its forms of organisation. Exactly how the process is viewed depends upon the perspective brought to it. A prediction that can safely be made is that the empirical evidence will remain insufficient to produce agreement on the broader issues.

The UK Labour Market

Industrial Change

Whatever one's view of the world, and how it came to be what it is, there is no doubt that observable and identifiable changes have taken place in the past 30 years in the UK industrial structure and the general economic environment. Hobsbawm (1994) refers to the end of a golden era in the advanced capitalist economies, beginning in the early 1970s, followed by crisis decades. Here we can only identify some of the changes in the United Kingdom in this period of crisis. Most of these changes have been detrimental to trade union membership growth or retention. Nevertheless, since the previous edition of this book was published in 1997 there have been significant changes in the direction of the economy and these have affected the UK labour market.

The Level of Employment

At the time that Hobsbawm's book, referred to above, was published, unemployment in the United Kingdom was registered as 9.3 per cent. Having remained at below 2 per cent between 1941 and 1961, it crept up to 3.2 per cent in 1975, continued increasing until it reached a peak of 11.6 per cent in 1986, then declined to 5.8 per cent in 1990 and then rose again to a peak of 10.4 per cent in 1993. At the time of writing the previous edition of this book – 1996 – unemployment was registered as 7.8 per cent. In April 2005, the rate was registered as 4.7 per cent. Figure 2.1 shows the trend over the previous ten years.

FIGURE 2.1 *Unemployment rate; United Kingdom; November–January 1995 to November–January 2005*

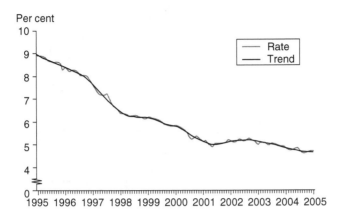

Source: *Labour Force Survey.*

FIGURE 2.2 *Working age employment rate; United Kingdom; November–January 1995 to November–January 2005*

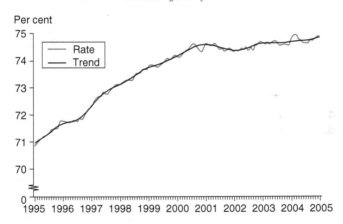

Source: *Labour Force Survey.*

The employment rate, as we would expect, has been moving in the opposite direction as illustrated in Figure 2.2.

In February 2007 the number of people in employment in the UK stood at 28.98 million. Unemployment had risen to 5.5 per cent.

The rate of change of unemployment in the 20 years from 1975 and the rate of change since 1995 could be associated with a longer-term trade cycle. (Figure 2.3)

FIGURE 2.3 *UK unemployment rates, 1881–1995*

Rates (per cent)

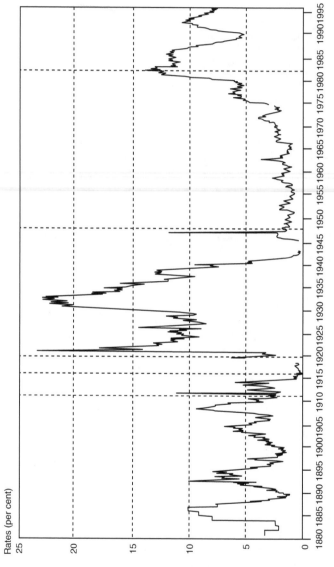

Notes: Vertical dotted lines indicate beginning of new series. Not seasonally adjusted.
Source: *Labour Market Trends*, January 1996.

This could be described as a tighter labour market than that which existed at the time of the previous edition of this book. However, there are certain offsetting factors. Between 1998 and 2002 net migration into the United Kingdom rose to 790 000 people with the vast majority aged between 15 and 44 years. In that period, this accounted for 75 per cent of the increase in population and 60 per cent of the rise in employment. Most of these migrants came from outside the European Union, but recent expansion of the European Union has extended the labour market available to the United Kingdom. At the time of writing the Government was predicting net migration of 130 000 per year.

Since 1998 women have accounted for over two-thirds of the increase in participation rates. There has been an increase in the activity rate of people above retirement age. In fact, since 1998 these two groups account for the whole of the increase in the activity rate. The trend in the increase in self-employment noted in the previous edition has continued along with the growth in part-time working, although in recent years this latter trend is more indicative of choice than it was in the earlier period. It is worth noting that recent growth in the labour market has come predominantly from the growth of the public sector, in particular in the National Health Service (NHS) and education.

A tightening labour market is associated, historically, with increases in trade union membership – a matter explored in Chapter 3. At the time of writing the view of the Bank of England is that the offsetting factors referred to, plus the potential for 'pressurising' the economically inactive into work, are sufficient to suggest that the labour market is not quite as tight as the general employment and unemployment data suggests.

Conclusion and Further Reading

This chapter has sought to describe some of the theory underpinning recent economic policy. In the previous edition, readers were referred to Hobsbawm (1994) who referred to a 'world crisis' and the impact of monetarist policies across the whole of the world economy. This was in tune with the way the United Kingdom looked in 1997. The current economic situation in the United Kingdom looks benign. However, if we look abroad in early 2007, France has an unemployment rate of 9.4 per cent; Germany 9.8 per cent, Italy 8.5 per cent and Spain 11.1 %.

For historical context, read Hobsbawm (1994), especially chapter 9.

3

Trade Unions

The opening to Chapter 1 pointed to the paradox of large numbers of people belonging to apparently unpopular organisations. Recent years have seen a substantial decline in trade union membership. No doubt the perceptive reader will predict that several explanations exist as to why this should be so. Even more perceptive readers will anticipate that the decline in membership could be put into the kind of historical context which makes it possible to argue that there has been no decline in relative terms.

This is not to suggest that the arguments put forward to support various interpretations of what has happened are unimportant. They most certainly are important. It has already been suggested that these have been used to rationalise the policies of governments, and no doubt they will be used in the future to similar effect. We must, therefore, understand the arguments. However, before undertaking an examination of these, a brief account of the origins and growth of trade unions is helpful. This will focus on the United Kingdom.

The Origins and Growth of Trade Unions

In the literature trade unions generally are defined either according to their functions or by reference to the current legal definition. The fact that there is a legal definition and that it has varied over time, is not independent of their perceived functions – it can be a barometer of these perceptions. For the moment they are best defined in terms of their functions. An early, and often quoted definition of a trade union, is that of the Webbs: 'a continuous association of wage-earners for the purpose of improving the conditions of their working lives' (Webb and Webb, 1902:1). In the United Kingdom, *collective bargaining* has been one of the main methods used by unions to achieve this. This was noticed by the Webbs, but they did suggest that trade unions had other methods – *mutual insurance* and *legal enactment*. Mutual insurance consists of providing friendly benefits – for sickness, superannuation, burial purposes – and trade benefits – replacing tools, and 'out-of-work pay'. Legal enactment is a method that aims to secure changes in the law to support the aspirations of trade unionists.

That the trade union movement in the United Kingdom was instrumental in forming the Labour Party is indicative of the view that legislation is seen as important by it. Recent support for the European Union is similarly indicative of this view – EU law was seen to be more sympathetic than UK law under a Conservative Government. In different periods of time and in different countries what the Webbs described as the 'proportionate use of these methods' by trade unions varies.

Regardless of their history of political involvement, their obvious interest in such things as labour law, health and safety, unemployment benefits, sick pay, pensions, local and regional industrial policy and so on, trade unions are often criticised for trying to exert a political influence. There are those who suggest that trade union interests are expressed too widely and those who suggest that they are expressed too narrowly. Trade unions are inevitably interested in politics, but this is rarely expressed in a coherent fashion. Individual unions and individual trade unionists differ in broad political perspectives and are often in competition with each other – there is competition between and within unions. There is competition for jobs and there is competition between unions for members. Such competition can be damaging, as unions recognise, but is not always controllable. Pressures from the wider structure of society and the day-to-day exigencies of earning a living lead to sectionalism. Trade unions discriminate between workers on grounds of race and sex and so on, much as do employers. Many of these divisions can be traced historically by looking at the role trade unions have played in trying to influence the employment relationship.

The Early Unions

A recent text Reid (2005: xi–xii) states the following:

> Thus collective bargaining power and trade-union membership fluctuated in relation both to short-term trade cycles of roughly seven years in length and to longer-term economic waves of roughly fifty years in length. Indeed, it is the latter which have been the most decisive for trade unions in Britain since the eighteenth century: producing four distinctive phases of expansion, in the 1790s to 1820s, 1850s to 1870s, 1890s to 1920s and 1950s to 1970s, separated by equally marked phases of instability and decline, in the 1820s to 1840s, 1870s to 1890s, 1920s to 1940s and once again from the 1970s to the 1990s.

In terms of the overall history it is possible to identify the 1850s as a kind of 'takeoff' stage in that from that date there emerged unions which developed forms of administration which secured continuity. Reid's analysis will be returned to.

The 'Model Unions'

Beatrice and Sidney Webb in their great book *The History of Trade Unionism* (1902:162–3) summarise the points made above as follows:

> From 1850 industrial expansion was for many years both greater and steadier than in any previous period. It is no mere coincidence that these years of prosperity saw the adoption by the Trade Union world of a 'New Model' of organisation, under which Trade Unionism obtained a financial strength, a trained staff of salaried officers, and a permanence of membership hitherto unknown.

The actual union seen by the Webbs as the archetype of the new model was the Amalgamated Society of Engineers (ASE), which was formed in 1851. It later became the Amalgamated Engineering Union (AEU): part of the Amalgamated Engineering and Electrical Union (AEEU).

It is not the purpose of this section to give a detailed history of one union in particular or of trade unionism in general. The significance of the ASE was that it became a prototype. National unification through amalgamation of a large number of local unions in the industry was a major achievement and an example to be followed. The union developed efficient systems of administration, subscription contributions, democratic decision-making processes and, above all, the basis for continuity. Equally important, it controlled entry to membership by requiring apprenticeship qualifications or experience and tried to enforce similar requirements on employers. The ASE set the pattern of exclusive, male-dominated, craft organisations (for a definition of this and comparable terms see the section 'British Unions Today' below). It also set the pattern associated with such organisations of political conservatism which was reflected in a search for benefits and status within the existing organisation of production. An alternative, and perhaps fairer, characterisation would be to see it as pragmatically pursuing the aspirations of its membership. When formed, it had 5000 members. By 1880 it had 45 000 members. Many such unions developed and became known as occupationally based craft unions.

The 'New Unions'

The term 'new model union' comes from the Webbs. Nearly 40 years after the formation of the craft unions by skilled workers there came a growth in the formation of more generally based unions by unskilled and semi-skilled workers, also on a permanent basis. These were described simply as the 'new' unions. Gas workers and dockers, for example, organised into general unions. Similar developments took place in other industries and among the unskilled and females in industries which had previously had organisations solely of skilled male workers. Membership in these general unions tended to be of the low paid, with low subscription rates. Unlike those of the model unions, the expenditures of these unions were concentrated on financing industrial action rather than giving some emphasis to friendly society benefits.

Leaders of these unions had often been influenced by socialist thinking and they expressed objectives which went beyond seeking benefits and status within a capitalist society. Often these were expressed in revolutionary form and generated antagonisms between the newer and older unions. While the rhetoric was stronger than the action, it did help to push the unions to seek political alliances and to press more strongly for legislative reforms. The Trades Union Congress (TUC) had been formed in 1868 and by the 1890s had become not only a forum for the expression of conflicting views and sectional interests but also a base for pressure-group activities.

Overlapping these developments was the formation and growth of the so-called white-collar unions. The National Union of Elementary Teachers (NUET, now the National Union of Teachers (NUT)) had been formed as early as 1870 and by the turn of the century had 23 000 members. Unions had also been formed among clerical and telegraph workers. By 1900 the main types of unions as we now know them had become firmly established in the United Kingdom. So also had the main features of collective bargaining – centralised and decentralised bargaining arrangements combined with multi-unionism at the industry and plant levels.

British Unions Today

The brief summary above indicates the long and deep-rooted history which lies behind the current organisation of trade unions in Britain. This section is concerned with classification and quantification of types of union as they are perceived today. Emerging from the references to the Webbs is an element of classification into craft and general unions.

Conventionally a system of classification emerged which added to these the category of industrial unions. It is possible to add to the list or create subdivisions within each category on the list. Dichotomous categorisations are often used – white-collar/blue-collar unions, private-sector/public-sector unions, manual/non-manual, manufacturing/service sector, skilled/unskilled and so on. Some substantive meaning can be given to each of the above, but there is no combination of terms which allows for a coherent classification of unions either now or in the past which would suit all purposes of analysis. Here we will begin by focusing on the traditional classification.

Craft Unions

At the simplest level such unions organise workers who perform a particular craft. There is a notion of possession of a skill, by training or experience, on the part of members of such unions, and that this provides a basis for eligibility for membership. What we do know is that certain unions were traditionally referred to as craft unions – the ASE and the early model unions having set the pattern. Sometimes such unions have been associated with the use of certain methods. For example, trying to regulate the supply of labour independently of the employer and then using control over this supply to determine wages independently of the employer on a 'take it or leave it' basis. This rarely happened and was rarely successful.

More recently such unions as the AEU (in engineering), the Electrical Trade Union(ETU) (electrical workers) and the National Graphical Association(NGA) (print workers) were referred to as craft unions. This reflected the nature of the membership and, to some extent, an emphasis on restrictive practices and rigorous control over entry into the union. Entry might be controlled by a combination of skill requirements, locality of origin and even family connections. Sometimes employers would collaborate on control of labour supply to secure the continuity and protection of their monopoly positions. Such controls have been considerably weakened in traditional craft areas by changes in technology, lowered union strength and employer emphasis on flexibility. It is significant that all of the unions referred to above have merged with other unions and are now more like general unions, even in terms of recruitment policies.

It is possible to argue that what might be called the professional unions in the NHS – the British Medical Association (BMA), the Royal College of Midwives (RCM) and the Royal College of Nursing (RCN), for example – display traditional craft union characteristics. They require qualifications for entry and jealously guard demarcation lines.

General Unions

These are unions which are very open in their recruitment – they are basically willing to recruit without any restriction. Unions such as the GMB and Transport and General Workers' Union (TGWU) fell into this category. The suggestion here is that most of what were traditionally referred to as craft unions are now general unions.

Industrial Unions

The industrial union is more an ideal type than an actuality. The term could refer to a union trying to organise all workers in an industry regardless of occupation or a union confining itself to one industry. The National Union of Mineworkers (NUM) came close to the first, as did Ceramic and Allied Trades Union (CATU), but both had to allow exceptions. Health service unions, such as the BMA and RCN, come close to the second, but even these have members in other industries. Perhaps the RCM is the closest example of the second, along with unions in the education sector such as the NUT.

Other Classifications

When we look at other classifications, they all overlap the traditional ones discussed above. Membership based on occupation would include craft, clerical and professional unions. White collar is a different order of classification, and as suggested above, would be contrasted with blue collar. Most unions combine the two, however elaborate the attempt at delineation. Perhaps more important is the question as to why white-collar workers are seen as somehow distinct from the mass of employees. Many now belong to general unions; many, even among those referred to as professionals, such as nurses and midwives, work in relatively low-paid occupations, with little managerial responsibility.

In the increasingly distant past the term white collar did suggest individualism and an unwillingness to organise. This has been much less the case in the past 30 years. The growth in the so-called white-collar sector areas of employment simply reflects changes in technology and production methods, on-going features of capitalism. For these workers the employment relationship is similar to that of most other workers. The majority are simply performing routinised manual tasks and have a traditional relationship to the means of production. Equally, older professions, such as doctors, teachers, nurses, midwives and so on are beginning to place more emphasis on the trade union activities of their organisations as current managerial styles clarify their relationship to the means of production. Many managers have discovered their status as agents of the owners as information technology has allowed for the 'delayering' of whole areas of supervision. The attribution of special characteristics to white-collar unions probably obscures more than it clarifies.

Classification should be a function of purpose. Why do we want to classify? The craft-general approach was and still is very useful. It helps us to understand history, and if a union is currently described as craft oriented, it tells us something of the behaviour being ascribed to it. In the NHS, for example, equating the BMA and RCN with craft unions is one way in which management attempts to downgrade their status and make them more vulnerable – see Caines (1992). The industrial union as a form of classification perhaps helps to understand the aspirations of such groups as miners, railwayworkers and steelworkers, seeking vertical integration of all staff. As a descriptive category, it lacked content. Similarly, as an antidote to multi-unionism, it was always handicapped by the difficulty of defining an industry, and this objective is best seen in terms of achieving one union at each place of work (see Chapter 4). General unionism is compatible with this objective, and the predominance of this type reflects the impact of a whole range of forces (see the following sections).

Turner (1962) introduced a classification of unions into 'open' and 'closed', which allowed for a more dynamic analysis of trends in union structure as they were then developing. Closed unions were seen as restricting entry, and open unions as those which did not. This explained, and anticipated, the emergence of general unions as the dominant type. Professional unions in the NHS are still predominantly closed, but there has been some loosening of boundaries – see Burchill (1995). With unions emerging as predominantly open and general, Undy *et al.* (1981) identified unions in more or less exposed and sheltered environments with more or less positive or passive attitudes to recruitment. Interestingly, these approaches could be applied to the remaining enclave of professional unions, but it is difficult to see their relevance to the main body of unions in the light of recent mergers and membership searches. If we examine these processes, it might be more helpful to classify on the basis of current union locations in the industrial structure. Unions currently located in declining or growing areas of the economy, or straddling both, might be an initial basis of classification which allows for some prediction.

Reid (2005), in probably the first historical text on trade unions written in the past 100 years that makes no reference to the Webbs, and that also makes no reference to the more recent work of Turner, provides an additional classification which he describes as linked to 'occupational experience'. His objective is to establish clearly that trade unions consisted of people who were integral to society and not from some unique segment of the population – they were a cross-section of society. This is an excellent text which here can only be strongly recommended. What it does demonstrate is the use of a classification designed for a purpose. In terms of its purpose, it has a traditional omission – no reference is made to a significant section of trade union membership contained in unions such as the RCN, RCM, BMA and so on which clearly demonstrate that both professional and highly paid people have recourse to trade unions. The British Airline Pilots' Association (BALPA) also fits this category.

The Condition of the Unions

Table 3.1 shows total union membership in the left hand columns and union density in those on the right. Tables 3.1a and 3.1b bring the

TABLE 3.1 *Union membership and density*

	Union membership		Union density	
Year	Number (000 s)	Annual change (%)	Level (%)	Annual change (%)
1892	1 576	–	10.6	–
1900	2 022	–	12.7	–
1910	2 565	–	14.6	–
1913	4 135	–	23.1	–
1917	5 499	–	30.2	–
1920	8 348	–	45.2	–
1921	6 633	–	35.8	–
1926	5 219	–	28.3	–
1933	4 392	–	22.6	–
1938	6 053	–	30.5	–
1945	7 875	–	38.5	–
1948	9 363	–	45.2	–
1949	9 318	20.5	44.8	20.9
1950	9 289	20.3	44.1	21.6
1951	9 530	12.6	45.0	12.0
1952	9 588	10.6	45.1	10.2
1953	9 527	20.6	44.6	21.1
1954	9 566	10.4	44.2	20.9
1955	9 741	11.8	44.5	10.7
1956	9 778	10.4	44.1	20.9
1957	9 829	10.5	44.0	20.2
1958	9 639	21.9	44.2	21.8
1959	9 623	20.2	44.0	11.9
1960	9 835	12.2	44.2	10.5

TABLE 3.1   *Continued*

Year	Union membership		Union density	
	Number (000 s)	*Annual change (%)*	*Level (%)*	*Annual change (%)*
1961	9 916	10.8	44.0	20.5
1962	10 014	11.0	43.8	20.5
1963	10 067	10.5	43.7	20.2
1964	10 218	11.5	44.1	10.9
1965	10 325	11.0	44.2	10.2
1966	10 259	20.6	43.6	21.4
1967	10 194	20.6	43.7	10.2
1968	10 200	10.1	44.0	10.7
1969	10 479	12.7	45.3	13.0
1970	11 187	16.8	48.5	17.1
1971	11 135	20.5	48.7	10.4
1972	11 359	12.0	49.5	11.6
1973	11 456	10.9	49.3	20.4
1974	11 764	12.7	50.4	12.2
1975	12 026	12.2	51.0	11.2
1976	12 386	13.0	51.9	11.8
1977	12 846	13.7	53.4	12.9
1978	13 112	12.1	54.2	11.5
1979	13 447	12.6	55.4	12.2
1980	12 947	23.7	53.6	23.2
1981	12 182	25.9	51.0	24.9
1982	11 593	24.8	48.0	25.9
1983	11 337	22.2	47.2	21.7
1984	10 994	23.0	45.7	23.2
1985	10 716	22.5	43.0	25.9
1986[a]	10 539	21.7	43.6	11.4
1989[a]	9 100	213.7	39.0	210.6

Notes:
a Certification Officer's Annual Reports, GB, and 1989 Labour Force Survey (prelim results), United Kingdom.
Source: Bain and Price in Bain (ed.) *Industrial Relations in Britain* (Blackwell, Oxford).

TABLE 3.1(a)   *Union membership in Great Britain, 1989–95*

Year	*Number of members (000 s)*	*Percentage change since previous year*	*Union density of all in employment (%)*	*Union density of employees (%)*
1989	8964	–	34.1	39.0
1990	8854	21.2	33.4	38.1
1991	8633	22.5	33.3	37.5
1992	7999	27.3	32.1	35.8
1993	7808	22.4	31.3	35.1
1994	7553	23.3	30.0	33.6

TABLE 3.1(a)   *Continued*

Year	Number of members (000 s)	Percentage change since previous year	Union density of all in employment (%)	Union density of employees (%)
1995	7275	23.7	28.8	32.1
Change since 1989	21 689	218.8	25.3	26.9

Notes:

1 Includes all those in employment, except for the final column which is employees only, excluding members of the armed forces.

2 Figures differ slightly from those reported in previous articles due to revisions in population estimates. See *technical note.*

3 From 1989–91 union membership questions were asked in the spring. Since 1992 they have been asked in the autumn quarter.

4 Those who did not report their union status, or who were not contactable in the autumn quarter, have been allocated on a pro-rata basis.

Source: Labour Market Trends, May 1996.

TABLE 3.1(b)   *Trade union membership and density for the United Kingdom, autumn 1995 to autumn 2004 (Thousands not seasonally adjusted)*

	In employment[a]		Employees[b]	
	Members[c]	Density	Members[c]	Density
People				
Autumn 1995	7070	29.0	6791	32.6
Autumn 1996	6918	28.4	6631	31.7
Autumn 1997	6911	27.5	6643	30.6
Autumn 1998	6890	27.2	6640	30.1
Autumn 1999	6911	27.2	6622	29.8
Autumn 2000	6924	27.2	6636	29.7
Autumn 2001	6846	26.8	6558	29.3
Autumn 2002	6840	26.8	6577	29.2
Autumn 2003	6820	26.8	6524	29.3
Autumn 2004	6784	26.0	6513	28.8
Change from 1995	−286	−3.0	−278	−3.8
Change from 2003	−36	0.6	−11	−0.5
Men				
Autumn 1995	3936	29.9	3727	35.3
Autumn 1996	3797	28.8	3579	33.6
Autumn 1997	3788	27.8	3600	32.4
Autumn 1998	3730	27.3	3545	31.4
Autumn 1999	3730	27.3	3528	31.1
Autumn 2000	3652	26.7	3457	30.4
Autumn 2001	3636	26.6	3426	30.1
Autumn 2002	3531	25.8	3354	29.4
Autumn 2003	3500	25.5	3297	29.4
Autumn 2004	3432	24.7	3243	28.5
Change from 1995	−504	−5.2	−484	−6.8
Change from 2003	−58	−0.6	−54	−0.9

TABLE 3.1(b)   *Continued*

	In employment[a]		Employees[b]	
	Members[c]	*Density*	*Members*[c]	*Density*
Women				
Autumn 1995	3134	28.0	3064	29.9
Autumn 1996	3121	27.0	3051	29.7
Autumn 1997	3124	27.0	3043	28.7
Autumn 1998	3160	27.0	3100	28.7
Autumn 1999	3181	27.1	3100	28.5
Autumn 2000	3273	27.7	3180	29.1
Autumn 2001	3210	27.0	3132	28.4
Autumn 2002	3307	27.6	3223	29.0
Autumn 2003	3320	27.8	3227	29.3
Autumn 2004	3353	27.6	3269	29.1
Change from 1995	219	−0.4	205	−0.6
Change from 2003	33	−0.2	42	−0.2

Source: Labour Force Survey, Office for National Statistics.

a Excludes members of the armed forces, unpaid family workers and those on college-based schemes.

b Excludes members of the armed forces.

c These figures have been revised from last year's publication and no longer allocate those who did not report their union status on a pro-rata basis. Note the figures for men and women may not sum to the total due to rounding.

membership and density figures up to date. Union density is aggregate membership as a percentage of potential membership – potential membership being the labour force, including the unemployed but excluding the self-employed, employers and the armed forces. It is possible to measure density by excluding the unemployed from potential membership. However, both sets of statistics indicate similar trends over the longer-term period. Similarly, inaccuracies which arise from methods of collecting the data do not obscure general trends.

Figure 3.1 shows a series of peaks of trade union membership approximately 30 years apart. It also shows a continuous upward trend. This suggests a trade union membership emerging from each phase of decline even stronger. However, given the very limited number of such occurrences, it would be dangerous to predict the future from such a pattern. There is no obvious reason why the past should repeat itself; equally there is no obvious reason why it should be assumed that trade unions are fundamentally in decline.

The longer-term cycle of trade union membership growth and decline does seem to link to the longer-term business cycle. Similar relationships have been identified in shorter-term cycles (Bain and Elsheikh, 1976). Unemployment seems to be a major factor – as unemployment grows, union membership declines. Employment, wages and

FIGURE 3.1 *Trade Unions, 1898–1988*

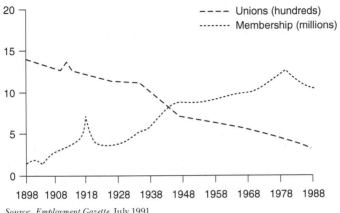

Source: *Employment Gazette,* July 1991.

prices tend to move in the same direction – with the 'stagflation' of the 1970s proving something of an exception. Unemployment causes a direct loss of membership as workers leave jobs and unions, but it also weakens the capacity of workers to organise and strengthens the capacity of employers to resist and evade union recognition. It also makes it easier to enforce labour legislation and to increase its credibility thus making it easier to add to and develop.

Between 1979 and 1986 trade union membership declined by 3 million in the United Kingdom. During this period there was a rapid growth in unemployment. Union membership continued to decline after 1986, while the number of employees declined. Both periods were accompanied by a fall in union density, regardless of the measure used.

It has to be acknowledged, however, that in the short run a number of factors are at play. Changes in industrial structure are redistributing labour from highly organised sectors to less organised ones. The growing number of females, part-time workers and workers from ethnic minorities is also regarded as having an effect – these are groups of workers generally seen as less willing to organise. Similarly, the privatisation of parts of the public sector, where trade unionism has been stronger, weakens the position of unions. Traditionally organised workers are finding their jobs subcontracted out to unorganised firms; there has been a growth in what was earlier described as secondary employment. Much of this reflects government policy, which in the 1980s was backed by anti-trade-union legislation and an assault on collective bargaining. Managerial strategies have been encouraged in both the public and private sectors, which emphasise individual pay and performance packages. These also have an effect on trade union membership, especially if accompanied by derecognition.

Size of firm and establishment are both said to affect the density of trade union membership. Generally it is suggested that the larger these two are, the greater trade union density will be. The proportion of the labour force employed in smaller firms and establishments has grown in recent years.

The surveys which produced these data also showed that union density was greater in the north than in the south of the country, with employment concentrations being higher in the south and growing. It also showed that density was higher among older workers than among younger workers and lower among ethnic minorities. Again all the trends in activity rates militate against a growth in union membership if these activity and density relationships persist.

There is no doubt that the extreme recession periods of the 1980s and 1990s in the United Kingdom, referred to in Chapter 2, have been factors in promoting union decline. These have occurred in the midst of the second largest long-term depression of the past 100 years. A feature of all of this has been the major developments in information technology, which have had a universal impact on industrial structure. It is possible to argue that industrial restructuring, or transformation, has taken place before, and that it is important that a distinction between long-term and short-term trends be borne in

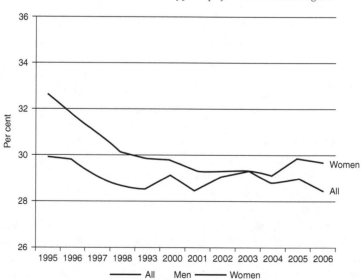

FIGURE 3.2 *Trade union density for employees in the United Kingdom*

TABLE 3.2 *Trade union density by industry, 1995 to 2006 United Kingdom employees*[a] *(per cent, not seasonally adjusted)*

	Autumn											Q4
	1995	1996	1997	1998	1999	2000	2001	2002	2003	2004	2005[d]	2006
All employees												
Agriculture, forestry and fishing	7.4	8.6	9.0[b]	12.3	9.0	10.5	8.8	8.9	9.3	c	8.5	9.0
Mining and quarrying	35.8	37.7	32.1[b]	29.9	36.2	31.8	25.3	23.6	28.0	27.3	21.2	23.5
Manufacturing	32.7	31.2	30.4[b]	29.9	28.5	27.7	27.2	26.7	26.2	24.6	24.8	22.2
Electricity, gas and water supply	67.0	61.6	62.7[b]	57.7	52.4	53.9	53.4	50.5	47.4	46.9	47.9	49.3
Construction	26.2	25.5	21.8[b]	20.6	21.1	20.1	19.2	17.5	18.9	16.7	15.7	15.8
Wholesale, retail and motor trade	11.4	10.8	10.8[b]	10.9	11.7	11.4	11.7	11.3	11.7	11.5	11.0	11.1
Hotels and restaurants	8.1	6.8	7.2[b]	6.7	6.2	5.4	5.4	5.9	5.4	5.0	4.2	5.6
Transport, storage and communication	48.8	47.6	45.7[b]	42.5	42.2	42.5	42.2	41.5	42.3	41.3	42.2	41.2
Financial intermediation	37.2	36.4	33.7[b]	31.1	30.2	29.9	27.0	27.2	25.9	26.6	24.4	24.3

Continued

TABLE 3.2 *Continued*

	Autumn											Q4
	1995	1996	1997	1998	1999	2000	2001	2002	2003	2004	2005[d]	2006
Real estate and business services	13.3	12.8	11.7[b]	11.3	11.4	10.3	10.6	10.6	11.0	10.5	10.1	10.0
Public administration and defence	58.8	60.7	62.8[b]	60.7	60.7	59.4	59.3	59.5	56.9	56.2	57.1	57.3
Education	56.1	54.9	54.8[b]	53.8	54.1	54.0	53.2	54.7	54.8	54.9	56.0	55.1
Health and social work	48.1	47.2	47.2[b]	46.1	45.0	46.3	44.7	44.9	44.4	43.8	44.2	43.4
Other services	23.8	21.6	21.1[b]	21.1	22.1	21.8	21.2	20.9	22.2	18.0	18.6	20.3
Male												
Agriculture, forestry and fishing	9.1	10.2	10.0[b]	13.7	10.3	11.2	10.7	9.2	10.4	c	9.9	9.0
Mining and quarrying	38.7	41.1	36.5[b]	36.2	40.4	34.4	28.3	25.9	32.0	29.4	24.2	25.5
Manufacturing	36.7	34.5	34.0[b]	33.4	32.3	31.4	30.9	30.4	29.6	28.2	27.7	25.2
Electricity, gas and water supply	75.4	67.3	71.2[b]	67.6	59.5	58.7	58.8	56.7	55.3	52.1	50.8	57.7
Construction	28.9	28.2	24.0[b]	22.0	22.7	21.5	20.9	18.7	20.3	18.2	16.9	17.0
Wholesale, retail and motor trade	10.1	9.9	10.7[b]	9.5	11.5	10.8	10.9	10.6	11.1	11.1	10.8	10.9
Hotels and restaurants	7.4	5.5	6.1[b]	4.9	5.5	3.8	3.9	5.2	4.7	4.0	2.8	5.0

Transport, storage and communication	54.9	53.5	51.9[b]	48.2	48.0	48.1	47.3	46.9	47.7	47.1	47.4	46.3
Financial intermediation	34.7	32.4	30.1[b]	26.6	25.3	25.5	23.0	22.3	21.9	21.9	19.8	21.1
Real estate and business services	15.9	13.8	12.4[b]	12.4	12.9	10.7	12.7	11.4	11.7	11.4	11.2	11.0
Public administration and defence	64.0	65.3	68.5[b]	66.3	66.4	63.1	65.0	63.4	59.8	58.4	58.9	58.8
Education	66.9	65.1	64.7[b]	60.1	62.0	62.1	60.8	60.5	60.6	61.1	60.9	58.5
Health and social work	55.1	53.8	55.7[b]	53.0	50.7	53.6	51.8	52.2	50.5	48.0	49.5	46.1
Other services	32.8	30.4	28.1[b]	29.5	29.2	28.9	28.6	27.0	28.8	24.1	23.5	26.3
Female												
Agriculture, forestry and fishing	c	c	c	c	c	c	c	c	c	c	c	c
Mining and quarrying	c	c	c	c	c	c	c	c	c	c	c	c
Manufacturing	22.8	22.6	21.0[b]	20.7	18.3	17.9	17.2	16.2	16.5	13.9	16.2	13.3
Electricity, gas and water supply	43.1	42.0	39.3[b]	30.8	36.6	41.9	37.8	31.0	24.6	34.0	38.4	29.1
Construction	12.1	12.1	8.3[b]	10.7	9.7	10.5	7.9	9.4	9.6	7.7	9.3	8.8
Wholesale, retail and motor trade	12.4	11.6	11.0[b]	12.0	11.8	12.0	12.4	11.9	12.2	11.9	11.3	11.2
Hotels and restaurants	8.5	7.6	7.7[b]	7.8	6.6	6.4	6.4	6.4	5.9	5.8	5.2	6.1

Continued

TABLE 3.2 *Continued*

	Autumn											Q4
	1995	1996	1997	1998	1999	2000	2001	2002	2003	2004	2005[d]	2006
Transport, storage and communication	30.3	30.5	28.6[b]	26.5	27.1	27.4	29.3	26.9	26.9	24.4	27.4	28.1
Financial intermediation	39.3	39.6	36.8[b]	34.7	34.4	33.8	30.5	31.4	29.7	30.9	28.5	27.4
Real estate and business services	10.7	11.8	10.9[b]	10.1	9.7	9.9	8.3	9.6	10.2	9.5	8.7	8.9
Public administration and defence	53.2	55.8	56.7[b]	55.0	54.8	55.8	54.2	55.8	54.2	54.2	55.4	55.9
Education	51.5	50.9	51.1[b]	51.4	51.2	51.3	50.4	52.7	52.7	52.7	54.3	53.9
Health and social work	46.8	45.9	45.4[b]	44.5	43.8	44.8	43.2	43.3	43.1	42.8	42.9	42.7
Other services	16.4	14.9	15.4[b]	14.7	16.0	15.9	15.0	16.0	16.4	13.0	14.0	15.0

Source: Labour Force Survey, Office for National Statistics.

a excludes members of the armed forces.

b indicates that data have been revised. The period marked is the earliest in the table to have been revised.

c sample size too small for a reliable estimate.

d results for 2005 and earlier are based on seasonal quarter LFS microdata.

TABLE 3.3 *Trade union density by major occupation group,*
2001 to 2006 – UK employees* (per cent, not seasonally adjusted)

	Autumn					Q4
	2001	2002	2003	2004	2005**	2006
All employees						
Managers and senior officials	17.9	18.0	19.0	18.6	18.9	17.0
Professional occupations	48.8	47.1	48.7	48.6	49.3	47.2
Associate professional and technical occupations	41.9	42.5	43.1	42.5	42.2	43.0
Administrative aad secretarial occupations	23.8	25.0	24.2	23.8	24.7	23.7
Skilled trade occupations	30.1	29.7	28.8	26.0	24.7	24.0
Personal service occupations	29.1	31.2	30.1	29.7	29.9	30.5
Sales and customer service occupations	13.0	12.9	12.5	12.8	11.6	12.7
Process, plant and machine operatives	36.7	36.6	34.4	34.2	34.2	33.4
Elementary occupations	21.9	21.2	21.6	20.8	20.9	20.5
Male						
Managers and senior officials	16.8	16.2	17.6	17.2	17.0	15.2
Professional occupations	39.5	36.9	38.9	38.3	38.8	36.4
Associate professional and technical occupations	37.6	38.3	37.8	38.3	36.6	37.4
Administrative aad secretarial occupations	30.3	31.4	29.8	28.7	31.6	29.1
Skilled trade occupations	31.2	30.1	29.4	26.7	24.8	24.6

Table 3.3   *Continued*

	Autumn					Q4
	2001	2002	2003	2004	2005**	2006
Personal service occupations	39.2	37.5	40.6	36.4	37.7	36.9
Sales and customer service occupations	10.8	12.7	10.6	11.2	8.7	11.8
Process, plant and machine operatives	38.4	38.4	36.2	36.1	35.7	34.7
Elementary occupations	26.6	25.5	26.0	25.0	25.4	24.4
Female						
Managers and senior officials	20.3	21.7	21.9	21.6	22.3	20.3
Professional occupations	60.3	60.5	61.0	61.2	61.8	60.1
Associate professional and technical occupations	46.3	46.5	48.2	46.4	47.3	47.9
Administrative aad secretarial occupations	22.2	23.4	22.9	22.7	23.0	22.2
Skilled trade occupations	19.6	25.2	23.1	18.4	24.4	16.9
Personal service occupations	27.3	30.1	28.1	28.4	28.5	29.3
Sales and customer service occupations	13.9	13.0	13.2	13.5	12.8	13.2
Process, plant and machine operatives	28.8	27.5	25.6	22.9	25.0	26.2
Elementary occupations	16.9	16.7	16.7	15.9	15.7	16.0

Source: Labour Force Survey, Office for National Statistics.
** results for 2005 and earlier are based on seasonal quarter LFS microdata.
* excludes members of the armed forces.

mind. New types of workplace and worker have emerged both here and abroad in earlier periods and have ultimately organised. For example, as women become a more dominant and permanent feature, their propensity to organise might grow. This is a speculative proposition, but so also are those propositions which suggest a fundamental and irreversible decline in union membership. In the short run, longer-term trends can be exacerbated by such things as changes in the law.

As suggested earlier, most theorising on trade union density focuses on rates of change in individual countries, rather than on differing degrees of density between countries. Country comparisons show that although the rate of change varies widely (as does the absolute level referred to above), virtually all are moving in a downward direction.

Reid (2005:418) takes a very deterministic and optimistic view of the future of UK trade unions:

> We have seen the unions hitting low points in the 1870s to 1880s and in the 1920s to 1930s, suggesting that the same was likely to happen again in the 1970s to 1980s. This did indeed occur and, though that downswing has lasted longer than the previous ones, it has not taken union membership levels anything like as low as before, suggesting that the unions may now be well placed for a rapid recovery.

Trade Union Recognition

Becoming a trade union, remaining a trade union and retaining and increasing membership are not generally seen as ends in themselves. As recognised earlier, a central method of UK trade unions has been collective bargaining – they wish to bargain with employers to secure benefits for their members. Success will of course help to achieve membership growth and retention. Bargaining is made easier for unions if they can secure recognition for such purposes by the employer. This has usually been achieved by the use of power – threatening to withdraw labour, or doing so, for example. Employers in such circumstances might consider recognition to be more cost effective than open warfare with trade unions. As already suggested, when unions were strong, then recognition and collective bargaining were rationalised by governments as the best way to deal with conflict. At such times employers might recognise without real resistance. Some employers might choose to recognise what they consider to be a 'responsible' trade union to preempt the incursion of a more 'militant' one. Foreign companies – there are Japanese examples – might choose to recognise a union on a greenfield site to avoid multi-unionism or conflict that could generate cultural antago-nisms in the belief that unions are manageable anyway.

Recognition implies formal negotiations and agreements. A union might be recognised for bargaining purposes across the whole range of substantive and procedural matters or for some of these. For example, they might be recognised for health and safety matters but not for oth-ers. They might be recognised for grading issues or they might be rec-ognised in some parts of a company but not in other parts.

Statutory rights to time off for trade union duties and those associ-ated with health and safety, or for disclosure of information, require recognition of the trade union by the employer. At the time of writing, recognition was predominantly a voluntary matter. If an employer chooses to derecognise a union, the union loses such statutory rights. The 1980s saw a decline in the extent of union recognition, and this no doubt accelerated the decline in union membership. Millward *et al.* (1992). Statutory recognition provisions which existed for a brief period in the 1970s were removed in 1980. In the year 2000, following the implementation of the 1999 Employment Relations Act, a procedure for securing statutory recognition via the Central Arbitration Committee (CAC) was introduced.

The CAC dates back to the Industrial Court of 1919. For the 20 years before its relaunch in 2000 it had the remit predominantly of dealing with disclosure of information for collective bargaining pur-poses. Its arbitration role was rarely called upon – Advisory, Conciliation and Arbitration Service (ACAS) being the main pro-vider. In June 2000, its membership grew from a committee of 12 to 42, consisting of a Chairman, eight Deputy Chairmen, 16 members with experience as employers' representatives and 16 with experience as workers' representatives. It took on responsibility for statutory rec-ognition and disputes over arrangements to establish European Works' Councils. Since then it has grown in size to include 11 Deputy Chairs and 23 each of employer and worker representatives and has taken on some responsibility for the Information and Consultation of Employees Regulations 2004.

Between June 2000 and December 2004, 1730 new recognition agree-ments were signed covering 788 500 employees. Only 206 of these came via the CAC and these covered 36 500 agreements. There is probably a relationship between the willingness to establish voluntary agreements and the statutory procedure, given that failure to voluntarily agree could lead to use of the alternative. It is also probable that the proce-dure has lessened the rate of decline of union membership.

The Closed Shop

Unions traditionally sought to create situations where it became a condition of employment that employees join a trade union. The requirement would usually be that the employee joined that union which was recognised for bargaining purposes for the category of employee concerned. Such agreements used to have legal effect. Obviously a closed-shop agreement strengthened the union and prevented dilution of membership by the employment of non-union employees. The counter argument, that workers forced to join might become simply 'card-carrying', inactive members and therefore weaken the union, was never convincing. Employers might be attracted by the closed shop as an antidote to union competition, stabilising bargaining, or even to preserve monopoly positions.

According to Millward *et al.* (1992), closed-shop arrangements reported by managers covered five million workers in their 1980 survey but only half a million in their 1990 survey.

Opposition to the closed shop is often expressed in moral terms, relating to the freedom of the individual. Suffice to say that the case for the closed shop can equally be argued on a similar basis. Employers tended to oppose it for obvious reasons. From the end of the Second World War until the late 1970s it appeared to be growing as an arrangement, but has declined since. The current situation in the United Kingdom is such that any contractual requirement to join a trade union is unlawful.

Union Responses

Many unions have found themselves in a declining spiral of membership and finances. One response has been to seek mergers, often rationalised in terms of economies of scale. Some of these mergers have had an obvious logic in terms of union structure – patterns of 'job territory' – and industrial structure. Others display no such logic and reflect historical patterns of inter-union competition. The merger of National Graphical Association (NGA 82) and Society of Graphical and Allied Trades (SOGAT 82) in 1992, to form the Graphical, Paper and Media Union (GPMU), fitted the logic of industrial structure. It also overcame differences between craft and unskilled workers in the printing industry. The Banking, Insurance and Finance Union (BIFU) and Manufacturing, Science and Finance Union (MSF) became more competitive in search of unions and staff associations in banking and finance. The MSF accepted declining unions such as the Tobacco

Workers' Union (TWU), but also absorbed the Health Visitors Association (HVA), an NHS union. The GMB became more active, absorbing textile unions and Association of Professional, Executive, Clerical and Computer Staff (APEX). In 1992, the Electrical, Electronic, Telecommunications and Plumbing Union (EETPU) and AEU merged to form the AEEU. Mergers often reflected political alliances between left- and right-wing unions, although such political bases could shift fairly rapidly.

An interesting case study is the NUM. Doomed to rapid decline as a result of government energy policy, alternative sources of supply and new technology (regardless of the strike of 1984–5 and the enmity of the government to mines, which probably served to accelerate the process) the NUM initially approached the National Union of Railwaymen (NUR) to consider a merger. This made neither strategic nor industrial sense. However, the notion of an energy sector combining power, nuclear energy workers, refinery workers and coalminers within the TGWU could be of long-term significance. Following industrial logic, the National Communications Union (NCU) and Union of Communications Workers (UCW) combined in 1995 to form the Communication Workers Union (CWU). Also in 1995 the National Union of Civil and Public Servants (NUCPS) and Inland Revenue Staff Federation (IRSF) voted for a merger to take effect from January 1996 forming the Public Services, Tax and Commerce Union (PTC). This was seen as a step towards rationalisation of the remaining civil service unions.

Privatisation has had an effect on traditionally public sector unions. The Institution of Professional Civil Servants (IPCS) became the Institution of Professionals, Managers and Specialists (IPMS) in anticipation of this. In 1993, the largest merger of all formed The Public Services Union (UNISON) from National and Local Government Officers' Union (NALGO), Confederation of Health Service Employees (COHSE) and National Union of Public Employees (NUPE). UNISON can follow its members into the private sector as well as forma formidable alliance within the NHS. Here it competes with nursing unions; in the private sector it competes with the GMB and Unite. Until recently, the largest union was Amicus created from a merger of the AEEU and MSF in 2002, followed by the absorption of UNIFI in 2004 and the GPMU in 2005. In 2007 Amicus merged with the TGWU to form Unite with over 2 million members.

A consequence of this process is that many unions are converging in terms of their organisation. They are becoming predominantly general unions made up of separate 'trade groups'. Merging unions are often promised autonomy as part of the inducement to attach themselves to larger unions. A short-run effect, presumably, is to create expensive administrative structures including separate conferences, and rivalry for power within, which works to offset potential economies of scale. Decentralisation of bargaining in the public sector is creating problems for unions geared to centralised bargaining and thus lacking a local infrastructure. In the NHS, the British Association of Occupational Therapists (BAOT) has reached a service agreement with UNISON, the RCM with the MSF and the Community and District Nursing Association (CDNA) with the GMB. Other smaller unions are in search of similar alliances (Burchill, 1995). Here, as in parts of the banking sector and higher education, the arrangements are of a federal nature. History would suggest that this kind of alliance is a step towards merger.

A difficulty with all of this is that economies of scale can only be secured with job losses and other resource rationalisations. Unions are not structurally, or temperamentally, inclined to efficient pursuit of such objectives. Widening the potential for membership recruitment offers the hope of some relief for lost membership, but this is likely to be overshadowed by internal power struggles arising from mergers for the foreseeable future. The cycle of membership and income loss could be exacerbated.

The House of Commons Employment Committee in its Report on *the Future of Trade Unions* (1993–4, Vol. 1: xx–xxii) discusses trade union mergers. Cases 'for' and 'against' are presented through summaries of views of employers and trade union officers, raising issues of democracy and representation. These are presented as technical rather than political issues – predominantly in unitarist terms. Metcalf is quoted as having 'pointed out that mergers are unlikely to increase total membership'.

Mergers have not been the sole response by unions to their current problems. As their evidence to the Employment Committee indicates, there has been some embracing of the 'new realism'. Unions are keen to demonstrate their capacity to work with current management practices and to point to evidence which suggests a relationship between the existence of trade unions in companies with modern management practices. They have sought to do deals with companies under the heading of 'partnership' which have considerably modified traditional approaches to collective bargaining. In their own organisations they have applied modern 'quality' techniques, taking on NVQ structures, offering skill training, adopting Investors in People, sending their officers to management training schools, such as Cranfield, and adopting dress codes, logos and 'mission' statements. In some cases there have been 'modern' developments of 'mutual insurance', such as credit card facilities and cheap loans.

More important, unions have recognised that they have to pay more attention to previously neglected sections of the workforce such as women and racial minorities. Similarly, policies have been developed to attract part-time workers and isolated groups of workers with virtually non-existent employment rights. Since 1998 the Trades Union Congress (TUC) has run an 'Organizing Academy' designed to promote the skills of organizing workplace union presence for long-term development and the maintaining of union membership. As suggested earlier, this awareness has led to greater emphasis on individual rights at work.

This emphasis on legal enactment led to a more compliant relationship with the Labour Party before the 1997 election. The mere commitment of that party to remove the requirement to renew permission every three years for the employer to deduct contributions to unions at source offered some relief on administration costs and membership loss. Further promises on statutory recognition, rights of representation and a minimum wage, plus the prospect of a less antagonistic legislative environment, proved sufficient to sustain this compliance until the 1997 election.

Multi-unionism

At the beginning of the twentieth century, there were approximately 1300 unions in the United Kingdom. In 1989, the Certification Officer listed 314. By 1994, this number had reduced to 267, and by 2004, it had fallen to 195. In comparative terms, this remains a large number of unions, although, as the next section indicates, membership is highly concentrated in a small number of these.

A consequence of the large number of unions has been competition for recognition and membership. It has also meant that in many workplaces the existence of a multiplicity of unions has led to complex bargaining arrangements. A recurrent critique of this phenomenon has been that it was costly in terms of demarcation and recognition disputes, restrictive practices, leapfrogging wage claims and managerial time. It can also be costly for trade union members in terms of duplication of administrative structures – factors referred to above in the discussion of trade union mergers.

Size of Unions

Regardless of the merger process, union membership in the United Kingdom has for a long time been concentrated in a relatively small number of unions. In 2004, the 16 largest unions, those with over 100 000 members, accounted for 84.1 per cent of the total membership of 8 230 543. Ten of these, with over 250 000 members, accounted for

73.9 per cent. The formation of Unite has reinforced this trend. The foreseeable future, as illustrated by Unite, seems to be one in which the trends towards concentration continue, combined with a decline in both aggregate union membership and density.

Conclusion

This chapter has sought to give a basic introduction to trade union structure. The section on the state of the unions introduces an important debate – in particular the role of the trade cycle – and this is followed by reference to union responses. There is no particular theory which can help us to come to any definitive conclusion about the future of unions *per se*.

Kessler and Bayliss (1995) supply additional statistical material. Waddington and Whitston (1995) provide essential additional material on union membership and responses. McIlroy (1995) is the key text to read on the whole subject of trade unions and should be read to supplement this chapter and the next one.

The Government of Unions

How are unions governed? In other words, what kind of constitutions and rules do they have? Do they have elections and secret ballots? To what extent do members participate? Are they democratic institutions? In recent years, Conservative Governments have interfered with union constitutions through legislation. Part of the rhetoric of such intervention has been the notion of 'giving unions back to their members'. Popular debate has often characterised unions' policies as being unrepresentative of their membership. Such debate may explain this in terms of the apathy of union members or, as reflected in the legislation referred to, in terms of union procedures. More academic debate might focus on the tendency for elites to develop. Is there an 'iron law of oligarchy' whereby the few always take power?

How unions are viewed in these terms is often a matter of perspective. Given the nature of many important institutions in our society – especially the large business corporations – the focus on union democracy could be seen as something of an impertinence. Nevertheless, to their credit, union constitutions do set out to be democratic, and there are basic similarities in these which derive from this simple fact.

From 'Primitive' to 'Representative' Democracies

The Webbs' book Industrial Democracy (1897), referred to earlier, was a pioneering study of union constitutions and the origins of such constitutions. In it they give a clear exposition of the move from fully participatory systems of organisation to more representative systems. Organisations of workers grew from gatherings of those with common problems arising at the place of work or in the community. Originally such gatherings might be spontaneous reactions to these problems seeking some kind of common action to resolve them. Given that problems often continued to exist, or recurred, it became obvious that some

50

kind of continuity of organisation was required. This would clearly be the case where funds were collected to be made available when cases of distress arose. These funds would need to be administered and audited. Meetings would be called to make a variety of decisions. In the early days of union formation, these might be called on an ad hoc basis. Gradually, such gatherings would be scheduled in advance for those who made contributions; notions of membership would emerge, along with formal rules for the conduct of business and the rights of members to participate in this.

At first these meetings would be open and accessible to all members. The nearest to what might be called an officer of the union would be the president of such a meeting, and each meeting would select a president for the purposes of that meeting. In other words, these early trade unions were governed by general meetings of the whole membership. Essentially, the Webbs use the term 'primitive democracy' to describe such a system of continuous universal access to participation in the running of such bodies. The development of secretaries to write letters and keep accounts came later, and members, under penalty of fine, were often expected to accept positions by rotation.

Naturally as trade unions grew in membership, geographical base and complexity, such a system of government became impracticable. Specialist skills were often required, and along with elected representative assemblies, paid, and ultimately salaried, officers emerged. This was not a sudden transition, and many unions continued to maintain referenda on special issues. Representative systems were also seen as more compatible with the notion of 'warfare' with the employer which required some kind of command structure. Not surprisingly, systems of government with common elements, but by no means identical, developed. Some of the common elements are described below. 'Representative democracy' characterises virtually all unions.

The Branch

Union members are allocated to membership of a branch. Historically, such allocation was usually based on where a person lived – often referred to as geographically based. Increasingly the place of work has become the basis for branch allocation. Branch meetings are the source of trade union government, policy and rule-making – according to union rulebooks. It is the unit of organisation which provides a forum for the rank and file membership to participate in determining all of the above. The branches nominate candidates for elections; they vote for such candidates; they propose motions to bodies elected to make decisions; they propose rule changes and so on. Because they are national organisations, unions tend to have regional, district and national bodies (see below). Again these are notionally structured and elected according to branch preferences (see below). It was the development of such structures which led the Webbs to refer to representative democracies, with an elected representative assembly at the pinnacle, the conference, becoming the rule-making and policy-determining body on behalf of all members.

The increasing location of branches at the place of work has tended to result in them dealing with workplace issues and not simply acting as a unit of union government. Obviously the two may overlap and coexist, but universal access to branch meetings may cause problems where unions are vertically organised – that is, where managerial and non-managerial staff are members of the same union – and based on the workplace.

Districts, Regions and Trade Groups

Unions vary in size and origins. Many of the larger unions had their origins in federations, and ultimately mergers, of both local and regional organisationd either in the same trade or industry or in different ones. Some were more homogeneous than others. The NUM was based in the coal industry but was very much a federation of regions; the TGWU organised nationally among many trades and across numerous industries. As organisations merged, constitutions developed to protect local, regional and trade interests. The NUM constitution was designed to protect smaller regions from being dominated by larger ones; the TGWU was designed to do the same and to protect some trades being out-voted by other trades and thus having their interests submerged. Each trade in the TGWU was allocated to a group – a trade group. Such groups had their own structure from local to national level.

Local interests were represented by district and regional committees. These developed policies to reflect such interests at national level. In terms of their relationships with the national union, these groups varied in their degrees of autonomy and strength. The same is true of different trade interests. The merger process described earlier is producing general unions with sections similar to those which operated within the TGWU but in what appear to be more federal structures. In other words, unions incorporated wholesale into larger ones often need some guarantee of independence. However, this can be expensive – separate conferences, specialist full-time officers and so on – thus hindering the benefits of merger.

On the other hand, strong district and trade groups not only provide constitutional protection. They can provide the kind of expertise required for decentralised bargaining. Many of the smaller but nationally based unions in the NHS are seeking federal links to provide help for bargaining and representational purposes at local level (Burchill, 1995).

Conference

Most unions are governed by their delegate conference – generally held annually. This system of delegation and representation has replaced the general assembly of all members for obvious practical reasons. Notionally the agenda of conference are determined by the members via their branches and intermediate structures. Each union has a system of providing for the election of delegates on the basis of constituencies determined by the geographical and trade group structure. The objective is to secure representation in proportion to numbers of members, their interests and so on, while maintaining protection of minority concerns.

As suggested above, membership proposals emerge from the branches. However, most of the important suggestions will tend to come from the executive – see below. The executive will usually dominate the platform of the conference, exercising further control over the content of debate. The major issues raised at conferences can be divided into three main categories – constitutional, policy and collective bargaining matters. Constitutional matters will relate to such things as the union's rules, election procedures, district and regional structures, trade group constitutions and so on. Policies will relate to broad issues such as attitudes to a minimum wage and its level, government policies on unemployment benefit, general welfare provision and the European Union. Where unions are affiliated to the Labour Party, decisions will be made on which policies to support, reject or amend.

Collective bargaining issues are more difficult. On a day-by-day basis these are at best the province of professional negotiators at the levels at which such issues arise. Nevertheless there will be related matters in which the broad membership have an interest, and they may mandate the executive to achieve broad pay targets, perhaps to oppose performance-related pay, to achieve maximum working hours or to oppose local bargaining.

In the NHS many unions are also professional bodies (professional unions) and are often registered as unions, companies and charities. The latter require annual general meetings, with conference being associated with the union. Professional unions include the RCN, the RCM, the Chartered Society of Physiotherapy (CSP), the Society of Radiographers (SoR), the BMA and so on. Their conferences mix professional matters with all those other matters referred to above. With the reforms of the NHS, collective bargaining and other industrial relations matters have taken on a greater significance for these unions.

Generally, the conference is seen as the supreme governing body, although in some unions the Executive has been able to overrule conference. This is still true of the RCM, for example.

The Executive

This body is responsible for the day-to-day running of the organisation. Its duty, according to the model, is to execute the policy of the union as determined by conference. Unions usually acted on the basis that the executive should be elected from the lay membership. The law now requires regular elections of executive members. These bodies vary in size and composition and the distribution of part-time and full-time members. Day-to-day running will involve the appointment of full-time officers, spending decisions, disciplinary matters, the organisation of industrial action and its sanctioning, and so on. They are responsible to the membership through conference or through specially called delegate conferences to deal with emergencies, or the conduct of strike action, for example.

The Officers

Writing in 1920 the Webbs tell us that 'The actual government of the Trade Union world rests exclusively in the hands of a class apart, the salaried officers of the great societies.' Unions have a chief executive – usually a general secretary or president – in a full-time position. There are other full-time officers, described by the Webbs as the civil service of the unions. In the model their role is to bring expertise to the bargaining process, recruitment and associated matters, and to the administration of the union. Most unions – about two-thirds – appoint their officers; the remainder elect them (Kelly and Heery, 1994). Recent legislation has required the election of officers on the governing body, whether full-time or not, every five years – except in the case of the professional unions in the NHS. This was part of the process of 'giving back the unions to their members' referred to earlier.

In the early days, many officers were appointed simply on the basis of their secretarial skills – they could read and write – and as a consequence they often came from outside the trade being organised. As Kelly and Heery point out, the distinction between elected and appointed is not clear cut. Some are elected for life, some for periods after which another ballot takes place, some appointments are confined to the trade and so on. In CATU, members have to 'pass' examinations before being allowed to proceed to candidature for election.

The debate between election and appointment is usually conducted on crude grounds contrasting the relative importance of expertise and accountability. Election is part of the process of ensuring accountability and overcoming some of the dangers implicit in the quotation from the Webbs above. On the other hand, it is said to generate insecurities, 'playing to the gallery' and takes little account of the skills required to perform the duties, thus creating organisational instabilities. There is no overwhelming case for any of the arguments, especially when posed so simplistically. The arguments also presuppose choices which can be made in some kind of historical vacuum. The trend towards larger unions through merger is shifting the balance towards appointed officers.

In the model these officers are like managers, responsible to the board (the executive) and ultimately to the shareholders' meeting (conference).

Democracy at Work

The above is the model of trade union government – a model designed to facilitate participation of the membership as a whole in the rule- and policy-making process. Rulebooks represent contracts with members which can be enforced through the courts in accordance with the principles of natural justice. There are critics of the model as it is seen to apply in practice, and such criticism can be classified according to our model of perspectives. However, there are common elements within the perspectives.

Participation at branch meetings is very low – usually less than 10 per cent of the membership. Executives become self-perpetuating oligarchies with vested interests manipulating the union through control of conference – compositing members' motions to dilute or subvert their objectives. They, along with the officers, become self-interested bureaucrats remote from the objectives and needs of the membership. Elections have low turnouts.

How one views these facts is usually a matter of perspective. There is a considerable literature available on the extent to which trade unions operate democratically – the extent to which their activities are fully representative of members' interests. This is a difficult concept to evaluate empirically, and the academic literature inevitably falls back on speculative debate about the interpretation of what facts are available. Contributions to these debates usually rest on political foundations.

A unitarist perspective places emphasis on the extent to which apathy is a consequence of the capture by activist minorities of the union bureaucracy. Apathy is seen as a consequence of unrepresentative groups pursuing unrepresentative policies and using and determining the rules to minimise participation. These groups are generally identified as left wing. Branch agendas are used to pursue political objectives and the meetings are manipulated to alienate participation and restrict democratic inputs. This process is pursued at all levels within the organisation and members are manoeuvred into actions they would not consciously choose. Their unwilling support is enforced by union rules and the use of the closed shop.

This form of unitarist rhetoric has been used to justify legislative intervention in union rule-making processes, the ballot requirements before industrial action, the election of officers, the outlawing of the closed shop, prohibiting the disciplining of members for refusing to take part in industrial action and so on. Many of these measures could be seen as making it more difficult for trade unions to organise and be effective, rather than as making a contribution to the creation of more representative bodies. The alternative rhetoric of the free market outlined in Chapter 2 could be used to justify such measures on the grounds that unions engage in monopolistic practices and that they ought to be weakened. Giving back the unions to their members and freeing the market are just different forms of unitarist rationalisation. If unions are cast in the role of friendly benefit clubs, the two sets of rationalisation are not mutually incompatible.

A crude conflict perspective would perceive the lack of democracy as inevitable. Trade unions participate in an economic system which itself is thoroughly undemocratic and their leaders are offered inducements to collaborate in the perpetuation of such a system. It is not left-wing activists who dominate union government but right-wing bosses seduced by power and money. At various times, depending upon the state of the economy, leaders are enticed into cooperating with state policies designed to preserve the system or are rejected and excluded from involvement because market conditions deprive them of potential power. This view is a consequence of a belief that the state simply serves capitalism and any attempts by trade unions to collaborate with the state will only be at the expense of their members' interests.

Within this view democracy among trade unionists is not simply a function of trade union government. The essential battle is at the place of work, where the rank and file confront the employer, and this confrontation regularly throws up challenges to union leadership where it matters. This of course depends upon a degree of organisation and confidence at shopfloor level.

Generally, pluralist and unitary perspectives tend to converge. In this debate, the convergence is more between pluralist and conflict perspectives. The optimism of the 1960s and1970s, based on the regular examples of rank-and-file trade union activism challenging employers, trade union leaders and governments has given way to newer rationalisations. These have emerged as a result of the impact of unemployment and the assault on trade unions which has been linked to this. Traditional conflict theorists are beginning to acknowledge that a battle on the terrain of capitalism might require some collaboration with a more sympathetic government, which need not be predominantly in the interests of capitalism. Such a government might require cooperation, or at least no sign of opposition, from trade unions to secure and maintain office, thus enabling it to develop policies which could be in the longer-term interests of labour.

Pluralist perspectives have tended to emphasise a conflict between democracy and administrative efficiency. An updated 'rationalisation' appears in Kelly and Heery (1994: 204):

> The multiform threats to trade unionism during the past decade arguably required a co-ordinated response since no individual union possessed the resources to meet them (as the miners discovered in 1984–5). Such coordination entails a degree of centralisation of power within individual unions (and within the TUC) if resources are to be conserved, mobilised and targeted on priority issues such as membership recruitment or campaigns over women's rights. Yet the very decentralisation set in train during earlier decades which equipped the movement so well at that time only served to inhibit the centralisation required in the very different conditions of the 1980s and 1990s.

Essentially, Kelly and Heery are telling us that the notion of conflict – whether explicit or implicit – between officers and rank-and-file membership can be exaggerated. Economic circumstances also seem to be important in determining the appropriate role for the bureaucracy. Similarly, the values officers bring to their work are important, and these often reflect those secured as activists. The Webbs recognised that officers might abuse their power. In the Webbs' account, leaders often lose their way with regard to their members' interests not because they pursue individual objectives but because their detachment from the disciplines of the workplace offers freedoms to their lifestyle which leads to many of them becoming drunkards.

This last comment is not meant to trivialise the debate. It is designed to show something of its complexity. Kelly and Heery are right to emphasise that we are not considering a relationship which is static and that values and personalities are of some significance, and also that there might be an inter-generational dynamic worthy of some analysis. What can be said is that union constitutions have developed with clear notions of democracy and membership participation in mind. Union officers, and activists, are constrained by these constitutions, by the actions of members at the place of work and by the possibility of members voting with their feet.

An account of the firefighters' dispute of 2002–4 is given in Seifert and Sibley (2005). It provides an interesting case study of a union's democratic processes under pressure – how they work and the impact of external forces, along with the role of factions. Not long after the fire dispute concluded, and therefore not included in the account, its General Secretary was voted out of office. Seifert and Sibley produce the kind of detail which is rarely available, allowing for the kinds of interpretation proposed above. It touches on most of the theoretical issues and concepts raised in respect of this section and should be referred to. It does attack a breakaway faction as acting undemocratically and therefore contrary to the interests of the union. Interestingly, from a perspectives point of view, their conclusions on some of the events in respect of factional conflict within the union were attacked in a review in the British Journal of Industrial Relations – apparently the subject's leading UK journal. The reviewer tells us '...it is important to note that the authors, as supporters of the Communist Party of Britain/Morning Star (although we are not informed of this in the preface) present a politically partisan viewpoint that happens to mirror that of the dominant faction in the union leadership in terms of conduct of the dispute.' A question you might consider is: why would an academic journal review a 'politically partisan viewpoint'? What was the 'political partisanship' of the reviewer? This is not revealed in the review. Is it relevant?

Shop Stewards

Shop stewards are officers of unions but in practice often not regarded as such. The reason for this is that their role is not directly linked to the governing of the union but is primarily linked to the role of the union at the place of work. Their prime responsibility is to represent members in dealings with their employers, with duties ranging from, in some contexts, acting on behalf of members in full-scale pay negotiations to representing members in grievance and disciplinary matters. They may be referred to as stewards, representatives, fathers and mothers of the chapel. Here the term shop steward is used to cover all of these.

Shop stewards as we know them are very much a twentieth-century development. They first came into some prominence as a consequence of the First World War. Capital needed the cooperation of labour not only to fight the war but also to produce the necessary goods and services. Those workers required to fight the war directly often had to be replaced on the shopfloor by untrained labour. The trade union movement sought to oversee such developments to prevent skills from becoming diluted and to maintain relative pay rates. Full employment gave power to those at the place of work and this power was asserted.

It was also in the interests of employers that 'green' labour be properly inducted and supervised, and shop stewards could play a role in this. Shop stewards both called and led industrial action independently of their trade union officials. In the engineering industry they organised across factories and trade unions, securing recognition by the employers in advance of securing recognition by the ASE. This led to the notion of a 'shop steward movement', with independent political objectives. In the main, however, these representatives concerned themselves with industrial matters. The labour surpluses brought about by the depression of the interwar years undermined the role of shop stewards and they declined in number and influence. Their revival began with the Second World War for reasons similar to those which operated in the First. Employment conditions following this war continued to be favourable to their continued growth and development until the mid-1970s.

Stewards are generally elected at the place of work by the people they represent. According to Millward *et al.* (1992), in 1990 the average steward represented 20 members, although constituencies varied considerably in size. According to Kersley *et al.* (2006), the average in 2004 was 24. Union rulebooks also vary in the extent to which they recognise and delineate the role of the steward. Nevertheless, they are seen as a key component of union activity and are vital to recruitment. No union can afford to ignore their needs and virtually all unions put considerable effort into servicing these.

Where there is more than one shop steward for a particular union, one of the stewards is usually recognised as the senior steward by the members. The fact that more than one union is recognised in many establishments has led to the setting up of joint shop stewards' committees, consisting of stewards from the different unions. The chairperson of such a committee is often referred to as the convener.

There are variations in the relationship between the steward and the union government. In the NUM, officers of the branches – the branch secretaries and chairmen – also act through their office as representatives at the place of work. In theory, although branch members, stewards are there to deal with workplace issues. They are expected to raise and deal with grievances, handle disciplinary matters, represent members on joint consultative committees and negotiating committees, and so on. Where unions are recognised, there is usually provision for stewards to have time off for training and the performance of their duties as stewards. Millward et al. (1992) reported a reversal in the trends suggested for the larger part of the post-war period. There was a widespread fall between 1984 and 1990 in the number of workplaces reporting the existence of shop stewards. These trends have continued according is Kersley *et al.* (2006).

The Trades Union Congress

The TUC is unique among national trade union centres. Not only was it the first to be formed, it quickly became and remained the one organisation through which the vast majority of trade unionists in the UK are represented in an inter-union forum. Approximately 85 per cent of all trade unionists in the UK belong to affiliated unions. There is no competing centre in the United Kingdom, although there have been attempts to form one. The latest of such attempts followed the expulsion of the EETPU in 1988.

The expulsion of the EETPU from the TUC indicates the only power which it has over affiliates. This is a very negative form of power, and the capacity of the TUC to retain its membership does indicate that the membership sees real advantages in remaining affiliated. Established in 1868, initially as a forum for debate of common issues, it rapidly became a body which spoke on behalf of the trade union movement as a whole.

The TUC has always seen itself as a pressure group trying to influence governments to pursue policies in line with the interests of trade unionists. Its influence on governments has varied over time mainly as a consequence of the relative strength of trade unions in relation to the trade cycle and the national requirements of capital during wartime periods. In the aftermath of the General Strike of 1926 and the continuing recession, it lost influence until it was revived by the Second World War. Labour Governments regularly wooed the TUC in pursuit of pay restraint. The past two decades have been periods in which the government has made a point of dismissing the role of the TUC, and the depression has helped this process. Nevertheless, it has played an important role in tripartite bodies of government, employers and trade unions such as NEDC, and has provided representation on bodies such as ACAS, the HSE and industrial tribunals. It is also affiliated to international bodies such as the International Trade Union Confederation

(ITUC), the European Trade Union Confederation (ETUC) and the International Labour Organisation (ILO).

Representation at the TUC, on its council and various committees is based on membership size of affiliated unions, as also are contributions and general voting rights. Its constitution is very similar to those of the trade unions it represents. An annual conference determines policy, which is placed in the hands of the General Council for day-to-day purposes. Such policies are based on attempts to establish common views on political, industrial, legal and economic issues. It has subcommittees to deal with these, as well as providing research and educational support for trade unions and their officers. Committees may be established to research and report on special topics.

The focus of the media is usually on the political divisions which emerge at the annual Congress – a focus which can produce a distorted image. It would be extremely unlikely that a body representing such diversity of interests should not produce a diversity of opinion. However, the Congress is at its neglected best when discussing technical issues such as health and safety, industry and the environment, and working conditions. Recent conferences have become more 'stage managed' in the fashion of Party conferences.

A major concern of the TUC is dealing with competition among affiliated unions and settling demarcation disputes. A resolution passed by Congress in 1939, when it met at Bridlington, incorporates what have become known as the Bridlington Principles, which affiliates are expected to observe when recruiting members. Essentially these require affiliated unions to ensure that members recruited by them from other affiliated unions have their membership, and any arrears in subscription, cleared by such other unions, and that no attempt should be made to recruit members in employment covered by recognised, affiliated unions. Nor should workers be recruited from such unions during a strike.

These rules were amended in 1985 to take account of the growth of single-union agreements. Such agreements should not be made at the expense of previously recognised unions, and on greenfield sites they should not be in breach of relevant existing industry negotiating arrangements. These principles are overseen by a disputes committee, which manages to settle most disputes through conciliation, thus avoiding a full hearing and an imposed settlement. The expulsion of the EETPU, previously referred to, was as a consequence of a failure on its part to observe a decision of the committee under this amendment. Trade Union Reform and Employment Rights Act (TURERA) 1993 introduced a provision which undermined the powers of the disputes committee – workers were given the right to join any union organising the appropriate class of employee.

It was suggested at the beginning of this chapter that the role of the TUC is generally underestimated. The literature tends to emphasise its weaknesses. However, its longevity and basic cohesiveness – even the EETPU found its way back through merger – testify to its perceived usefulness by those affiliated to it. Probably the main threat to the TUC in its present form is the scale of some of the current union mergers being discussed – especially the scale of the one between Amicus and the TGWU.

During the 2002–4 fire dispute, the TUC played an important role in the negotiations and a crucial role was played by the then General Secretary, Brendan Barber, in its ultimate settlement.

Chapter 12 examines some of the international relations engaged in by the TUC.

Conclusion and Further Reading

This chapter has suggested that the government of trade unions is best understood in terms of historical development and a concern by trade unionists that their institutions should embody democratic access to participation by members in their governance. Generally they have succeeded in achieving this. Kessler and Bayliss (1995) and McIlroy (1995) provide good supplementary material.

5

The Employers

Employers may be classified according to whether they are small or large; in the private sector or the public sector; in the primary, secondary or tertiary sector; whether they are conglomerates, bestriding sectors and markets; whether they are nationally based with or without multinational connections, or whether they are foreign-based multinationals with locally or nationally based units. The characteristics, in these terms, displayed by an employer, are said to have some effect on the nature of industrial relations in their organisation.

In the United Kingdom, the 1980s witnessed a decline in employment in the primary sector, especially in mining; a general decline in the secondary sector, in manufacturing; and a growth in the tertiary sector, in services and distribution. This process has generally continued into the present with some decline in the financial services sector. There has been some increase in the labour force of small employers and a growth in the intrusion of foreign-owned multinationals in manufacturing and the utilities. Employment in the public sector remained static in the 1980s, with some decline in the 1990s. However, as pointed out in Chapter 2, recent increases in the employed labour force have come predominantly from the public sector – a trend continuing into the twenty-first century. In the secondary sector there has been a rise in part-time and subcontracted labour. All of these trends – apart from recent change in the public sector – have been seen as detrimental to the future of trade union organisation and as challenging traditional collective bargaining and labour relations arrangements.

New technology – information technology in particular – is seen as underpinning these changes. Such technology has facilitated the reorganisation of markets on an international basis and promoted their deregulation. It also allows for the decentralisation of responsibility by the development of cost centres or divisional units. This should not be confused with a decentralisation of power.

How fundamental all of this is to the relationship between capital and labour is a matter for debate. Much of the identified change has been associated with a depression in economic activity during the 1980s and 1990s on a scale only surpassed in the past 100 years by that of the 1930s. Employers in the United Kingdom have certainly been using the combination of new technology and economic circumstances to establish greater control over the workforce. Government policy and legislation have encouraged employers to do so. Similarly, the government as an employer has promoted privatisation and the decentralisation of responsibility.

Management

Ownership of the means of production confers legal rights on such owners. This is true of such ownership whether it is public or private. The nature and location of ownership might affect the manner in which these rights are exercised but such rights exist regardless of this. On a day-by-day basis these rights are usually exercised by management. Whether or not management legitimacy is perceived as deriving from this source or from management expertise will depend upon how legitimacy is defined.

For the purpose of this text the terms manager and employer will be used interchangeably to designate those who exercise power and line authority on behalf of those who own. Like shop stewards, they act in a representative capacity. Historically employers have organised themselves by alliances which have joined them across and between industries, and this is our starting point.

Employers' Associations

Employers have organised both for the purpose of regulating relationships with trade unions and employees and for the purposes of combining in the market place to fix prices and control competition. We are mainly concerned with the first purpose. Employers' associations concerned with regulating the employment relationship generally emerged in response to trade union organisation in the nineteenth century. Early trade unionists often referred to them as 'unions of masters'. Employers were sometimes faced by the tactic of being singled out by unions to secure gains which could then be forced on other employers. This would also allow unions to fund such actions from contributions of the employees of those employers still operating. A response by employers was to come together and lock out all employees in an area of the trade and thus cut off funds to strikers. It followed from this that employers would combine to try to enforce terms and conditions in line with their own objectives. Like trade unions, they often had conflicts of interest between them, within their associations, and thus developed membership rules and requirements to secure solidarity.

It was not always possible to separate out trade functions from wage and conditions regulation. Standardisation of wage costs could be an important prerequisite for preventing price-cutting competition in the product market. Often, as union organisation declined, so did the employer association relationship. As unions became permanent organisations, so did the employers' associations. Similarly, as trade unions moved from being locally based to nationally based, so did they.

Implicit in the above are the reasons why employers joined such associations. They were designed to protect individual employers against union demands and they provided a basis for adopting common policies on wage levels and control of the workforce. There is a history of lockouts, strike insurance funds and attempts to force employees to withdraw from unions. Sometimes employers' associations encouraged the development of collective bargaining machinery by taking the initiative on the formation of what were then called boards of conciliation and arbitration. Employers' associations also took initiatives on the development of procedure agreements for dealing with grievances and disputes. As one would expect, they also acted as pressure groups for political and other purposes.

The government of employers' associations also mirrors that of trade unions. They have chief executives, executive committees and conferences. Along with their bargaining and general market functions they provide a range of information and research services. There is also a general body – the Confederation of British Industry (CBI) – to which most associations are affiliated. Like the TUC, it acts as a pressure group and provides a major source of employer representation on tripartite bodies.

In recent years, the growth of single-employer bargaining, with an emphasis on company and plant levels, has resulted in a decline in association memberships. Similarly, large multinational companies have tended to withdraw from the kinds of bargaining arrangements fostered by such associations as well as wishing to remove themselves from the influence of small employers sheltering under the umbrella of the associations. The CBI has been seen on the other hand as largely concerned with the interests of a declining manufacturing sector and not representative of the growing service sector. In the 1980s, the government displayed less sympathy to the corporate orientation of the CBI, and, like the TUC, it has felt its influence waning.

Membership of employers' associations

1968	75% of firms
1980	25% of establishments
1994	13% of establishments
1998	18% of establishments

Number of employers' associations

1968	1350
1989	293
1994	117
2004	95

Sources: Donovan (1968); Millward *et al.*
(1992); Certification Office.

If employers' associations are seen as a reaction to trade unions, the decline indicated above does appear to match that of trade unions.

In a survey of employers' associations (IRS, 1994), more than half the respondents identified a decline in their membership over the previous three years. The membership of the associations was reported to consist mainly of small employers, evenly split between those employing less than 20 and those employing up to 500. A growing role was advising, and lobbying, on EU legislation. Just under one-half of the respondents saw their associations as predominantly employers' associations, rather than trade associations, with most playing a dual role.

Two-thirds of the respondents reported that they represented employers in multi-employer bargaining (see Chapter 6). Three-quarters of these bargaining bodies set minimum rates of pay, with the remainder setting actual rates. Ninety-two per cent of these established industry-wide agreements on holidays and holiday pay, with the length of working week and overtime premia also being widely determined by these bodies. Three-quarters of these also had industry-wide disputes procedures. Members involved in such bargaining saw saving of management time and the prevention of leapfrogging pay claims as the main advantages of this.

The Enterprise

In the early days of industrialisation, the unit of production was usually specific to one location – ownership coincided with production at the equivalent to a plant. The owner built up the business and managed it in all respects – including both production and marketing. Revenues from sales generated surpluses over production costs, providing the owner with an income which could be partly or mainly invested in the growth of the business. A classic entrepreneur of the late eighteenth century – such as Josiah Wedgwood – built up a large business by even modern standards using just these methods. He eventually brought in outside sources of finance, mainly from borrowing, but retained full control of the business. Wedgwood thus pioneered the growth of the business, managed all aspects of its finance and production, controlled and disciplined the labour force and was an inventor.

Many such enterprises remained small, and still do. However, during the nineteenth century, other enterprises expanded and became nationally based, with plants and units of production in many locations, including abroad. This process was helped by the growth of banking as a source of finance and the development of the joint-stock company which followed from the introduction of limited liability for shareholders. Corporate ownership began to succeed single-person or family ownership, although such ownership remained concentrated in few hands.

The Private Sector

The above illustrates something of the origins of the private ownership of industry, as opposed to state or some other form of public ownership. Company law in the United Kingdom requires the directors of a company to give priority to the interests of the shareholders. The interests of those who own are given explicit priority over those of the providers of labour. From a unitarist perspective, this does not matter because these interests actually coincide.

Although there is a mix of ownership forms, what is owned varies considerably in size and variety. The large enterprise predominates. As suggested earlier, the location of ownership can vary from the small local enterprise to the large multinational; the enterprise might produce a variety of products or services. Purcell and Ahlstrand (1994) place considerable emphasis on the recent growth of multi-product, or conglomerate, enterprises and the need for divisions specialising in particular products. If a single enterprise combines the production of newspapers, pottery, books, ladies' underwear and so on as a consequence of buying up other enterprises, what will the decision-making process be in the total unit? Is industrial relations affected by the arrangements for overall government of the enterprise?

These questions are generally asked but not answered. All that can be said is that elaborate management and shareholding structures will tend to generate coalitions which may create interests in conflict with those of the shareholders. In the neoclassical model, enterprises aim to maximise profits. Critics of the model suggest other possibilities – to maximise growth or secure stability, for example. The difficulty with such objectives is that they are not mutually exclusive. Size and profitability might go together; on the other hand, if the pursuit of size or stability weakens profitability then shareholders may take their money elsewhere. Another major problem in making such distinctions is the difficulty of offsetting short-run considerations against long-run ones. Maximising in the short run might conflict with maximising in the long run and vice versa.

There is a considerable debate about the extent to which the owners of capital exercise power over those who manage it. A classic scenario portrays expert managers persuading ignorant, but key, shareholders to accept policies which serve the interests of the managers (Galbraith, 1967). (This is replicated in the public sector through 'Yes, Minister' style scenes – gullible cabinet ministers bamboozled by clever civil servants at the expense of the electorate.) Opinion on where power lies in terms of this particular debate again often depends as much on the perspective held as on the evidence, given the difficulty of devising empirical tests for such propositions. Unitarists and conflict theorists tend to assert the primacy of capital – unitarists explain it in terms of the market which will punish the less profitable, and conflict theorists in terms of the nature of ownership, associated power and the need for control. Given that power is regarded as an important variable in labour relations, perceptions of where it lies and how it is exercised are of some importance.

What can be said is that the size, nature and complexity of ownership will affect labour relations. Millward *et al.* (1992: ch. 3) showed that union membership had a strong positive relationship with size of establishment (basically plant or workplace); it also noted that the decline in recognition of trade unions was more marked in establishments independent of larger organisations, although greater in foreign-owned ones; UK-based multinationals were more likely to have a greater number of bargaining units than those owned by UK companies solely based in the United Kingdom. It is not possible to explore these variations in detail here. Suffice it to say that size and ownership structure were linked to labour relations variables. It has always been difficult for unions to organise in markets dominated by small outlets, such as retailing and agriculture, although both contain large and multinational corporations.

Whatever the market model, varying degrees of market power and structure are identified. Monopoly conditions might allow for higher pay and inefficiencies. Millward *et al.* (1992: 247) identified some relationship between lower pay and greater levels of competition. A difficulty, of course, with this kind of analysis is that the size of establishment – company, corporation or whatever – is not independent of the market structure.

The Public Sector

Chapter 3 gave data showing a much higher level of union density in the public sector than in the private sector. There are other differences. For a clear delineation of what constitutes the public sector, and for detail, see Kessler and Bayliss (1995: ch. 7). In general terms the public sector comprises the central government, local authorities and public corporations. It is still a large sector, employing over 20 per cent of the UK total labour force, 60 per cent of whom are female, although the latter are disproportionately located in part-time and low-paid posts.

Winchester and Bach (1995: 308), following Fredman and Morris (1989) suggest '*The decline of the model employer*...Since the end of the First World War British governments have recognised the need to act as a good employer to promote stable industrial relations.' In this analysis 'model' has become synonymous with 'good'. The main ingredients of model/good employership are seen to be active support for trade unions; fostering of collective bargaining; 'fair wages' established through private sector comparisons; job security; good pensions and sick leave; and firmly established procedures on discipline, grievance matters and disputes.

Winchester and Bach (1995: 310) go on to tell us that from 1979 'the government abandoned its position of good employer and encouraged a more abrasive style of public-sector management.' They do admit that the good employer role was applied unevenly and that low pay was a feature of sectors of public employment. However, there are other weaknesses in this approach. One is that the characteristics of the good employer that they refer to were more part of the rhetoric of the post-1945 period than of that between the wars. The post-1918 consensus broke down very quickly.

Perhaps more importantly, what constitutes a 'good' employer is a matter of perspective. In Conservative Government rhetoric, the so-called model employer of the years up to 1979 is in fact a bad employer, who fosters inefficient employment practices which are to the detriment of all. The Conservative approach has been to introduce a new type of good/model employer. Now trade unions are seen as detrimental and to be discouraged. The closed shop inhibits individual rights, and collective bargaining distorts pay. Imposing wage conditions, minimum pay, and trade union recognition on contractors reduces employment levels by increasing costs. Employers must be able to take free advantage of the market place by securing the lowest cost deals – hence compulsory competitive tendering. Security of employment militates against employment on merit. Pay is to be related to individual performance, and employment must be as flexible as possible. Employees must have the right to purchase their own individual pension schemes, sick pay insurance and so on.

A paradox of the Conservative notion of a good/model employer is that it is based on an idealised private employer operating in a free market. Public-sector employment is inevitably 'bad'. Being 'privatised' is another essential feature of the conservative model employer. The public-sector employer mimicking the idealised private-sector employer is a stage towards full privatisation. Agency status, the internal market in the NHS, opting out of schools, private loans for higher-education students and so on are examples of this intermediate process. Privatisation can also be achieved by outright sale of public corporations on favourable terms – the sale of British Rail being a good example.

Sources of finance have important consequences for labour relations. Requirements to secure private finance through revenue-raising schemes force public-sector employers into activities which inevitably decentralise pay determination. This is reinforced by government pressures to decentralise activities via the breakup of utilities for the purposes of sale and by direct centralised pressures to decentralise in the civil service, health and education. We see highly centralised collective bargaining in traditionally public sector activities being decentralised, with a consequent devolvement of pay determination.

At the time of writing, Britain is left with a large and influential public sector, but it was in decline as an employer of labour and as a proportion of economic activity. We also see a devolvement or decentralisation of bargaining in what remains. This process of decentralisation of bargaining is much more marked in the public sector than in the private sector.

Management Strategy

In giving content to a concept such as management strategy, the definition of management is at least as important as the definition of strategy. The equating of management with employer at the beginning of this chapter implicitly emphasises the importance of structure – the need to

generate profit sufficient to survive in a competitive environment transmitted through the organisation by those who have been delegated line
authority. It would follow from this that a key role of management is to
minimise costs and especially labour costs. On the other hand, management itself is employed and is thus part of the labour force.
Management also needs to be controlled and prevented from pursuing
objectives of its own which may conflict with those linked to maximising profits. The process of management, and any associated strategy,
inevitably contains contradictions.

According to Hyman (1987: 27), 'In the literature on and for capitalist
management, the notion of strategy has become increasingly popular;
yet its meaning is often elusive and imprecise.' He goes on to quote
Chandler on strategy, which 'can be defined as the determination of
the basic long-term goals and objectives of an enterprise, and the adop-
tion of courses of action and the allocation of resources necessary for
carrying out these goals' (p. 28). This raises obvious questions in respect
of choices which seem to be a necessary component of the concept of
strategy. A structural definition of management implies some restriction on choice – they are constrained by the need for profit. Similarly
there are other constraints; Ormerod (1994: 197) says:

> Around any underlying growth rate, economies move in cycles...When a major
> shock takes place, such as the 1973–4 oil-price increases, the pattern of regular,
> cyclical behaviour is broken, and a period of irregular behaviour occurs, before
> economies settle into new, steady cycles.

There may, of course, be laws of both regular and irregular behaviour,
and ultimately of economic cycles, but it does appear to be implied that
within capitalism they have a life of their own. These must constrain
choice in terms of any notion of management strategy. Interestingly,
economists seem to believe that some control can be exercised, that
there is discretion. Nevertheless, they leave us with the odd conclusion
that 'In principle, policy-makers have the tools to reduce fluctuations
in the economy, but in practice they frequently make things worse'
(Lipsey and Chrystal, 1995: 856). This may be true of managers,
although 'worse' is clearly a pejorative term. Perhaps actions are best
described as having unintended and unwished-for consequences. See
Chapter 13 of this book for concepts of strategy linked to changing the
relationship between employers and trade unions.

As one peruses the literature on strategy it becomes apparent that
there is only agreement around the notion that the concept itself is prob-
lematic. It is a very short step from this to the belief that there is no such
thing as 'best practice' or to Hyman's suggestion that 'It is on this basis
that managerial strategy can best be conceptualised: *as the programmatic*

choice among alternatives none of which can prove satisfactory' 1987: 30; italics in the original). Storey and Sisson (1993: 71) quote Marginson et al. in respect of recent industrial relations practices as applied by companies they researched:

> They suggest, alternatively, that pragmatic and opportunistic responses to changing economic and labour market conditions appear a more valid explanation. Indeed, they observe, 'it is a moot point whether it is appropriate to dignify management's approach to industrial relations with the adjective "strategic".'

Indeed, one might ask, 'why not'? Opportunism and pragmatism may well be appropriate strategic responses – who knows?

Storey and Sisson go on to explain the difficulties of linking a human resource management (HRM) strategy to a business strategy, even if such a thing could be deemed to exist. In the end they reach what could be described as an opportunistic and pragmatic conclusion: 'We suggest, none the less, that they [managers] do have some "choice", and that there is often a great deal that can be done by managers who are prepared to question the conventional wisdom.' This comes as something of a relief. For further guidance, and as an oblique reference to the pervasive role of new technology, I would add for managers Joseph Heller's caveat that 'anything that can happen will happen'.

Rather than worrying about the applicability of tautological concepts of strategy it may be more appropriate to identify patterns of managerial behaviour and perhaps contextualise these in economic and historical terms. Responses to the recent economic crisis and the growth in competition, combined with the impact of information technology and increased globalisation of production – all linked – seem to have produced a focus on cutting labour costs, and this has had effects on the behaviour of functional managers within the field of labour relations.

If we examine the public sector, whatever the weaknesses of the concept of strategy, it is possible to suggest that its use there has some meaning. The NHS has witnessed the development of line management; the introduction of trusts and an internal market; a shift to primary care and the community; a massive planned, and actual, increase in day case interventions; some decentralisation of bargaining and the dismantling of Whitley and many other changes. During the Labour Government's period of office we have witnessed since 2000 the implementation of the NHS Plan – a 10-year-plan setting numerous targets in terms of outcomes in relation to various illnesses and conditions. This has virtually doubled NHS expenditure, has certainly improved UK healthcare provision whilst having unintended consequences in terms of pay and public support. To suggest that all of this is a hotchpotch of opportunism and pragmatism rather than calculated tactics in pursuit of objectives would be very odd indeed.

Functional Management: Personnel

The term 'personnel manager' is the one most associated with the manager who has responsibility for labour relations. This role began to develop separately out of a concern by employers with the difficulties arising from employing large numbers and the consequent lack of personal contact with individual employees. In 1896, Rowntree established a welfare department and employed a Miss Wood, a former teacher, to oversee it. She was described as a representative of the workforce who should give advice to workers on their work and personal matters, respond to grievances and encourage educational interests. The role further developed to include recruitment of unskilled staff and to suggest improvements in terms and conditions of employment.

This early origin is worth mentioning if only because there has been a notion that the personnel manager was an independent person acting as between management and the labour force, who would advise in some apparently neutral way between the parties. To some extent this is incorporated in notions of professionalisation of the function (see below). A residual belief is that the personnel role is somehow 'soft' on the employee, and this has made it vulnerable to attacks from 'macho'-style management.

The personnel function is seen as predominantly concerned with human resourcing – recruiting and selecting staff, human resource planning, health and safety, labour relations – bargaining, discipline and grievance handling, employee development, for example, training and appraisal, and so on. Enterprises have always required these functions which have gradually come together to provide some description of the personnel function. Theoretically, the personnel manager, or labour or industrial relations manager, is in a staff position acting as an adviser to line management – giving advice that may or may not be accepted. His or her line authority is thus confined to personnel department staff. In practice such managers may be board members with inputs into business planning and strategy.

In recent years the term 'human resource manager' has been widely used as a replacement for 'personnel manager'. Attempts have been made to establish a clear distinction between the two. Generally these revolve around notions that the human resource manager is more linked to strategy, is unitarist in approach and so on. HRM is often associated with the application of such things as total quality management

(TQM) and just in time (JIT) systems (see Chapter 12). In fact, in much of the literature, these terms – HRM, TQM, JIT – are used interchangeably (see Burchill and Casey, 1996). Associated techniques – psychometric testing, numerical, pay and hours flexibility, PRP, downgrading of collective bargaining and unions, the growth of individual contracts and appraisal and so on – could all be seen as current practices within the field of personnel management. All of these developments can be associated with market conditions related to the current phase of the economic cycle, with little new in them. In this analysis, the term HRM is simply a replacement for the term personnel management, perhaps being applied to give legitimacy to a resurgence of scientific management and more extensive exploitation of labour. The rhetoric of HRM, TQM and JIT thus becomes the rhetoric of current human relations approaches to rationalising the exploitation of labour. Again, in this model the 'hard' and 'soft' approaches to HRM (Storey, 1992) are seen not as competing or contradictory but rather as complementary – the 'soft' approach, rooted in human relations, is designed to make palatable and acceptable the underlying 'hard' approach, rooted in scientific management and structure, often producing a dual message of competition and collaboration: an emphasis on team working and PRP; loyalty, commitment and short-term contracts; statements to the effect that a company's human resources are its most valued assets combined with large-scale redundancies.

The professionalisation of personnel practices is fostered by the Chartered Institute of Personnel and Development (CIPD), and possession of its qualification, which requires both academic and practical expertise, is widely established as a prerequisite for posts in the field. Notions of devolving the personnel function to line managers would seem to conflict with this idea of professionalism. But, in practice, line managers have always made final decisions on such things as recruitment, selection, pay and so on, while on the other hand, if such decisions are made without professional personnel advice, or without being overseen by a centrally responsible department, then laws will be broken and nepotism will creep in.

The CIPD has buttressed the professional role by introducing codes of conduct for members. Nevertheless, its control over labour supply does not extend to statutory registers. Anybody can be allocated the role of personnel manager, but someone who has witnessed the activities of a well-organised and well-qualified group of personnel staff will recognise the need for expertise in this area and its value to an enterprise.

All managers to the extent that they have line authority will be involved in personnel functions and in our particular area of interest, namely labour relations.

Conclusion and Further Reading

The main purpose of this chapter has been to identify the role of management in labour relations at both the macro and micro levels. Management ideologies were discussed in Chapter 1, and an understanding of these can illustrate the fact that perceptions of the relationship between HRM and personnel management will very much depend upon the perspective which is brought to our analysis.

6

Collective Bargaining

The term 'collective bargaining' was invented by Beatrice Webb, and propagated by the Webbs, to describe the process of agreeing terms and conditions of employment through representatives of employers – possibly their associations, probably managers – and representatives of the employees, probably their unions. It was seen by them as primarily a substitute for the employer bargaining singly with each employee and establishing individual contracts of employment. Collective agreements are not substitutes for individual contracts. What is agreed collectively is implied, or inserted, into each employee's contract. From the employee's point of view, it helps to mitigate the uneven balance in bargaining power between an employer and an individual employee. It follows from the above that collective bargaining is essentially a representative process in which representatives of employers reach agreements, or compromises, with the representatives of employees.

Such bargaining is not a discrete process whereby agreements are reached on a periodic basis but a continuous process which calls for the maintenance, regulation, interpretation and supplementation of such agreements on a day-by-day basis. Where it does take place, it is a major determinant of the rules which govern the relationships between the parties at the place of work. However, it is not the sole determinant. Management makes some rules unilaterally, without bargaining; so, sometimes, do workers. Other rules are made by the government through legislation. On occasions, employers, unions and the government have established joint agreements. The literature often talks about 'unilateral' (one-sided), 'bilateral' or 'joint' (collective bargaining) and 'tripartite' (government, union and employer) rule-making. The latter is probably more consistently described as 'trilateral'.

In Chapter 1, collective bargaining was described as a pluralist concept *par excellence*. More accurately, it is better described as something encouraged by those who take a pluralist viewpoint. From this viewpoint, it is rationalised as efficient not only because it provides a mechanism for dealing with inherent conflict which could be destructive to all if not resolved but also because it can be an economic way of dealing with the labour force – common settlements make sense where there is a homogeneous labour force. According to the Donovan Commission (1968, par. 212), 'Properly conducted, collective bargaining is the most efficient means of giving workers the right to representation in decisions affecting their working lives, a right which is or should be the prerogative of every worker in a democratic society.'

From a unitarist perspective, such bargaining can inhibit the free flow of market forces by standardising terms and conditions of employment. It can prevent the proper use of incentives to the individual and thus reduce motivation and productivity. A worker will best have a say by directly negotiating a contract and having the ability to move elsewhere. The corporatist implications of collective bargaining generate inertia by legitimising the *status quo*.

This latter point could be incorporated within a conflict perspective, which would be more likely to see collective bargaining as an acknowledgement of power by both parties. It has no intrinsic merits, and attempts to identify these, especially by management, are simply a rationalisation, rather than admission, of its own impotence. Management, like the union, is forced to bargain out of weakness. As the balance of power shifts, so also dos the content of collective bargaining and the willingness, or otherwise, of employers to recognise unions. It is an expedient – a response to force of circumstance. Recognition (see Chapter 3) may be a prerequisite of collective bargaining, but the two should not be confused. Recognition may be a device, probably second best, for manipulating the labour force and transforming the bargaining relationship forced on the employer into something weaker – preferably consultation – see below. In times of national crisis the institutions of collective bargaining, especially the trade unions, provide a mechanism whereby the state might secure the cooperation of labour, to be discarded when possible.

Coverage of Collective Bargaining

Whatever our perspective on the institution, it is possible to describe the main features of collective bargaining. Although it is in decline, in terms of coverage, many employees in the United Kingdom are still affected by collective bargaining. Measurement of the extent of this coverage is complicated by the fact that collective agreements may be comprehensive and partial. For a discussion of the problems in respect of the United Kingdom see Milner (1995).

The coverage rate of collective bargaining relates to the proportion of workers covered by collective agreements. In 1993, according to the Organisation for Economic Co-operation and Development (OECD), with some exceptions which include the United Kingdom, the coverage of collective bargaining remained static for the previous decade. Where decline took place, it was most dramatic in the United Kingdom, with a fall of 20 per cent over 12 years. The rate for the United Kingdom in 1990 is given as 47 per cent, after a peak of around 70 per cent in the mid-1970s. The fall in coverage is attributed to the removal of statutory support for recognition and to the withdrawal of the government and employers from the presumption that collective bargaining was helpful (Millward, 1994).

The 47 per cent figure is derived from Millward *et al.* (1992). A difficulty with this survey is that part of the explanation includes the suggestion that 'two large groups of workers losing their negotiating rights – the teachers and nurses' – contributed to this (p. 94). If this is reflected in survey responses then the figure is underestimated. Nurses certainly did not lose their negotiating rights, even at national level. The Pay Review Body method of approaching pay determination is within the sphere of collective bargaining and not outside it (see Chapter 8, later, especially the discussion of mediation). Collective bargaining on other matters also takes place at local level. In the NHS we have recently seen the negotiation of a consultant contract, a GP contract and Agenda for Change all agreed directly with the relevant unions and independently of the Review Bodies. This surely constitutes collective bargaining. Similarly, firefighters were excluded from collective bargaining coverage statistics because of their pay formula. If they were not covered by collective bargaining how do we explain their recent industrial action?

The latest Kersley *et al.* (2006) places coverage of collective bargaining in all workplaces at 40 per cent. For the private sector the figure given is 26 per cent with unilateral pay setting given as the most widely used approach to pay.

Bargaining Levels

Bargaining levels relate to the location of bargaining which can take place in such a way, for example, that it covers a whole industry at national level or at regional or local level. Such bargaining may include several enterprises. On the other hand, bargaining might take place at the level of the enterprise; it may take place at divisional level within an enterprise or at the level of the establishment or plant or shopfloor. None of these levels need be exclusive. In the public sector, for example, nurses pay was traditionally negotiated at national level; now it has been partly devolved to the level of the trust, with an element at national level remaining.

In the early days, bargaining took place predominantly at local level, sometimes with industry-wide bargaining at this level. As the nineteenth century ended, more nationally based industry-wide bargaining emerged. Trade unionists were interested in establishing a rate for the job which offered some protection against the vagaries of the market place. Employers, as suggested in Chapter 5, often wished to standardise wages to protect themselves from low-cost competition and to prevent leapfrogging wage rates and the poaching of labour. The whole process was encouraged by the government through the Royal Commission on Labour's recommendations of 1891 and eventually by those of the Whitley Committee of 1917, both of which encouraged the notion of setting terms and conditions beyond the level of the factory or plant.

The real push towards more centralised bargaining came from the First World War. Rapid inflation and the need for government to take control of essential industries led to wage fixing at national level, as unions bypassed local arrangements and sought intervention. The Donovan Commission, reporting in 1968, saw the type of industrial relations which emerged from these pressures and recommendations – with strong employers and strong trade unions reaching detailed national agreements on all issues – as less relevant to the situation which existed some twenty years after the Second World War. What the Donovan Commission mainly identified was a dislocation between what was described as the formal arrangements for procedures and bargaining and what it called the informal arrangements. Twenty years and more of sustained full employment and economic growth had shifted the balance of power to the workforce, which had used this power at the place of work. The so-called official institutions, of which the industry-wide agreement was an output, had become remote from the reality of bargaining. Pay and terms and conditions as contained in these agreements were far from actual pay and terms and conditions because of all the additions negotiated at shopfloor level. These included not only straightforward additions to nationally negotiated rates, but piecework payments, overtime payments, bonuses and so on, all negotiated at the place of work. Shop stewards were seen to have wrested power from full-time officials and national negotiating committees.

National procedure agreements were being ignored by workers seeking solutions at the place of work and able to achieve these by the use of industrial action. The Commission made recommendations:

> Factory-wide agreements can however provide the remedy. Factory agreements (with company agreements as an alternative in multi-plant companies) can regulate actual pay, constitute a factory negotiating committee and grievance procedures which suit the circumstances, deal with such subjects as redundancy and discipline and cover the rights and obligations of shop stewards. A factory agreement can assist competent managers; many current industry-wide agreements have become a hindrance to them. Industry-wide agreements should be limited to those matters they can effectively regulate; but there would be an advantage in agreements between employers' associations and trade unions which set out guide-lines for acceptable company or factory agreements and exempt the latter from the obligation to uphold all terms of the existing industry-wide agreements.

The Commission was concerned with what it saw as the consequences of what it called 'disorderly bargaining'. Productivity and pay were said not to be linked to each other, thus producing an inflationary outcome and ultimately undermining the competitiveness of the UK economy. There was no adequate bargaining machinery to allow for the development of an effective incomes policy. Other aspects of the Donovan Commission are dealt with later. The Commission reinforced, through its recommendations, the concept of industrial relations in the United Kingdom, being a voluntary system. The law was seen to play a small part, and Donovan's view was that this should remain so. Essentially the institutions of UK industrial relations needed adjustment to bring them into line with decentralised bargaining.

An assessment of the extent to which Donovan's analysis matched any kind of reality is very much a matter of perspective, although its neglect of the public sector in the analysis was a glaring omission. By the mid-1960s, trade unions and strikes had become a central political issue. The mass media and the Conservative Party had developed the notion that trade unions had become too powerful and needed both reform and legislative control to deal with this. The Donovan Commission reported at a time, then, when trade union power had become a politically sensitive issue and trade unions were also closely related to the Labour Party, which was in office. A possible view of the Commission was that it was established by a Labour Government with the task of defusing the political issues associated with such a government introducing laws which the trade unions would strongly oppose. This is not to suggest that the conduct of labour relations does not have important economic consequences. What it does suggest is that the possibility of establishing some objective model of reform which is seen to be neutral in its consequences for the balance of power between the parties, and seen to be mutually beneficial to them, is non-existent. Reforms will ultimately be rationalised in terms which reflect the interests of those most likely to benefit from them.

As indicated in the introduction to this chapter, the structure of collective bargaining is a complex concept. The extracts from Donovan, and comments on these, also suggest that it is an important one. Manipulation of the level at which bargaining takes place is an important tactic in securing control and is used by the parties as such.

Bargaining may include more than one employer (i.e. be multi-employer); it may be single-employer and multi-plant; either of the above may be combined at national, regional or local level. It is possible, thus, to talk about single- and multi-tier bargaining, with separate issues being decided at different levels or tiers. Two-tier bargaining with multi-employer, industry-wide bargaining being supplemented at plant or enterprise level is an option used widely in Europe. According to Brown *et al.* (1995), using data from a variety of sources, the proportion of private employees in the United Kingdom covered by multi-employer bargaining declined from 60 per cent in 1950 to 10 per cent in 1990. There is also a trend away from plant bargaining towards enterprise bargaining. In the public sector, the trend has been away from national bargaining towards a more local system. In terms of factors which might determine bargaining levels in the private sector, ACAS (1983) tells us:

> In examining the factors that appear to be associated with particular bargaining levels in the private sector, the evidence suggests that industries which have highly competitive product markets, which are composed of a large number of small companies each with a small market share, which are labour-intensive or geographically concentrated will, other things being equal, tend to have multi-employer bargaining. To some extent representational factors will work in the same direction, with both employers and trade unions in industries characterised by a large number of small firms and a competitive market preferring multi-employer bargaining. Single-employer bargaining is likely to be preferred by a company which is dominant in an industry, in industries where there are relatively few firms each of which has a sizeable share and where companies wish to introduce their own wage payment system or productivity agreement.

Rationalisations of the above pattern are easy to devise. Where the product market is competitive, the argument that employers will want to standardise labour costs is one such rationalisation. It is possible to argue that the opposite would be true. The more competitive the market, the more the gains to be made by taking initiatives to minimise labour costs – especially if labour is in abundant supply. Leapfrogging is difficult for labour in such conditions. The Conservative emphasis on decentralisation, even away from collective bargaining at all, could reflect this.

Bargaining Units

This term defines the group(s) of employees covered by an agreement. It is closely related, but not identical, to the concept of level. For example, in the NHS all clinical staff might be grouped together even though they belong to separate unions. A grading structure might be negotiated which includes solely nurses, midwives and health visitors. Negotiations could then be undertaken solely with those unions which represent them – RCN, RCM, MSF, UNISON and so on. A bargaining unit could consist of a group of workers represented by one union or a multiplicity of unions. Where there is more than one union there is often competition for members. The NHS, for example, contains over 40 unions with membership divided between TUC and non-TUC affiliates. For a period, employers there were faced with a situation where TUC affiliates refused to 'sit down' with non-TUC affiliates at local level and this caused serious administrative problems for management.

Those who bargain on behalf of units are called bargaining agents. Employers will generally want to simplify bargaining units and agents – they prefer wider units and fewer agents, at whichever level bargaining takes place. A wider unit is not necessarily a larger one – it could mean at the level of an operation all members of a cost centre. Attempts to deal with all agents simultaneously is referred to as single-table bargaining. This may help prevent leapfrogging claims and reduce bargaining time. Where the agents represent a wide variety of staff such bargaining can be difficult because of the wide range of interests involved. Hospital trusts might prefer a single table for issues such as disciplinary and grievance procedures, but may prefer separate – or functional – negotiations on pay and conditions with doctors, nurses, ancillary staff and other groups.

The Content of Bargaining

Collective bargaining, as already suggested, is one process determining rules at the place of work. Its existence reflects the growth of organisations of workers, in particular trade unions, and the constraints placed on employers by such organisations along with acknowledgement of such constraints by employers. The outcome of collective bargaining is collective agreements, which contain rules covering a whole range of workplace issues. Such agreements are compromises based on the relative power of the parties. Collective bargaining machinery institutionalises conflict.

Where collective bargaining exists, the issues covered may vary from arrangement to arrangement and over time. Notionally anything is negotiable within collective bargaining. In practice agreements tend to cover such things as hourly pay, overtime rates, bonuses, hours of work, holiday pay, productivity payments, grading issues and related matters. Such items are referred to as substantive. Agreements are also reached to cover the procedures to deal with such matters as disciplinary issues, grievances and disputes – referred to as procedural matters. A distinction is thus made between procedure agreements and substantive agreements. This is useful, but it has to be recognised that procedure agreements can contain substantive elements – such as the range of sanctions, for example.

Over time there was some growth in the range of issues included in collective bargaining. The concept of managerial prerogative has been referred to earlier in this text. It refers to areas of decision making where managers claim the right to decide unilaterally – the 'right to manage'. Clearly, organised labour can inhibit such a 'right' by use of its power, and this power relationship has generally determined what is negotiable.

Given that notionally anything is negotiable, it is interesting that collective bargaining has remained largely confined to pay and terms and conditions of employment. Widening the scope of collective bargaining to include such issues as marketing and investment policy has rarely happened, although on occasion unions have tried to use their power to prevent both in such places as South Africa. If collective bargaining is a way in which workers can have a say in issues which affect them, then the content of collective bargaining could be seen to have some relevance to notions of industrial democracy – a point to be taken up later.

A theme throughout this text has been the shift in the balance of power from workers to employers in recent years. This has meant that employers have been able to extend bargaining to secure concessions from the workforce on productivity, for example. Such developments do not really widen the content of bargaining.

Joint Consultation

It has already been suggested that recognition of unions does not necessarily imply that collective bargaining will take place. Employers may simply wish to recognise trade unions in line with the unitary perception that unions may be a useful extension of the organisation's bureau-cracy. They can be used as a channel of communication, which becomes more open and freer because the views of the workforce may be more readily expressed through representatives, removing individual employ-ees from the firing line. In the consultative model, unions can be informed of management's plans and, after discussion with their mem-bers, possibly come up with useful suggestions as to how these may be modified to better secure objectives. In this model, the ultimate deci-sion remains with management. In the Whitley proposals, national bar-gaining was to be supplemented at the level of operation by the establishment of formal joint consultation machinery.

The word 'joint' before 'consultation' suggests a representative pro-cess, usually involving unions. It is thus distinct from direct communi-cation with individual employees. At face value, joint consultation is best seen as a method whereby the parties better understand each oth-er's problems to their mutual advantage. Management gains informa-tion from the workforce, which better enables it to refine its plans and objectives and to implement and achieve them more effectively. The workers are able to identify clearly the benefits of cooperation. On the other hand, it might be a device for pre-empting independent union development and manipulating the workforce leadership. It may be similarly used for bypassing collective bargaining and undermining the original purposes of union recognition. In the Whitley model, it is a direct supplement to collective bargaining, and in the NHS, this has been very much the case.

Whitley certainly saw the process as one of making more effective use of the expertise of the workforce and of educating it to the mutual benefit of the parties. Following the Whitley Report, many consultation committees were established, but most did not survive the 1920s. A difficulty with measuring the extent of joint consultation is that in practice it often does overlap with bargaining. Worker responses to information can contain implied threats, which may inhibit plans related to such information.

In 1976, as part of a general review of the Whitley Council System as operated in the NHS, Lord McCarthy highlighted all the problems associated with the concept. He certainly saw it as an important adjunct to collective bargaining and as an essential ingredient in the efficient running of the service. In his recommendations, he made a statement which actually became incorporated in the NHS Whitley agreement section on joint consultation:

It should be accepted that the mere passage of information is not consultation. Consultation involves an opportunity to influence decisions and their application. It is best conducted when some attention has been paid to alternatives, but they have not taken their final form.

This is as good a statement of the intent of joint consultation from a pluralist perspective as might be found. As far as the practice was concerned, McCarthy observed that the evidence he had received created an impression of the practice as 'immensely variable and not a little confusing'. Many managers were not sure what to consult about, and meetings often concerned themselves with trivia. Others found the process rewarding and constructive. These comments could be applied to experiences of joint consultation in general (see Marchington *et al.*, 1993).

There is no coherent evidence as to the extent of joint consultation practice. Some committees engage in negotiation, while some fail to meet regularly; agenda vary widely and, as suggested above, consultation inevitably overlaps with negotiation. In a period of rapid change, such as that occurring in the NHS, formal provision for consultation may be seen by management as unnecessarily delaying the decision-making process, and unions may use it for precisely that purpose. Managers often attempt to move towards more direct communication with the workforce in order to undermine joint consultation and, at the same time, trade union recognition. At the time of writing, the National Information and Consultation of Employees Regulations was having little impact in the United Kingdom.

Conclusion and Recommended Reading

Perhaps the main conclusion is that collective bargaining is still an important feature of labour relations both in the United Kingdom and in other European countries. This is not to deny that there has been some decline of its coverage in the United Kingdom, with the reservation that this has probably been exaggerated.

7

Procedures

Earlier in the book a distinction was made between procedural rules and substantive rules. It was suggested in passing that this distinction was probably oversimplified. Procedural rules contain substantive elements. For example, a disciplinary procedure may contain more or less severe sanctions or it may not allow for independent appeal. These are clearly matters of substance. Nevertheless, it does make sense to retain the distinction.

This chapter examines disciplinary and grievance procedures. Such procedures may be broadly characterised as the procedure used for disciplining employees (the disciplinary procedure) and the procedure used for disciplining the employer (the grievance procedure). This is not to suggest that they are evenly balanced in terms of their effectiveness. The chapter also comments on what are often referred to as Disputes Procedures.

Since the previous edition of this book was published there have been very substantial changes in the law relating to both discipline and dismissal.

Discipline

This section is concerned with discipline in the formal sense. Most workplaces have rules which are enforced by the use of sanctions against those who are perceived to have broken them, and it is the use of such sanctions in this connection that we have in mind when we consider discipline.

In the United Kingdom there is a legal requirement that employees receive a written statement of their terms and conditions of employment and that such statements must specify any disciplinary rules applicable to them and indicate the person to whom they should appeal if they are dissatisfied with any disciplinary decision.

Implicit in the above is the notion that the formal disciplinary procedure contains subprocesses. The first of these is the establishment of the rules themselves; the second is the establishment of sanctions; the third is the identification of the breaches of such rules and the fourth is the application of the appropriate sanction. Essentially we have all the ingredients of a legislative and judicial process. The determination of the rules and sanctions is a law-making process. Accusations of law breaking will lead to possible 'prosecution', a 'trial', possibly followed by 'conviction', a 'plea in mitigation' and the allocation of an appropriate 'sentence'.

From a unitarist perspective it will generally be argued that such a process is in everybody's interest; the rules reflect shared norms and have been designed to facilitate the achievement of commonly agreed objectives. A pluralist perspective will emphasise a degree of compromise implicit in the whole process, with the rules, and the rigour of their application, shifting with the balance of power. A conflict perspective might argue that the development of such procedures, with their apparently constitutional flavour, is designed to secure legitimacy for the coercive actions of the employer and to inhibit collective action.

Whatever the perspective, there is no doubt that such procedures have become much more widespread, formalised and standardised in the United Kingdom over the past 30 years. The introduction of legislation relating to unfair dismissal in 1971, and consequent decisions of the associated labour courts, has been a major factor in promoting these developments. These trends are confirmed by the research literature – especially the Workplace Employee Relations Surveys.

According to a survey conducted by IRS (1995, no.591) of the organisations which responded, on average 0.6 per cent of their workforce was dismissed for disciplinary purposes in any one year and 2.2 per cent had disciplinary action short of dismissal taken against it. Over half the respondents had faced an employment tribunal on unfair dismissal claims. Most organisations that responded ranked absenteeism as the main reason for dismissal, followed by performance, timekeeping, theft/fraud, sexual/racial harassment, verbal abuse, health and safety infringements, fighting and alcohol/drug abuse.

In 1977, the secretary of state approved a code of practice issued by ACAS pursuant to the relevant clauses of the Employment Protection Act 1975. The code, entitled *Disciplinary Practice and Procedures in Employment*, provided guidelines on these matters. Breach of the code by an employer did not in itself render the employer liable to proceedings before an employment tribunal, but where such proceedings do take place, tribunals take into account observance of the code. This code helped to reinforce the establishment of standardised procedures in workplaces, and this was further encouraged by the publication of the ACAS handbook, *Discipline at Work*, in 1987. The handbook offered general guidance on practice in a whole range of areas related to the matter of discipline and dismissal – how to deal with gross misconduct, long-term sickness, absence and so on.

The Employment Act of 2002 brought in extensive changes to the law relating to Unfair Dismissal by introducing statutory dismissal and disciplinary procedures linked to statutory grievance procedures. A concern of the Government was that although such procedures were more orderly than they had ever been, a number of employers, in particular those employing few employees, were the source of an unduly large number of Employment Tribunal cases. Statutory procedures were seen as a way of potentially reducing Employment Tribunal costs, without causing too much strain on mainstream employers, most of who already complied with what was introduced.

Before the 2004 Act there was no statutory obligation to have either a disciplinary procedure or a grievance procedure. Failure to have such procedures, or to properly manage them, could be taken into account by Employment Tribunals in reaching their decisions. Since the Act was introduced, an employer is expected to follow a defined sequence of actions before dismissing an employee. Where an employee qualifies for unfair dismissal and is dismissed without the employer following the defined sequence, the employee will be able to claim that the dismissal was automatically unfair. However, the employee is also expected to cooperate with the procedure – for example, to complete the procedure to appeal level before applying to an Employment Tribunal. Compensation could be increased, or reduced, by between 10 and 50 per cent depending upon the behaviour of the parties.

The statutory procedure is supported by guidance from ACAS Code of Practice 1 *Disciplinary and Grievance Procedures*, published in 2004. This Code points out that the statutory procedure is a minimum requirement and that even where followed the dismissal may still be unfair if the employer has not acted reasonably in all the circumstances. That Code and the *ACAS Discipline and Grievances at Work Handbook*, also published in 2004, provide a lot of guidance on what 'acting reasonably in all the circumstances' might mean.

The Statutory Procedure

Step 1 Write to the employee specifying allegations in terms of conduct, performance, capability- inviting them to a meeting, informing them of the right to be accompanied.

Step 2 Hold the meeting, discuss the grounds for any allegations, notify them of the decision and their right to appeal.

Step 3 If requested hold an appeal meeting, with a right to be accompanied, and inform them of the final decision.

The statutory procedure is clearly minimal. The ACAS Handbook provides a sample disciplinary procedure – described as for 'any organisation'. Essentially, it is simply a list of sanctions with some guiding principles. This is the case with most written procedures. However, they are usually supplemented by guides, designed to help managers, to the proper application of the process and subprocesses. Where trade unions are recognised, the whole process is usually negotiated and agreed. Nevertheless, however the process is determined, there is wide scope for variations in practice, even where procedures are very similar or with the same procedure over time. Many organisations go through phases of tightening up on discipline and this can be done 'judicially', that is by stricter interpretation of the rules, as well as 'legislatively', that is by making the rules more rigorous. References to 'macho' management often suggest that such changes are taking place. Where labour is in abundant supply it is easier to apply disciplinary sanctions without provoking organised reaction.

Emphases on equal opportunities, and associated anti-discrimination legislation, have led to more rigorous rules and applications of sanctions in these areas. Reduction of government subsidy of statutory sick pay has led to more control over sickness absence. Evidence relating to the effects of passive smoking has led to many more employers introducing rules inhibiting smoking at work. As suggested above, the decisions of labour courts, along with changes in the law, all influence discipline at work, along with shifts in the balance of power. The current exclusion of most employees with less than one year's continuous employment from the protection of the largest part of unfair-dismissal legislation, along with many part-time employees, means that a large part of the labour force is unprotected. It is precisely this section of the labour force that is most vulnerable to the arbitrary use of sanctions by the employer.

'Doing the Right Thing'

Whatever the underlying motive behind the establishment of formalised disciplinary procedures, such a procedure will require some
apparent consistency of application, at least in the short term, if it is to
acquire legitimacy and to satisfy the demands of tribunals. The procedure above grants both a right to accompaniment and a right of appeal.
These are requirements under statute. However, the right of accompaniment does not extend to formal legal representation within the
procedure. It is hard to imagine any rationalisation, within any of the
perspectives, which could give credibility to the involvement of 'lawyers'
at the place of work in such situations, and accompaniment is usually
confined to using a trade union officer or a colleague. The right of
appeal is to a higher level of management not directly associated with
the issue. Whether a right of appeal to an independent body, such as
ACAS, is included is a matter for agreement between the parties.
According to the Workplace Employee Relations Surveys such provisions are in decline. Again, this is probably a reflection of the shift in
the balance of power in favour of the employer, who probably feels that
there is less chance of collective reactions to individual decisions, and
prefers to act without external interference, with less need for external
legitimation.

As implied above, employers in a continuing relationship with their
employees will at least seek to legitimise formal disciplinary processes
in order to maintain and secure motivation. One way of doing this is
to appeal to wider sources of authority, such as the decisions of employment tribunals, as to what constitutes fairness. Before the unfair-dismissal legislation was enacted there was no legal requirement even to
give a reason for dismissal. It would seem to be a basic requirement
that any employer who wishes to be seen as fair in taking disciplinary
action should give a reason. However, there are plenty of examples of
employers behaving arbitrarily and eccentrically in their choice of
reason and it is not enough, therefore, simply to give one: the employer
should give a *potentially fair reason*. Misconduct, poor performance,
incapability are the main headings under which formal disciplinary
action is taken and legitimised. Dismissal may also be legitimised
under the heading of redundancy. Two things follow from this. First,
the reason given should be the actual reason. In tribunals, applicants
often argue that the employer had a reason other than the one given.
Redundancy might be used to hide the dismissal of an undesirable
employee – such as a trade union activist. Second, the sanction should
be appropriate. Theft may be good reason for dismissal but perhaps
not theft of a paper-clip.

Having a reason and applying an appropriate sanction are not enough. The employer should be able to demonstrate that there is sufficient evidence, properly gathered, to substantiate the accusations made. Essentially what is being said is that the employer should have good reason for taking disciplinary action and should act reasonably in all the circumstances. If discipline goes as far as dismissal and a tribunal is asked to decide whether or not the employer behaved fairly, then the employer will have to show that a reason was given; that it was the actual reason; that it was a potentially 'fair' reason; that the employer acted reasonably in the choice of reason – that it was not trivial and that the employer acted reasonably in the manner of the dismissal.

It is this last requirement of acting reasonably in the manner of the dismissal that needs to be explored. It is further being suggested here that any disciplinary action should be dealt with similarly if legitimacy is being sought. This requires three things of the employer:

1. that there has been a proper investigation;
2. that a properly constituted disciplinary hearing takes place;
3. that any action taken is consistent with the facts and previous practice.

The Investigation

This will normally be conducted under the supervision of the manager immediately responsible for the person concerned. All relevant facts will be collected, and where there are witnesses these will be interviewed. If a charge is made and this is denied, then it is expected that the person concerned will be given full opportunity to challenge all the evidence. This might warrant an investigatory hearing. If such a hearing is to take place, then the employee should be given notice of the hearing, be informed of its nature, be informed of the nature of the evidence and be given in advance any documents which might be used. There should be a right for the employee to be represented. The employee should also be told of the possible consequences – a disciplinary hearing, and the possible sanction, given the nature of the offence being investigated. Finally, the employee should be notified of a right to appeal.

Failure to act in accordance with the above could itself lead to an appeal against any action taken. If gross misconduct is suggested, suspension on full pay may be applied, depending upon the circumstances, pending the outcome of the whole procedure. Suspension on full pay will be regarded by an employee as a very serious matter in such circumstances – the employee is presumed to have a right to work where work is available – and it thus follows that there should be no unreasonable suspension on full pay or delay in bringing the matter to its conclusion.

The Disciplinary Hearing

Where an employee accepts guilt when accused, a disciplinary hearing may be the main process. It follows that an investigatory hearing that leads to a finding of 'guilty' will generally be followed immediately by a disciplinary hearing. A disciplinary hearing is simply a plea in mitigation.

If we assume that the manager conducts an investigation, calls in the employee and presents the evidence, and that the employee accepts it, then certain things should follow. The employee should be given notice of a disciplinary hearing and be informed of the right to be represented, of the possible sanction and of the right to appeal. At the hearing, the employee and/or the representative will make out a case for minimising the sanction on the basis of the employee's previous 'good' record and so on. The employer will take this into account, along with any current, unexpired, warnings.

Consistency

At the very least it would be expected that any sanction applied would be proportional to the offence and consistent with previous patterns of discipline. There should be no suggestion of victimisation or discrimination. Employers who feel that approaches to discipline have been lax and wish to change, should give notice of such change. As suggested earlier, employers recently have been introducing new policies on such things as sickness absence and smoking. Notice should be given of the implementation of such policies.

Warnings in procedures are usually given time limits – natural justice does in fact require this. The implication is that warnings can expire, and, when expired, not be taken into account in disciplinary hearings. 'Going rates' for expiry appear to be three months for an oral warning, six months for a first written warning, and one year for a final written warning. These are best expressed as 'normally up to x months, or x years' to allow for flexibility in extreme cases.

The term 'oral warning' is a little misleading, and procedures now tend to refer to stages; the terms 'stage 1 warning' and 'stage 2 warning' refer to severity of sanction. Where 'oral' denotes the first level of formal sanction, it still needs to be transmitted in written form to allow for clarity and record. There should also be a right of appeal against such a warning – if it is too trivial to be appealed against then it is probably best regarded as too trivial to give.

Given the nature of misconduct in particular, it is possible that, depending upon its seriousness, it might, even in a first instance, warrant the application of any sanction up to summary dismissal. On the other hand, poor performance might warrant progress through all levels of sanction, with clear indications at each stage of the degree of improvement required.

Provision for appeal is usually made on the basis that a level of management remote from and unconnected with the issue will hear such appeals with the person or incidents concerned. In multi-divisional organisations, for example, a manager from another division might hear an appeal. In a hospital trust, non-executive directors of the board of that trust might hear it. What is certain is that the overturning of a decision will affect the credibility of the manager or managers involved in that decision.

Grievances

The concept of a grievance is much misunderstood. It has also been further complicated in the United Kingdom by the recent legislation, the content of the 2004 Code of Practice and the ACAS Handbook – see below. It is essentially a technical term when used in connection with employment relationships and goes beyond the notion of simply feeling aggrieved or upset. A grievance is always registered 'against' management and not some other individual or group. An individual or group might be the source of a grievance. For example, if one employee sexually harasses another then the grievance would not be registered against the individual but against management for not protecting the harassed individual. Obviously in a case such as this management may not be directly responsible, but the onus is nevertheless on it to take appropriate action.

A useful definition of a grievance is the one incorporated in the ILO Recommendation, number 130, adopted in 1967:

> the grounds for a grievance may be any measure or situation which concerns the relations between employer and worker or which affects or may affect the conditions of employment of one or several workers in the undertaking when that measure or situation appears contrary to provisions of an applicable collective agreement or of an individual contract of employment, to works rules, to laws or regulations or to the custom or usage of the occupation, branch of economic activity or country, regard being had to principles of good faith.

This highlights the fact that the best approach to a grievance is to try to identify which rule, regulation, agreement, custom or practice the employee believes the employer is in breach of. One of the difficulties of identifying a grievance in the United Kingdom arises from the fact that agreements, rules and especially custom and practice are not clear. Collective agreements are generally written but usually in language which is imprecise and open to interpretation by outsiders. Millward *et al.* (1992: 212) state: 'The duties and obligations which agreements placed on the parties remained imprecise.' The parties usually understand the intentions of provisions at the time that they are written, but these intentions can become obscured by time and by changes in the participants and those affected. The potential obscurity or ambiguity derives to some extent from the fact that the agreements are not generally legally binding – although, as the courts demonstrate daily, even where agreements are legally binding differences in interpretation emerge.

In the UK labour relations context many written agreements are supplemented by unwritten agreements – custom and practice – at the shopfloor level. Although courts might dismiss such 'agreements' as 'void for uncertainty' when asked to interpret them as parts of individual contracts of employment, or impose interpretations that neither party could have imagined, there is on a day-by-day basis the expectation that the parties will abide by known intentions, however ambiguous the letter of the agreement.

Where an individual feels that he or she has a right under any of the categories of agreements or rules, and management disagrees, we have what is generally referred to as a 'dispute of right'. This differs from a dispute that arises where the parties attempt to change the rules. For example, parties at regular intervals renegotiate agreements, and a demand for a pay increase when a previous agreement is subject to review or has expired would be an illustration of such a situation. A disagreement in such a case can lead to what is called a 'dispute of interest'.

A dispute of right is about what an agreement actually means; a dispute of interest is about what an agreement ought to contain. Given that a grievance is about rights, arguments will revolve around the meaning of agreements, whether written or based on custom and practice. If somebody is described as entitled to 'reasonable' time off to perform certain duties – as a shop steward or councillor, for example – there will often be argument about what the word 'reasonable' means. Grading of jobs is a classic area of grievance issues: does a job fit into a higher or lower grade given its content and the definitions of job requirements (which can be highly generalised)? (See Chapter 11 later.)

The 1999 Employment Relations Act introduced the statutory right to be accompanied at Disciplinary and Grievance hearings by a colleague or trade union officer – even where no union was recognised.

The 2002 Employment Act introduced statutory Disciplinary and Grievance Procedures. It is difficult to involve statute in grievance issues without some meaningful definition of a grievance. In its examination of the right to be accompanied, the Code of Practice, page 33, states that ' For the purposes of this right, a grievance hearing is a meeting at which an employer deals with a complaint about a duty owed to them by a worker, whether *the duty arises from statute or common law (for example contractual commitments.'* (My emphasis). On page 23, for general purposes, it asserts that 'Grievances are concerns, problems or complaints that employees raise with their employers.' This really gives two inconsistent definitions of a grievance. Considerable management and union time is spent dealing with so-called complaints that are totally unsuitable for processing through a grievance procedure. The definition based on contract and implied duties is the only sensible way forward.

Grievance Procedures

The procedures for dealing with grievances vary considerably between organisations. When the Donovan Commission reported, such procedures were identified as being a cause of industrial action because they were often too longwinded and there was, therefore, a temptation to take such action rather than await the outcome of what could be a long and indeterminate process. Many procedures were nationally based, and these tended to match the following structure:

1. The employee raises the grievance with the employee's immediate supervisor.
2. If the grievance is not settled, the employee sees a representative – a shop steward, where the employee is a union member. Where the steward agrees that there is a grievance, or fails to persuade the member otherwise, they both take it back to the supervisor.
3. If this fails to settle the matter, it is taken to the next level of manager – possibly a departmental head.
4. If the matter is not settled then it is taken to the plant, works or unit manager.
5. If there is still no settlement then local or district full-time officers of the union and representatives of employers consider the issue.
6. If the case is still not settled, then it is dealt with at national level.

Such agreements are now rare. Donovan argued that grievance procedures would ideally end at the level of operation – the plant or the unit. The report also proposed that time limits should apply to each stage. In 1971 a code of practice was issued pursuant to section 3 (1) of the

Industrial Relation Act, with a section on grievance procedures which was very influential. It had the same status as the disciplinary code in respect of industrial tribunals. Although this status was revoked in 1991 as part of the then Government's policy of downgrading collective bargaining, it is worth reproducing for the insights it gives into grievance and other procedures.

GRIEVANCE and DISPUTES PROCEDURES

---

120 All employees have a right to seek redress for grievances relating to their employment. Each employee must be told he can do so (see paragraph 60).

121 Management should establish, with employee representatives or trade unions concerned, arrangements under which individual employees can raise grievances and have them settled fairly and promptly. These should be a formal procedure, except in very small establishments where there is a close personal contact between the employer and his employees.

122 Where trade unions are recognised, management should establish with them a procedure for settling collective disputes.

123 Individual grievances and collective disputes are often dealt with through the same procedure. Where there are separate procedures they should be linked so that an issue can, if necessary, pass from one to the other, since a grievance may develop into a dispute.

INDIVIDUAL GRIEVANCE PROCEDURES

124 The aim of the procedure should be to settle the grievance fairly and as near as possible to the point of origin. It should be simple and rapid in operation.

125 The procedure should be in writing and provide that:

i. the grievance should normally be discussed first between the employee and his immediate superior;
ii. the employee should be accompanied at the next stage of the discussion with management by his employee representative if he so wishes;
iii. there should be a right of appeal.

COLLECTIVE DISPUTES PROCEDURES

126 Disputes are broadly of two kinds:

i. disputes of right, which relate to the application or interpretation of existing agreements or contracts of employment;
ii. disputes of interest, which relate to claims by employees or proposals by management about terms and conditions of employment.

127 A procedure for settling collective disputes should be in writing and should:

i. state the level at which an issue should first be raised;
ii. lay down time limits for each stage of the procedure, with provision for extension by agreement;

iii. preclude a strike, lock-out or other form of industrial action until all stages of the procedure have been completed and a failure-to-agree formally recorded.

128 The procedure should have the following stages

i. employee representatives should raise the issue in dispute with management at the level directly concerned;
ii. failing settlement, it should be referred to a higher level within the establishment;
iii. if still unsettled, it should be referred to further agreed stages, for example, to a stage of an industry-wide procedure or to a higher level within the undertaking.

129 Independent conciliation and arbitration can be used to settle all types of dispute, if the parties concerned agree that they should. Arbitration by the Industrial Arbitration Board or other independent arbitrators is particularly suitable for settling disputes of right, and its wider use for that purpose is desirable. Where it is used, the parties should undertake to be bound by the award.

CODE OF PRACTICE

INDUSTRIAL RELATIONS ACT 1971 S3(1)

As clearly indicated we now have a new Code of Practice which covers both disciplinary and grievance procedures.

According to Millward *et al.* (1992: 212), in the 1980s 'Procedures for resolving individual grievances were also widely introduced.... They showed increasing precision and uniformity across all industries and types of establishment.'

Chapter 6 of Millward *et al.* (1992) is titled 'Procedures for Resolving Disputes'. In it the authors identify the following procedures: pay and conditions; discipline and dismissal; individual grievances; health and safety. Other texts make reference to redundancy procedures and recognition procedures, collective grievance procedures and disputes procedures. All of this can be confusing. These confusions partly arise because the procedural arrangements can vary in respect of particular issues within organisations, and because what is called a procedure might simply be a substantive rule or a policy statement.

For example, a grievance on time off, or expense entitlements, might be dealt with through an individual grievance procedure which is carried through general line management – supervisor, departmental manager, plant manager, with appeal to the manager of another plant. In principle, it makes no difference whether one or more persons are involved, and therefore collective grievances could be dealt with in the same procedure. Separate procedures for dealing with collective and individual grievances existed in the NHS under Whitley, with the collective procedure being referred to as a disputes procedure. Trusts are tending to have just one procedure for dealing with grievances. In fact, if a grievance is about rights under agreements and rules then decisions relating to individuals will set collective precedents.

Where a grievance relates to grading under a job evaluation scheme, there will tend to be a separate arrangement, involving those with job evaluation expertise, usually an established joint panel. Nevertheless, it remains a grievance. What is not clear within the Millward *et al.* classification is whether a procedure dealing with job evaluation appeals is a pay-and-conditions matter or an individual grievance matter. For the purpose of analysis, we should treat it as a grievance matter, without adding either individual or collective as an adjective, or requiring a designation such as pay-and-conditions procedure. Similarly, there might be separate procedures for health and safety grievances, bullying, or harassment. All that we are identifying under the separate headings are grievances over issues relating to particular sets of substantive rules. It is important that this is borne in mind.

What is often referred to as a redundancy procedure – the need to give notice, the method of selection, the determination of redundancy pay, and so on – is really a substantive agreement rather than a procedure agreement. Again, grievances may arise out of the way this agreement is applied, and there may be a separate procedure for dealing specifically with redundancy grievances. They remain, nevertheless, grievances.

It could be said that if a matter is in procedure then the parties are in dispute until the matter is resolved. On the other hand, it could be argued that a dispute arises if the parties fail to agree at the end of a procedure. At the final stage, a union, for example, might reject the decision that is made – they might disagree with a dismissal or sanction, or disagree with management's rejection of a grievance. Similarly, there may be a failure to agree at the end of the periodic renegotiations of pay and terms of conditions. The procedure for such negotiations usually consists of a rather flexible timetable rather than a series of specified steps or stages. In all of these cases it is relatively rare that provision is made for automatic settlement by independent arbitration, although there is more frequent reference to conciliation, and occasionally to mediation – see Chapter 8. Millward *et al.* (1992) do not present data which is sufficient to allow for a clear distinction between the different forms of access to third-party intervention – again, see Chapter 8. This is also true of subsequent Workplace Employee Relations Surveys.

If there is a failure to agree at the end of the procedure then the most common situation is that the parties could fight it out – the union might take industrial action. On the other hand, the union might fail to agree, but reluctantly live with the outcome. In the miners' strike of 1984–5, the union returned to work without an agreement, and conditions were imposed upon the miners, along with a new, but unagreed, disciplinary procedure. There is usually a provision that a procedure should be followed through to its final stage before industrial action is taken – a course of events often described as 'the procedure being exhausted'. Where action is taken before the procedure is exhausted such action is described as 'unconstitutional' or as 'in breach of procedure'.

Grievance procedures usually require that what is called the *status quo* is preserved until the procedure is exhausted. For example, management may feel that they have the right to introduce a change in practice that the union challenges as being in breach of existing agreements. Workers who have had free car parking at the place of work might feel that the introduction of parking charges is in breach of custom and practice, with management arguing that it had simply been a concession, and that there was no formal agreement. Until this matter had been settled, the understanding might be that no charges are imposed – that the *status quo* is maintained. Where management unilaterally breach an agreement – they might impose substantive changes detrimental to workers before the annual agreement has expired – workers may take industrial action and claim to have been 'locked out'.

Statutory Grievance Procedure

Step 1 Inform the employer of the grievance in writing.

Step 2 Be invited by the employer to attend a meeting to discuss the grievance with the right to be accompanied. The employee must take all reasonable steps to attend the meeting. The employer must notify the employee in writing of the decision.

Step 3 Be given the right to appeal and to attend a meeting where the final decision will be made.

In practice, grievance procedures will generally have a right of appeal to a person not involved directly in the earlier stages. There will also be elaborate guidance at the place of work on how grievances should be investigated and handled. The ACAS Handbook provides clear examples – subject to some of the comments above on their general definition. Where an employee fails to initiate and follow the statutory grievance procedure to appeal level they may be barred from bringing an Employment Tribunal case in relation to the issue. This applies to jurisdiction under Schedule 4 of the Employment Act 2002 which includes discrimination matters, consultation rights, unlawful deductions and so on. Depending on whether or not the employer responds compensation to the employee may be increased or reduced where a claim is upheld.

Chapter 8 extends the discussion of procedures to examine the use of third parties in dispute resolution.

The statutory disciplinary procedures described in this chapter are referred to as 'the standard procedures'. These will be applicable to the vast majority of relevant disciplinary actions. The Employment Act 2002 also introduced 'modified procedures' applicable to a small minority of cases. The purpose of this chapter is essentially to communicate the key issues related to discipline and grievance handling, not to explore the minutiae of the law. This is best left as the preserve of labour law courses and literature.

Conclusion and Recommended Reading

The literature on procedures is limited and the concept of a procedure is ill-defined. This leads to some ambiguities in the research conclusions in respect of their extent, growth and content.

The ACAS advisory handbook, *Discipline and Grievances at Work* (ACAS: London), is an essential document for the understanding of discipline and grievance issues.

8

Settling Disputes

In Chapter 7 it was pointed out that there was some confusion over the term 'disputes procedure', which historically, in practice, tended to be used to describe collective grievance procedures. It was further argued that distinguishing between collective and individual grievances did not make much logical sense. In practice, organisations are tending to use one procedure for general grievances, with variations for specific grievances, such as those relating to job evaluation or redundancy. It is possible, for analytical purposes, that the term 'disputes procedure' could be reserved to describe those provisions which are made for the use of third parties. Such provisions are far from universal and vary considerably. Third parties may be used to act as conciliators, mediators or arbitrators.

There is a long history of state provision in this area of third-party intervention and there has been considerable variation in government attitudes to it. It is not a purpose of this chapter to examine this history – its purpose is to examine the options and recent developments. Procedural forms will be examined first and then the content or substance of the three devices referred to above. It must be recognised also that, although there may be no provision or reference to such devices in procedures, the parties may decide to try any one or combination of these devices on an *ad hoc* basis. In other words, the parties might fail to agree and choose to refer the matter to a third party.

Procedural Forms

With respect to the use of these devices the terms 'compulsory' and 'voluntary' are often used to distinguish between arrangements which are imposed by the state and those which are agreed voluntarily by the parties. This can be misleading. Here, the terms are used regardless of whether or not the state is involved. The significance of these distinctions is probably best illustrated by giving examples of provisions from procedures:

Compulsory   'If the parties fail to agree, the matter *will* be referred to . . .'.

Unilateral   'If the parties fail to agree, *one* or *other* party *may* refer the matter to . . .'. An implication of this is that if one party decides to refer the matter to a third party, then the other party will participate in the process. However, there is no compulsion for either party to refer the matter.

Voluntary   'If the parties fail to agree, the matter *may* be referred to . . . if *both* parties agree to do so . . .'. This is probably best seen as a clause which simply reminds the parties that some form of third-party assistance is available.

Where the state imposes a requirement, the word 'statutory' is probably best used. Given the limited intervention of statute in respect of the use of third parties these will not be discussed here. Our main concern is with the principles related to and the consequences of the use of third parties. Third parties, in respect of disputes, are used in three main ways, and any of the above formulations may be used as a preliminary to access any one of these.

Conciliation

A distinction must be made here between individual and collective conciliation. Individual conciliation is associated with the settlement of individual cases submitted to Employment Tribunals as a substitute for a formal tribunal hearing. ACAS is obliged to offer conciliation in such cases. Here we are concerned with collective conciliation, which implies some kind of representative process arising out of failures to agree. As implied above, we are essentially talking about a voluntary process which requires the consent of both parties. This is also true of the other two forms of intervention referred to below. Conciliation of the type we are referring to is almost invariably provided in the United Kingdom by ACAS. ACAS employs staff who specialise in this process. Also, given that it is a representative process, it is almost inevitable that unions are involved.

Generally ACAS is invited by the parties to offer the service, but ACAS might, where it becomes aware of a problem, remind the parties that its services exist. A conciliator has no powers over the parties. Generally the role of the conciliator revolves around clarifying the issues that divide the parties, offering advice and information, suggesting possible ways forward and perhaps facilitating the reopening of negotiations. This can be done through chairing joint meetings and discussing matters separately with the parties or both. Proposals from one party to another can be communicated by the conciliator, thus ensuring responses in good faith to such proposals.

Where unilateral recourse to conciliation exists, it might be used as a face-saving device that allows for the reopening of negotiations. It can be used to overcome some of the problems associated with intra-organisational bargaining – see Chapter 9. Because conciliators have no powers, conciliation provisions do not commit the parties to any outcome. Where agreements are compulsory or unilateral, ACAS will be concerned to establish that there is a possibility of a settlement before getting involved and that one or other party is not simply going through the motions of abiding by an agreement. Even where there is no provision, *ad hoc* use of the process may be agreed by one or other party simply for public relations purposes – to suggest a willingness to be reasonable as a mask for intransigence.

There is no doubt that such conciliation is of value and this is reflected in the extent of its use – see below. Less experienced parties might discover options they would not have conceived of alone. For the more experienced parties it can provide a means of having second thoughts without losing face.

Mediation

Where ACAS mediation services are used, the mediators are drawn from a list of names held by ACAS – these include such people as academics, retired conciliation officers and lawyers. Arbitrators (see below) are selected in the same way. In both cases, the parties may choose a single individual or a panel and will agree that the person or persons will act in whichever capacity is appropriate.

A mediator has the power to make recommendations and is generally expected to do so. Recommendations do not bind parties – they simply provide a basis for an acceptable settlement or for further negotiations. Mediation requires the drawing up of terms of reference, usually quite broadly expressed. For example, a mediator might be asked to make recommendations with regard to items in an overall substantive pay agreement. The process of mediation usually begins with a conciliation process, which attempts to bring the parties to an agreement. Where agreement is reached, the parties may still require that their agreement is presented by the mediator in the form of recommendations. Again this reflects the intra-organisational bargaining process (see Chapter 9). The parties will have been mandated to secure recommendations, and therefore any agreement will have to be 'sold' to the

union members and to the board of the organisation. What the mediator is seeking is confirmation from the parties that they believe that
those they represent will accept the recommendations. If the parties
are unable to agree the recommendations of the mediator, it is highly
unlikely that their constituents will. Where the parties do agree, the
fact that a mediator is recommending what they agree will give it more
credibility.

The Pay Review Bodies (PRBs) which deal with the pay of professional groups in the NHS, with teachers, the armed forces, and the
prison service, for example, are mediators. They receive evidence from
the parties, gather other evidence they deem relevant and make recommendations to the government. These may be accepted or rejected, but
given the nature of the process moral pressure is brought to bear on the
government. Similar pressure is brought on the parties if the government accepts PRB recommendations. If, for example, the unions reject
the recommended offers – not being bound by them – they will be
exposed to criticism. In the past, the government occasionally set up a
court of inquiry into high-profile disputes – the one in the case of the
Grunwick dispute in 1977 being one of the most recent – in the hope
that publishing facts and recommendations might bring pressure for a
settlement. These forms of mediation do not contain the conciliation
process which seeks agreement, but recommendations will tend to be
based on considerations of the attitudes of the parties and the overall
political implications of different outcomes. The Review Bodies will
make rigorous attempts to evaluate the evidence given to them as a
basis for recommendations, but the evidence will never be sufficiently
refined to allow for an indisputable set of recommendations.

Arbitration

ACAS (1989: 21) states:

> In all cases ACAS explains to the parties that, while awards from voluntary arbi-
> tration are not legally binding, nevertheless they are regarded as morally bind-
> ing and the arrangements for arbitration are made only on the clear
> understanding that the award will be honoured by the parties. In practice
> awards are invariably accepted and implemented.

Implicit in the definition of arbitration, then, is that the parties agree
to be bound by the decision of an arbitrator when they submit a dispute
to settlement by arbitration. It follows from this that the issue has to be
submitted in such a way that a clear decision is possible. The parties

submit terms of reference, and the arbitrator must make a decision that does not exceed these. For example, if an arbitrator is asked to determine the date from which a pay award should be granted, the arbitrator is not expected to determine anything other than this – the size, or length, of the pay award would be seen to be outside of such terms of reference.

When the parties go to arbitration they are usually taking a calculated risk. On pay awards they know that the arbitrator will not choose more than the union has demanded, or less than the company, or organisation, has offered. In fact, the arbitrator could be specifically confined in the terms of reference to such limits. There are conventions which are known to constrain arbitrators, and the parties understand this. Where ACAS is used, conciliation will be attempted. If there is failure to secure a negotiated settlement then ACAS will help the parties to draft the terms of reference so that they are clear and unambiguous and the parties are aware of the possible outcomes.

It is possible for the parties to devise their own machinery. In such cases, or where ACAS is involved, they may require a panel or tribunal. Sometimes persons who are generally referred to as assessors may be incorporated. These have expert knowledge of the industry, service or issue, which they can make available to the arbitrator. They have no say in the decision. Whatever the form used, the parties make the choice by agreement and similarly decide the persons to be involved in whatever capacity. Where ACAS is used, it will supply names of people with experience in the relevant roles. Whatever the structure, a decision will be made.

In cases involving dismissal or equal opportunities issues in respect of any individual, there may be cases where the individual chooses not to be bound by the decision and takes the matter to an industrial tribunal. Since arbitration is inevitably a representative process, the parties are the union and the employer – not the people they represent. It is expected that the parties are able to influence the people they represent and that they play no part in supporting any attempt to overturn the decision.

The Extent of Third-Party Intervention

The discussion of the procedural forms and the processes relating to third-party intervention illustrate at one level the simplicity, and usefulness, of the associated devices, while at the same time suggesting a complexity which prohibits meaningful generalisations about the extent of their use. ACAS Annual Reports illustrate the extent to which its services are used under the headings listed above (see below). However, Millward *et al.* (1992: 209–10) attempt to describe the extent to which what they call 'fully external third-party intervention' is used in general. They tell us that

> management reported that ACAS was *referred to* in a third (31 per cent) of pay and conditions procedures . . .Where ACAS was mentioned over half *referred to the possibility* of both conciliation and arbitration with the bulk of the remainder *allowing* conciliation alone. Only one in 25 establishments where procedures *envisaged the possibility of ACAS assistance* in pay and conditions disputes *allowed* for arbitration alone . . . We estimate, on the basis of management responses, that a maximum of 3.5 of the 15.6 million workers covered by our survey *were in the scope* of such provisions in 1990. [My italics]

Given the procedural forms of entry into the use of a third party, it is difficult to know what much of the above means. 'Allowed for arbitration' could mean compulsory, unilateral or voluntary access. It is difficult to imagine that a procedure would forbid the use of arbitration or conciliation – they probably all allow for *ad hoc* recourse to either or both. The general data provided hide more than they reveal.

That there is some confusion among respondents to such surveys seems to be illustrated by the comment: 'Only two fifths of our respondents said, for example, that the decision of an arbitrator must be final and binding on the parties' (Millward *et al.*, 1992: 211). Given our definition of arbitration, this could only mean that if an arbitrator makes a decision that both parties disagree with, then they can reject it. Such an interpretation could be treated as commonsense or utterly meaningless. If it can be rejected by either party, then it sounds more like a mediator's recommendation that the authors and respondents have in mind. They could, of course, mean that recourse to arbitration is binding – compulsory, in our definition.

According to the ACAS *Annual Report* (1996), there had been a falling trend in arbitration and mediation cases conducted by the service. In the 1970s such cases averaged around 300 per year, falling to 200 in the 1980s and 170 in the 1990s. This decline could reflect less willingness on the part of employers to hand over responsibility in a period when they feel they can settle differences without workers having recourse to industrial action – possibly a reflection of a changing power base. Following a similar trend, collective conciliation cases fell between the 1970s and 1980s, but remained relatively stable into the 1990s. In 1975, there were 2017 such cases, in 1985 there were 1448 and, in 1995, 1229.

The ACAS *Annual Report* of 2005–6 showed a continuation of the above trends. In the year 2005–6, 57 cases were referred to mediation and arbitration, with 936 being referred to collective conciliation. The year 2003–4 showed 1271 referred to collective conciliation.

Related Issues

The 1980s saw increased reference to the negotiation of no-strike deals. To some extent, this was a debate which related to something with very little content. A no-strike deal implies third-party intervention in the form of arbitration. This is the only way a final settlement could be achieved in all cases without any resort to industrial action. Furthermore, it would seem to require compulsory arbitration – unilateral and voluntary access do not guarantee that there will be recourse to the process and that strike action is not excluded from the agreement. Where compulsory arbitration is introduced to cover all failures to agree, then the union is often said to have given up the right to strike. The TUC guidelines on no strike-deals suggests that unions should 'not make recognition agreements which remove the right to take industrial action . . . this is not meant to deter unions from agreeing to procedures for arbitration' (quoted in Salamon, 1992: 385). Since there is no 'right' to take industrial action, this presumably refers to the 'right to organise industrial action', which still exists to a limited extent (see Chapter 10). Where unilateral recourse to arbitration is allowed in all failures to agree, the employer can veto the union's right to organise industrial action. Where compulsory arbitration exists, or where unilateral arbitration exists and the employer uses the veto, any industrial action will be unofficial.

That the debate had little content is reflected in the fact that such deals were very few and far between. The Government also opposed the automatic use of arbitration in the public sector, and many agreements incorporating this were dismantled. There is a popular view that 'rational' people would not allow a situation to develop which resulted in industrial action – see Chapter 1 and the comments on unitarist approaches to labour relations. This can lead to the view that arbitration is an obvious way of settling disputes, hence no-strike deals. An enlightened third party should, it is argued, be able to demonstrate to the other parties the error of their ways and persuade them to a mutually beneficial and sensible solution; after all, it is urged, industrial action benefits no one.

In 1989, a minister exhorted the union to go to arbitration during a railway dispute; the union refused. In the same year, another union exhorted another minister to go to arbitration during an ambulance staff dispute; the minister refused. The same reasons for refusal were given in both cases – it was a problem for the parties to resolve between themselves. In the first case the union saw itself as winning the dispute, while in the second case the minister saw the Government as winning, and neither party could see any reason why a third party would achieve a better result for it. What these cases imply is that while a losing party will usually raise the question of arbitration to win public support by appearing more reasonable than their opponent, arbitration is resorted to on an *ad hoc* basis only where both parties see the continuation of the dispute as mutually destructive.

All this suggests that arbitration and provisions for it are intimately linked to the power the parties perceive themselves to have. Why should employers allow arbitration to settle disputes when they have the upper hand? No-strike agreements seem attractive to employers, but why should they concede any power when there is very little prospect of workers taking industrial action? Hence the lack of real substance to the debate surrounding such deals. Employers were less willing to make concessions; trade unions have never really had principles in respect of no-strike agreements, but respond to them pragmatically. After all, the unions offered such a deal to resolve the issue of union existence at Government Communications Headquarters (GCHQ) – the offer was turned down. Later, under a Labour Government, recognition of unions at GCHQ was re-established with an arbitration agreement.

The rationalisations for dismantling provisions for compulsory or unilateral arbitration will usually include insistence that the parties should solve their own problems. To this a Conservative Government may add the assertion of the desirability of a free market. Actual reasons could include the argument that such arrangements take away the resolve of the parties to negotiate a settlement. For example, if the convention is that the arbitrator will never award less than the employer's final offer, and the union knows that a failure to agree will go to arbitration, why should it settle? It might get something extra from the arbitrator, however little. An employer knowing that this will happen is likely to minimise their final offer. This is known as the 'narcotic' or 'freezing' effect of compulsory arbitration – the negotiations are frozen or deadened by the knowledge that arbitration will take place. The long-run outcome might be detrimental to both parties. In the public sector, the Government could end up financing inflationary outcomes, with the parties to negotiations disclaiming any responsibility.

These are very powerful arguments against compulsory arbitration. A counter argument is that a degree of inflation might be a price to be paid where industrial action could be particularly damaging – education, health or news for that matter cannot be stockpiled in anticipation of industrial action. Another factor influencing the Government in the 1980s was its antipathy to collective bargaining implicit in its free market model. Arbitration is a representative process and almost invariably implies union recognition. The same is true of collective conciliation and of mediation. Setting up the NHS PRB in the early 1980s was basically a short-term response to labour relations problems in the industry.

Neither shade of government has found an opportune time to dismantle them although, at great cost, deals were negotiated outside of the NHS PRB, for most staff, between 2003 and 2006.

In the lead up to the firefighters' dispute which involved a sequence of strike actions in 2002–3 the union refused to respond to an employer request to go to arbitration. Their procedure allowed for unilateral access to arbitration – 'if either party wishes the matter might be referred to arbitration.' The employer accused the union of breaking the national agreement. The union accused the employer of being in breach of the spirit and intent of the agreement by trying to use arbitration to secure local determination of some terms and conditions and therefore undermining the National Joint Council. The Employer decided that the Union's position really meant that the national agreement no longer existed and decided it had the right to implement change independently of the union. The union decided to call a Delegate Conference and recommend all out industrial action.

In the final analysis, the arguments did not matter. This all came to a head in September 1999 raising the prospect of a Fire and Rescue Service strike taking place during the millennium celebrations. Both parties were 'got off the hook' by the setting up of an inquiry by the Government into procedures for determining the conditions of service of firefighters on condition that the National Joint Council (NJC) be re-established pending the publication of the Report – neatly scheduled for March 2000 and delaying the possibility of industrial action to beyond that date. Essentially, a mediation took place which 'tweaked' the existing agreement, and the parties accepted all of the Inquiry recommendations. The unilateral arbitration provision was retained but no party saw fit to have recourse to it during the 2002–3 dispute.

Pendulum Arbitration

Pendulum arbitration is sometimes referred to as 'flip-flop' arbitration or 'final offer' arbitration (FOA). It became a popular topic of debate in the United Kingdom in the 1980s, and very much associated with agreements of 'new-style Japanese' type. Although used more extensively under such circumstances than ever before, it was still used very little, and is now rare. The rationalisations for its use focused on some of the problems associated with compulsory and unilateral arbitration discussed above, especially the so-called narcotic effect.

Pendulum arbitration requires the arbitrator to choose the final position of one or other of the parties. For example, if the issue is a straight pay claim and the final offer of the employer is 2 per cent, with the final union demand being 4 per cent, then the arbitrator will be bound to choose an award of either 2 per cent or 4 per cent. The logic is that there will be an outright winner and loser, and that each party will try to approach the arbitration so as to appear the more reasonable of the two. Both parties will therefore be tempted to moderate their positions – the union to reduce its demand and the employer to increase its offer. The pressure of such an arbitration will pull the parties closer to a negotiated settlement. If they do not settle, the difference between the parties will be so small that there is less chance of an inflated award.

Although presented as innovatory in the 1980s, this approach to arbitration has a long history. It was used in the UK coal industry in the latter part of the nineteenth century and in the early part of the twentieth century (Treble, 1986). There was also a history of its use in the United States. However, its history was neglected by its latter-day 'innovators' and thus arrangements were introduced which recreated the problems which had led to its earlier abandonment.

Perhaps the major problem with such arbitration is just that there *is* an outright winner and an outright loser. Being the loser can have a serious effect on the standing of the party, especially with the workforce: its credibility is undermined. The very objective of removing the temptation to split the difference removes the possibility of a perceived compromise as an outcome. Arbitrators rarely split the difference; the outcome is usually close to the position of one party or the other.

Earlier in the book reference was made to disputes of right and disputes of interest. Disputes of right are by definition a matter of interpretation and often involve either–or decisions. This is particularly true of grading disputes. Paradoxically, such disputes are more amenable to third-party resolution than are disputes of interest, because they revolve around identifiable agreed parameters (though these themselves are open to interpretation) such as written agreements, custom and practice, grading criteria and so on. Disputes of interest, on the other hand, are about new agreements, and although there are conventional arguments, about the significance of inflation, productivity, differentials or profits, these are open-ended arguments. It is in this area that most problems with arbitration, whether conventional or pendulum, arise.

New agreements may relate to a package of items – pay, hours of work, pensions, holidays and other items. Bargainers often talk about having a shopping list. This raises the obvious question of how pendulum arbitration could be used to determine such a package. A pendulum arbitration on each item could undermine its purpose – items could be determined in such a way that a compromise emerged, thus defeating the object. Going the same way on every item would reinforce the winner–loser problem. Costing the claim and offer leaves the parties with a problem of distribution. Even identifying the agreed final positions of the parties may be difficult. Nevertheless, a professor at the London School of Economics, recommended pendulum arbitration as a means of settling the 2002–3 fire dispute. The arbitrator would have been in the absurd position of deciding between the contents of the Bain Report – subject to interpretation –and a 39.7 per cent pay increase.

Solving such problems may require supplementing the process with conciliation and possibly mediation. In the US literature reference is made to 'med-arb', which involves a mediator in the early stages. The mediator's role might be to clarify positions, encourage trade-offs, help reduce a package to an outstanding item, and to determine the terms of reference for arbitration if the matter gets that far.

Perhaps the main function of arbitration is to make available to the parties a face-saving device where a dispute is becoming mutually destructive. As such, it is more effective where it is entered into on an *ad hoc* basis. This very much embodies the pluralist approach, and with it the well-known 'rule' that the role of the arbitrator is 'to find out who the lion is and make sure he gets the lion's share'. In other words, it is not the role of the arbitrator to bring to the decision their own views of fairness and justice, but to recognise the politics of the relationship, and to try to reach a decision that allows the parties to move on from the dispute. The unitarist approach has already been mentioned. Its ultimate expression is that in a free market, without trade unions, rational 'economic men' will decide their mutual differences without the need for help. In a conflict model arbitration will be seen as a tactical retreat or simply as a defeat.

The popularity of the use of third-party intervention ebbs and flows. If it relates to the balance of power then it is possible to speculate that the flows reflect periods where a shift is actually taking place, while the ebbs occur once the balance becomes clear.

ACAS

Numerous references have been made to ACAS and it seems appropriate to say something about that institution at this stage. ACAS was established in 1974 and its legal basis was embodied in the Employment Protection Act 1975. Although financed by the Government, it is independent of day-to-day control and interference. Under the Act, the Secretary of State for Employment, who was then responsible for ACAS, appoints the chairperson. It also provides for the appointment of a council of nine members, which could be increased to 11. These appointments are also made by the Secretary of State, subject to advice from organisations of workers and employers. Until 1989, the council consisted of three TUC nominees, three CBI nominees, and three independents, normally academics. In that year two additional council members were appointed, one from the RCN, a non-TUC affiliate, and one as a representative of small employers. In 1995, the RCN representative was replaced by one from the Association of University and College Lecturers, along with other replacements.

ACAS has regional offices and local as well as national expertise. It has a duty to provide conciliation in individual employment matters covered by legislation, such as unfair dismissal, equal pay, sex discrimination and race relations cases. An objective is to try to settle these matters without them proceeding to the tribunals, although the parties are free to ignore an approach from ACAS. At a collective level it has a duty to try to settle matters arising out of disclosure of information provisions for collective bargaining purposes, and to make services available for collective conciliation, mediation and arbitration.

ACAS also provides an extensive advisory service on the whole range of labour relations and personnel issues, and will undertake visits, projects and investigations on behalf of the parties. It has published a range of booklets on matters such as payment systems, job evaluation, performance appraisal, recruitment and selection, absence, labour turnover and so on. It also publishes research-based papers, and is associated with the Millward *et al.* survey. ACAS may, if it sees fit, conduct an inquiry into any matter relating to industrial relations.

The Act also gives ACAS the power to issue codes of practice subject to approval by both Houses of Parliament after submission by the Secretary of State. Such codes are admissible in industrial tribunals (see Chapter 7). Currently there are three such codes produced via ACAS: 'Disciplinary practices and procedures in employment', 'Disclosure of information to trade unions for collective bargaining purposes' and 'Time off for trade union duties and activities'.

In January 1987, ACAS produced a draft replacement for the code of practice on discipline. This was rejected by the Secretary of State. However, it did provide the basis for the handbook *Discipline at Work*. The 1980s and 1990s saw a change in Government attitudes to ACAS. This is partly reflected in the broadening of its council, the rejection of the proposed code of practice and the withdrawal of the remains of the 1971 code of practice. Much more important were some of the provisions of TURERA 1993. This removed ACAS's duty to encourage collective bargaining, allowed it to charge fees for any of its services, and gave the Secretary of State power to order such charges.

That such changes might take place was speculated upon in the first edition of this book. Since the second edition of this book was published, changes to ACAS have taken place but the commercial pressures have persisted. At the time of writing ACAS consisted of a Council with a Chair and 11 members. The Chair and four of the members have a trade union background; four members come from an employer/management background, three are practicing lawyers and one is the Director of the Involvement and Participation Association. There are no academics *per se* on the Council. ACAS now also has a Chief Executive directing the day-to-day running of the organisation. In the year 2005–6, the organisation was faced with the requirement of having to reduce its workforce by 17 per cent.

Such a change might be seen to reflect some of the changes referred to above. However, dealing with collective disputes is only a small part of the ACAS programme. They attempt individual conciliation with those involved in Employment Tribunal cases. In 1999, they completed 99 826 cases. In 2005–6 they completed 130 711 cases. This is a major volume of work reflecting the growth of anti-discrimination law and the widening jurisdiction of Employment Law. ACAS staff have to absorb and become expert in all of this.They also play a role in CAC recognition jurisdiction and are involved in the implementation of Works Council legislation. On top of all of this they provide an extensive advisory and training service and are involved in Department of Trade and Industry (DTI) sponsored partnership negotiations. They also produce a wide range of publications.

In respect of the main theme of this chapter, ACAS now offers an individual mediation scheme. An implication of this is that mediators may deal with individuals rather than representatives. The objective is to try to avoid grievance and potentially disciplinary cases by trying to reconcile the differences between individuals. In 2005–6, ACAS dealt with 85 such mediations. Also, in 2001 the ACAS Arbitration Scheme was introduced. This allowed the parties to an unfair dismissal, or flexible working, case to submit their case to a single arbitrator with the power to award similar remedies to those awarded by an Employment Tribunal. It was felt that this might attract cases to a less costly process of settlement, whilst also simplifying the process for the parties. The scheme has not attracted many cases: unfair dismissal: 2003–4, 7; 2004–5, 4; 20005–6, 6. Flexible working is 1, 1, and 0, respectively, for each of the above years. There is no explanation for this low take up. The authors view is that the benefits and disadvantages for employers and the benefits and disadvantages for employees are probably assymetrical. If an employer wants privacy, the employee wants publicity; if an employee wishes to reduce potential costs, the employer may wish to increase them.

ACAS still retains a very high reputation within the working community and has a high reputation abroad. It is to be hoped that workload and financial pressures do not result in any compromise in the way ACAS has historically delivered its core business.

Conclusion and Further Reading

This chapter has suggested a theoretical point about how a disputes procedure could be defined. It has also shown some of the confusions relating to definitions of the forms of third-party intervention, which again lead to difficulties in interpreting survey reports about the extent of their use. The section on pendulum arbitration has indicated the nature of the bargaining process where compulsory arbitration exists, followed by some indication of the role of shifting power balances in determining its popularity. Pendulum arbitration, as a relatively recent but short-lived fad, also tells us something about 'innovatory' management techniques.

For a more comprehensive guide to the use of third parties, see Lowry (1990).

9

Negotiating

Chapters 7 and 8 have examined the procedures within which differences between the parties are resolved. Both within and beyond these procedures differences are settled by negotiation. The actual use of procedures and ultimately the threat and the use of sanctions are all linked to the negotiating process. If bargaining, and in particular collective bargaining, is seen to reflect power relationships, then what we have is a political process. Negotiation is the mechanism through which the parties bring to bear their strengths, or their weaponry, in pursuit of their objectives. Skilled negotiators will make more effective use of their power than less-skilled ones. However, skill in negotiations can only supplement power; it cannot act as a substitute for it. Skill in negotiations is about securing the maximum advantage from the distribution of power.

The terms 'bargaining' and 'negotiating' are not clearly distinguishable in common usage and one is often defined as the other. There is no agreed set of definitions within the labour relations literature. Here the distinction will be based on process and structure – bargaining theory will be used in relation to structure – levels, recognition, multi-employer and so on – with negotiating theory being to do with process. Negotiating theory is to do with the process by which the parties bring to bear their power relationships – it implies the use of threats and sanctions to secure objectives. From the above it would appear that negotiating theory is essentially concerned with the direct relationships between parties and individuals through which they try to achieve generally conflicting goals. It implies compromise by both or one of the parties.

A question which such theory seeks to find answers to is how do parties set specific objectives or strategies and devise tactics to achieve these? Earlier in the text it was suggested that what passes for theory in the field of labour relations seems to consist of poorly defined and often untestable hypotheses. Negotiating theory is equally limited. One of the most widely agreed hypotheses in negotiating theory seems to be that with any given distribution of power between the parties there is still a number of possible outcomes when it is used by the parties in attempts to determine the basis of their relationship. For example, when trade unions and employers meet to agree a pay settlement, there is a range of pay levels within which such a settlement may be achieved. Negotiating theory attempts to identify those factors within the relationship which work to determine the precise outcome. An implication of this hypothesis is the further hypothesis that there are skills which will help one or the other party to achieve, from a range of mutually acceptable settlements, the one which is more or most advantageous. Given the nature of the relationship, it is impossible to measure the effectiveness of such skills in achieving any particular outcome – there are too many variables at play. Models based on games theory are so remote from the complexity of reality that they do not help resolve this problem. For example, the games theory concept of the prisoners' dilemma is often used to suggest that cooperative relationships are more productive than competitive relationships in achieving outcomes for the parties (see Hutton, 1995). The difficulty with this is that it only allows such a conclusion to be drawn where the parties have equal power – not a helpful proposition for understanding real-world situations.

The Walton and McKersie Model

Intuitively, the notion of negotiating skills having an effect makes sense; scientifically, it is very difficult to test the proposition. Another part of negotiating theory lies in attempts to establish models of the negotiating process within the context of collective bargaining. The most important of these is that of Walton and McKersie (1965). They argue that labour negotiations can be broken down into four systems of activity which they call subprocesses and that it is possible to generate from this model, which is based on research into labour negotiations, 'predictive hypotheses about how people will tend to behave in various circumstances and under varying conditions'.

Texts on how to negotiate refer invariably to the Walton and McKersie model. This makes sense on the grounds that a better understanding of the process makes it easier to manipulate and to secure advantages within it.

Distributive Bargaining

This is described as a subprocess, where the goals of the parties are in fundamental conflict with each other. Each party can only attain its goals at the expense of the other. In games theory, such a situation is described as a 'zero-sum game'; a classic example is poker, where a player can only win at the expense of other players – all winnings and losses cancel out to zero. Walton and McKersie describe this type of game as the dominant activity in the labour–management relationship. They use the term 'issue' to describe an area of common concern where the parties are in conflict.

That the authors identify this as a dominant activity between the parties is of some significance. Most of the 'how-to-negotiate' literature and management training concentrate on what are usually described as 'win–win' situations – see below. This could suggest that the objective of such training is to shift the balance of activity. On the other hand, if the Walton and McKersie conclusion is rooted in the nature of the employment relationship then such an approach could be misguided at the worst and confusing at the best.

Integrative Bargaining

This term describes the system of activities or subprocess where the goals of the parties are not in fundamental conflict. It relates to the notion that there are common problems whose solution will benefit both parties – in fact, Walton and McKersie use the term 'problem' to identify areas of common concern where there is no fundamental conflict involved. Games theorists characterise such activities as 'positive' or 'varying-sum' games. At the end of such negotiations there are shared gains which derive from the joint solution of problems – 'win–win' situations.

During the 1960s, productivity bargaining was often described as integrative. Attempts to negotiate away restrictive practices such as demarcation lines – only plumbers could turn off taps or electricians switch on lights – were seen as ways of increasing productivity and generating gains which would be shared between the parties. Nevertheless, where such gains are accrued, there will still be distributive bargaining to determine the proportionate shares of these gains.

Attitudinal Structuring

In the field of labour negotiations, no one set or round of negotiations can be seen as distinct from any other, given the continuing relationship between the parties. Hence, the parties will attempt to use negotiations to influence both current and future negotiations, by trying to structure the attitudes of the opposing party. They may wish to develop or replace attitudes of trust, hostility, respect and so on. Expressions associated with Margaret Thatcher such as 'no U-turn' and 'the lady's not for turning' generated a belief that opposition would be vigorously fought and acted as a deterrent to it. Such a stance, with all its dangers, can be tempting in labour negotiations.

Intra-Organisational Bargaining

Negotiating theory generally relates to the relationship between workers and their representatives and employers and their representatives. In fact, a great deal of negotiating activity takes place within the organisations. Managers who represent employers will try to negotiate with the employer to secure clear mandates. The same is true of trade union representatives and their members. Clear mandates make negotiations easier when the parties meet – easier for the representatives, that is. Trade union representatives will want to influence the aspirations of their members, resolve differences of opinion that might fragment the bargaining process, and try to reach some accommodation with other unions. 'Divide and rule' is a common negotiating tactic, which is based on the knowledge of actual or potential divisions in the ranks of opponents across the negotiating table.

Intra-organisational negotiations are usually designed to generate common approaches from an integrated unit. It was suggested in Chapter 8 that the use of third-party intervention was often addressed to intra-organisational problems – negotiators are able to agree across the table but may need some additional device to persuade the people they represent. Although most training in negotiating techniques is focused on the union–management relationship, it is possible to argue that the techniques associated with intra-organisational negotiations are of greater importance.

The Model in General

The model outlined has been used to provide useful insights into the negotiating process, and some of these will be referred to in the following account of the stages of negotiation. However, the model does have problems when we examine it in terms of the different perspectives. As presented, the model is a pluralist one. It recognises the mutual dependence of the parties but separates out distributive and integrative bargaining. Distributive bargaining could be seen as rooted in problem solving in that it recognises this dependence and therefore a need to negotiate and compromise. Integrative bargaining may produce net gains but, as suggested above, these will need to be distributed. Such bargaining will include both costs and benefits, which may be very unevenly distributed. In practice it is very difficult to identify the aims of negotiators in such a way that the processes become clearly distinguishable.

From a conflict perspective, it is possible to accept the distributive process as pervasive and to regard the other processes as tactics to be used within it. Such things as joint consultation, quality circles and communications strategies are often associated with integrative bargaining. These could be seen as distributive bargaining via tactical devices aiming at manipulation and incorporation. The rhetoric of problem solving is a common negotiating tactic: 'We have a problem to solve, how can you help us?' Attitudinal structuring could be seen as a tactic designed to strengthen future bargaining power. Intra-organisational bargaining would focus externally on divide and rule, and internally on securing power. Third-party intervention could be seen as a form of 'fixing', which is used to obscure issues and transfer power to the representatives.

From a unitary point of view there is no need for distributive bargaining. In fact, the existence of parties is illogical, because the enterprise operates in everybody's interests. Problem solving ensures a 'win–win' outcome; attitudinal structuring is simply about educating the parties to identify their common interests and to learn the techniques of problem solving.

Given the different perspectives it does not make sense to talk about 'successful negotiations' in general. This is a term that is often used to describe those which are brought to a conclusion without overt industrial action. What follows is a description of the stages of negotiation with reference back to the subprocesses identified above.

The Stages of Negotiation

The Negotiators

In this case it is assumed that the stages discussed are linked to negotiations involving a union or unions and the representatives of an employer or employers. We know something of the structure of such organisations from the earlier text.

Setting Objectives

Most of the prescriptive literature emphasises the need to set clear objectives. Who sets the objectives, and how these are set, are complex issues when dealing with organisations of the type which are party to labour negotiations. Later we will be examining the concept of a negotiating team. At this stage it is necessary to remind ourselves that, in this context, negotiations are a representative process. Those who act as representatives may develop their own or hidden objectives, but their pursuit of these will have to be reconciled with the objectives of those people they represent.

In negotiations, management often says that it may be possible to persuade the board to accept a proposition put to them. The union representative may say the same of his or her union, branch or members. At the time, such statements might not be taken at face value, but they do imply some knowledge of the objectives of the organisations they represent. On the management side, annual negotiations will be discussed at the level of the operation responsible for the financing of the outcome. If this is a divisional unit of a company, then it will have to take account of company-wide objectives and principles. A trust in the NHS – usually a large employer, with around five thousand employees – will have to fund the outcome of negotiations but will be bound by national priorities established at National Health Service Executive (NHSE) level. Nevertheless, there will be an executive board team which will have to set objectives. Intra-organisational bargaining will take place with different managers seeking negotiating objectives that fit their individual interests, and they will advise and inform accordingly.

The research put into assessing and determining objectives will vary from organisation to organisation, but ultimately a view will emerge that will take account of its needs in terms of retention, recruitment and motivation, and compatible objectives will be set. Labour negotiations might be used as a forum to develop and implement longer-term labour relations strategies. Walton and McKersie discuss the tactic of 'last offer first' as part of a strategy of undermining the position of the union. They predict that where such a tactic is used it needs to be based upon elaborate research into the needs and aspirations of the workforce, probably achieved on a day-to-day basis by supervisors. The offer is set to fulfil these needs and aspirations, communicated directly to the workforce and presented to the union as a fait accompli. They further predict that such tactics will result in an openly abusive union frustrated at losing its main function. Meetings between management and union will become abrasive because they are pointless. The hierarchical structure of management makes it easier for the management side to develop clear objectives and tactics, although it does not follow that it will always do so. For the union side the membership's rights to participation create particular difficulties. Open and detailed debate about objectives, even at branch meetings, will alert management to these and allow them to weaken the union's bargaining strength by use of their advance knowledge. Often in national negotiations, union executives are simply mandated to secure a substantial improvement in terms and conditions. Where local bargaining takes place, branches may use a similar formula for their negotiating team. Members may simply restrict their overt participation to listing items in the employment package that they would like to see improved. Such general mandates make the bargaining position more difficult for union negotiators, compared with the more specific ones on the management side.

In both cases, the parties have varied knowledge of the parameters within which they are working. Both will have in mind a range of acceptable outcomes. For management, the main constraint may be the cost of a package, but often even it may have a principle in respect of linking pay to productivity indicators rather than, say, cost of living. Once a union claim has been formulated, the members will know its details but recognise that the claim is only a starting point. The stated claim and its cost will be a tactic designed to achieve objectives.

The process of formulating the claim will be part of the process of determining and achieving objectives. Union negotiators may wish to raise or lower membership expectations. This is part of the intra-organisational bargaining process. The closer the outcome to the claim presented, the more successful the negotiators will be perceived to have been by those they represent. Negotiators will generally hold official positions within the union structure and rivals may try to force unrealistic objectives to undermine these positions. On the same principle, negotiators may want to dampen expectations as part of the process of securing and maintaining such positions. According to Walton and McKersie, negotiators may settle for less than they know they could have achieved had they felt they could 'sell' the outcome. This tactic could be used to facilitate future negotiations. These methods are clearly rooted in the intra-organisational bargaining process.

Management negotiators will be faced with similar dilemmas. For both parties, negotiating meetings are part of a research process. They will be seeking out their opponent's objectives and trying to evaluate the strength of commitment which lies behind these. From the very beginning, negotiating theory suggests that the parties should set themselves clear objectives but recognises that these will need to be adjusted as the negotiations develop. This suggests that although adjusted, they need to be clear at each stage and set precisely in respect of specific objectives – the literature often refers to target positions. Usually three such positions are identified – the ideal, the realistic and the fallback.

The ideal is defined as that which can be achieved if everything goes right in terms of the analysis; the realistic is that calculated to be the most likely outcome; the fallback is the position beyond which the party setting the objectives will not go. For example, in pay terms, these may represent for management a total cost of 5 per cent, 7 per cent and 9 per cent, respectively, although the positions may need to be revised as the negotiations progress. Establishing such positions is probably the best illustration of what is described as the setting of objectives. The advice is that negotiators are more likely to achieve their objectives if these are both rigorously set and revised. Tactics will usually dictate that what is asked for or offered is beyond the ideal, because the ideal is perceived as obtainable. In other words, what is proposed is a tactical manoeuvre and not the expression of a target position. 'Last offer first' clearly defies such conventions, and where determinedly applied can, if representing a move away from such conventions, create conflict. It can also undermine problem solving which might be part of the compromise to be reached – trading productivity for pay, for example.

It is argued in the literature that where negotiations follow the conventional pattern, and are part of a continuing relationship, target positions will overlap, as illustrated in Figure 9.1. This is called the 'area of settlement'. Theoretically success in negotiations is measured by the extent to which a party achieves an agreement in that area of settlement that is closer to that party's target position. This has to be an abstract analysis – the parties will not know the extent of overlap. The same is true if there is a gap between the parties' positions – no area of overlap.

FIGURE 9.1 *Target positions*

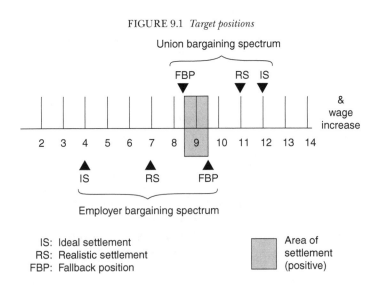

IS: Ideal settlement
RS: Realistic settlement
FBP: Fallback position

Area of settlement (positive)

In such a situation, it is generally concluded that one or both parties have not properly calculated their opponent's positions. This suggests that part of the process of setting objectives inevitably involves estimating your opponent's target positions.

A gap could arise if one or other party decides to break away from the historical relationships. As suggested earlier in the text, the miners' strikes of the 1970s reflected a shift in the balance of power as a result of oil price increases. This created a new and unpredictable relationship. The same could be said of the then new determination under Thatcher to cut public-sector costs. In such situations, the adjustments create a gap rather than an overlap in target positions, and the sanction of industrial action becomes less effective if there is a new determination to resist. Ultimately, the shift in the balance of power asserts itself, and this may be accommodated in future negotiations.

The above framework could be applied to the fire dispute of 2002–3. For example, see Burchill (2004). Why did the union break away from the pay formula that had determined pay for 25 years and put in a demand for a pay increase of nearly 40 per cent? According to Seifert and Sibley (2005: 76–81) the pay formula had resulted in a deterioration in firefighters' pay relative to comparator groups and there had been an increase in productivity. The firefighters and their leadership believed that all considerations justified a pay level of £30 000 for November 2002 – an increase of nearly 40 per cent on current rates of pay. This appears to have been the union's fall back, target and ideal position – according to the Fire Brigades Union (FBU) leaders quoted. What they were asking for they expected to get – 'last demand first', a unique approach. The text focuses on the arguments used to support the demand but does not analyse the strategy behind it. The author of this book was told that they really thought that 20 per cent was the ideal, giving £25 000, and to get this they chose double and the round figure of £30 000 as an opening demand.

Whatever the strategy, an increase of even 20 per cent in one go was unlikely to be secured. The scene was certainly set for distributive bargaining. A consequence of the approach was that productivity – referred to by the employers as modernisation – would become firmly on the agenda. The FBU's opening demand raised the expectations of the members creating the possibility of disillusionment if a settlement was seen to be too remote from that demand. Given the inevitable retreat from this position the door was opened for rivals within the FBU to challenge the credibility of the FBU leadership. In the immediate aftermath of the dispute, the General Secretary and Assistant General Secretary lost their positions in leadership ballots.

The Negotiating Team

Each organisation has its own formalities for selecting a negotiating team, which does not necessarily solely consist of those people meeting across the negotiating table. There is a strong case for having a team, which is referred back to by the direct negotiators after each round. Planning and developing a strategy might need skills quite distinct from those required to implement it. Having such a team allows more flexibility in selecting negotiators and it also allows for specialist knowledge to be available; it is rarely necessary to have specialist knowledge available at the negotiating table. Complex questions of detail can be taken away and probably discussed more effectively in adjournment.

The kinds of skills needed at the negotiating table are not those associated with specialisms. There are certain roles to be played, and one person may play more than one of these depending upon the circumstances. The roles identified in the literature – for example 'specialist' or 'analyst' – vary and are often ill-defined. However, one that is generally identified is that of chief negotiator, though a more accurate description would be 'lead spokesperson'. Somebody needs to take the lead and act as chairperson of the negotiating team. Each team will have its own chairperson; there is no overall chairperson to a set of negotiations. The order of items on an agenda will be negotiated and manipulated by the parties.

Research seems to have identified two basically extreme forms of the lead spokesperson role – the 'spearhead' and the 'conductor'. The spearhead would be a spokesperson who makes the main, if not total, oral contribution during the actual negotiations; the other members of the team would be generally expected to remain silent. The conductor is seen as leading the equivalent to an orchestra, calling on other members of the team to make contributions as appropriate. Within the orchestra concept there seems to be a notion of a gathering of experts.

In practice, the spearhead approach is the most used. This reflects the desire to avoid the divide-and-rule tactics that experienced negotiators tend to deploy; participants in a negotiating team may be made to appear to be contradicting each other by the use of this tactic. It is also easier for a single person to develop a line of argument or presentation in such circumstances. This kind of approach requires considerable discipline – which means it is more difficult for the union than for the employer. Often, particularly on the union side, there are people present simply as witnesses – ensuring that their constituent interests are being adequately pursued. This is another reason why the spearhead approach tends to be adopted. With this approach, the adjournment becomes the mechanism whereby intra-organisational differences can be sorted out. If any member of the team feels the urgent need to raise a point then a short adjournment can be taken and an agreement reached about how to continue.

Another role usually identified is that of notetaker. This is quite different from the role of minutetaker – such a role is very rare in negotiations in the United Kingdom. Each team has its own separate notetaker, and the purpose of such notes is to provide information in adjournments and between meetings. In adjournments, negotiators often try to recollect what exactly was said by members of the other team in an attempt to discover clues to the other party's overall position. Their use of language can be quite illuminating – 'we will never do x' is quite different from 'we cannot envisage the circumstances under which we could do x', but may be treated as the same if not properly analysed. It is therefore helpful when the full negotiating team meets between meetings to have as full a record of negotiations as possible.

During negotiations developments are usually monitored by the process of summarising positions on a regular basis – 'it is our understanding that the following indicates the position between us as it now stands.' This is often necessary before an adjournment. If it is said immediately after an adjournment, and the other party expresses a different view, it could mean that the debate in an adjournment is based on false premises and is therefore a waste of time.

Sometimes the literature identifies the roles of 'hard' and 'soft' persons. These are not necessarily allocated roles but may emerge from structural factors. A person on the management side from finance will always emphasise the great difficulties a concession offered may cause. On the union side, competitors for union positions may emphasise the reluctance of members to agree concessions. Such interventions suggest that the concessions being made are particularly difficult ones. A tactic is to ignore such interventions.

The fire dispute referred to above was of course a public sector dispute. Notionally separate and distinct local authority employers employed the firefighters. At the time of the dispute the fire authorities were represented in negotiations at national level by the employers' side of the National Joint Council (NJC). Although notionally autonomous, the Government provided Fire Service funding predominantly and this clearly restricted the freedom of the employers' side of the NJC. Furthermore the employers' side was made up of local councillors with various political affiliations. Where public sector bargaining takes place reference is often made to 'the ghost at the bargaining table'. Given the influence of the Government, the employers' side of the NJC had little power and even less knowledge of the Government's overall objectives during the strike. Walton and McKersie refer to the tactic of 'calculated incompetence' – having a negotiating team that is so lacking in knowledge and authority that it conceals strategy and resistance points. It was impossible to identify the real negotiating team on the employers' side.

The Negotiations

Negotiations of new agreements, as suggested earlier in the book, usually follow a timetable. This will tend to be flexible, although there will be deadlines laid down. A claim for a new agreement will usually begin with a written submission from the union. It will contain a number of demands, or propositions, usually supported by arguments (see below). The first meeting is then likely to consist of a 'state of the nation' presentation from management – the competitive position, the need to cut costs and so on – followed by an attempt by it to seek full clarification of the items submitted by the union, possibly backed by a request for details of the sources of information on which the union arguments are based.

A possible sequence is for management to adjourn when it believes it is clear about the union's claim, and then to offer a written response as a preliminary to further negotiations. At the next meeting, the union might respond in kind, seeking clarification and sources of information, and taking an adjournment to allow consideration of the overall response by management. What follows from then is difficult to generalise on. Each party is trying to discover the other's settlement areas and the degrees of commitment to target points implied. Previous negotiations between the parties offer clues – hence the importance of attitudinal structuring. Appointing new negotiators can be part of the process of signalling change from the past. In the case of the fire dispute, there had been no negotiations on pay between the parties for 25 years, and there had been a change in FBU leadership.

Walton and McKersie identify certain 'rules' and 'conventions'. There is a convention that concessions alternate – not in a mechanical sense but based on proper evaluation of the offers. The clearer the party is about its own degree of commitment to its targets, the fewer moves it will make before taking up a final position. Where the negotiations follow other, related, negotiations, which have established key settlement levels, then convergence will take place more quickly.

Various tactics will be used to elicit and secure degrees of commitment, and these may revolve around attitudinal structuring and intra-organisational bargaining. Public statements, television interviews and letters to the press may all be devices used in connection with these subprocesses. The legal requirement for pre-strike ballots may be used by the union to secure a degree of commitment from members that members might have resisted if the requirement had not existed. Members may be prepared to vote for strike action knowing that this is a future commitment that they can withdraw from.

At the negotiating table, a range of tactics will be used to express commitment, to avoid commitment or to persuade the opponent to abandon commitment. Threats can be responded to or ignored. If an opponent says 'Do this or else', the response 'Or else what?' may provoke a degree of commitment it was better to avoid. 'This is our final offer' implies a greater degree of commitment than 'We can see no reason to move any further.' The second leaves open the possibility of suggesting a reason. Moving away from a position of total commitment can be damaging to credibility. Attitudinal structuring following from 'final, final offers' leads to the belief that it is always worth pressing for more from someone who takes up more than one final position. Also making an offer which cannot be delivered will virtually destroy all credibility. No offer should be made without complete confidence that those who are represented will support it.

Argument and Proposition

In examining the negotiating process it is worth commenting separately on these two tactics, particularly the use of argument, which is often misunderstood. A proposition consists of a statement to the effect: 'We would like 8 per cent' – it is usually a demand or an offer. Argument is used to support such propositions. A feature of negotiations is that the argument put is often well known in advance by the party to whom it is put, so that union negotiators in pay claims, for example, will often tell the company what the current rate of inflation is and what is contained in the company's own annual report. Why is this done? Are parties persuaded by argument?

A major purpose of argument is to secure commitment from the people represented by those who put the argument. It is best seen as part of the intra-organisational bargaining process. If public support is being elicited then the public is more likely to respond to argument than to threats. An opponent will assess arguments not on their intrinsic merits or according to abstract or absolute principles but rather according to their potential impact on those represented – the principals, as they are called in the literature.

At the negotiating table itself, arguments allow for a phased move from one proposition to another, in addition to indicating commitment. Without argument the parties would be reduced to exchanging propositions. Notionally, there is no reason why the union should not simply signify a demand – say, 10 per cent – and the employer simply reply with an offer – say, 5 per cent. The parties could then adjourn and return with similar exchanges. Argument can be a device which allows transitions to be made, with apparent credibility. A danger in negotiations is that the parties simply become locked into argument. Debating the current inflation rate and the mode of construction of the index on which it is based can be very interesting, but there will be no progress without propositions. An implication is that parties need to consider carefully the purpose of argument to ensure that it is used purposefully and systematically to achieve objectives and not simply to score points.

The above indicates some aspects of the negotiating process. Understanding it helps the negotiator but in itself such understanding is not sufficient. Guides for negotiators often offer rules of conduct – do not be aggressive, be honest; do not threaten and so on. There are probably occasions where such rules are clearly broken and the interests of those so doing have been furthered. Power is an important parameter that can be supplemented by the other party's ignorance and by your own knowledge and skill. It is also something that is often used quite ruthlessly, regardless of the consequences for others and regardless of any apparent conventions.

The Agreement

Most negotiations are concluded without the use of sanctions. Formally, they end with an agreement, or treaty, which contains rules about the parties' future relationships. There will come a time at the negotiating table where both parties agree to recommend an identical set of proposals to their principals – the management to the board and the union to its members. If the principals of either party reject such a recommendation, then there will be a loss of confidence in the negotiators who have their recommendations rejected. There may come a point where one party refuses to move and the other agrees simply to put the propositions to their principals. This raises the strong possibility of a failure to agree. If management put propositions to the union's members where the union refuses to do so, then the union will probably recommend their rejection.

A failure to agree may bring into use a disputes procedure, or result in the immediate use of sanctions. When sanctions are applied – for example, a strike or lockout – the negotiations change dramatically. Both parties incur costs which they may believe they need to recover. The differences between the parties are thus likely to widen in the initial phase. Walton and McKersie believe that the display of completely credible commitment should avoid the need to carry through threats. They see the length of a strike as difficult to predict, but relate it to fatigue and resignation. As the sanction continues to be applied, the parties eventually move back to positions which are more amenable to a settlement and negotiations are resumed with arbitrary deadlines or no deadlines at all.

Understanding the structure of negotiations probably helps the negotiator. Participation and experience also help. So do the personal qualities brought to the negotiations by the negotiators themselves. These factors may help to mitigate the power of opponents, but will rarely be sufficient to overcome its determined use where there is an imbalance.

Conclusion and Further Reading

This chapter has suggested that negotiating in the field of labour relations is a process operating within strong structural constraints. These constraints work to produce fairly predictable and identifiable components within the process. An understanding of the process and constraints can have practical but unquantifiable benefits for the practitioner but never sufficient to overcome the constraints.

Walton and McKersie (1965) is the only text worth reading in this field. Fortunately, Cornell University issued a paperback reprint of it in 1991.

10

Industrial Action

The parties to both the employment relationship and the collective bargaining relationship have access to the use of sanctions to secure their objectives. Employees may quit individually, in groups or *en masse*. They can use the grievance procedure. Employers may use disciplinary measures. Either party may use the courts and legal sanctions. A whole range of sanctions is available to both parties.

Employers are constantly seeking means of exercising control over the workforce, and these will include systems of both reward and punishment. Sanctions may be applied on either an individual basis, a collective basis or both. Those on an individual basis will include such things as dismissal, suspension, transfer, downgrading, withholding of pay or promotion, and many other such actions. Those on a collective basis could include lockouts and mass dismissals.

Employees equally are constantly seeking means of resistance and may act individually or collectively. Absenteeism – often on sickness grounds – or quitting, working without enthusiasm, even sabotage, are often seen as sanctions used by individual employees. All these could be organised collectively, although collective action is usually associated with such activities as strikes, working to rule and overtime bans.

The literature often makes a distinction between organised and unorganised industrial action when referring to the workforce. It is of course possible for employers to act collectively or for individual employers to use their armoury in a more or less strategic manner. In the collective bargaining sphere, both parties use the threat of sanctions as a means of persuading their opponent. There is no conclusive evidence in the literature with regard to the relationship between different forms of industrial action, whether these are classified as individual and collective or organised and unorganised. Attempts to discover whether or not strike action, absenteeism, overtime bans or whatever are substitutable or complementary have been unsuccessful. A major difficulty in discovering a relationship between different forms of industrial action

lies in the fact that the only detailed and continuous i[n]
available relates to the size and frequency of strikes (in th[
subsumed within what are referred to as stoppages; see belo[w]
participation rate in terms of numbers involved. However, [
al. (1992: 309) do say that for the period of their survey all forms of
industrial action moved in a downward direction in the United
Kingdom. This trend has continued till the time of writing.

'Strikes'

As suggested above, statistical analyses of strikes in the United Kingdom
rely on the general statistical measure of stoppages. A consequence of
this is that the data are usually referred to as 'strike statistics' – strikes
and stoppages become synonymous. This is the convention followed in
this book. Before examining the data, it is worth defining the terms of
certain classifications. Strikes might be classified as official and unofficial, and as constitutional and unconstitutional.

Official

An official strike is one that is formally supported (sanctioned) by the
union. This would mean that those on strike would be entitled to any
benefits provided for under the union rules, such as strike pay. It would
also mean that the union could be held to be legally liable where the
strike was organised in breach of current labour laws.

Unofficial

If a strike is not supported in the above sense it is described as unofficial. To avoid any liability for such a strike the union must formally
repudiate such action by its members when such action takes place. It is
insufficient that it has not been declared official. This also applies to
industrial action short of a strike.

Constitutional

A constitutional strike is a strike which takes place after relevant procedures for resolving disputes, as agreed with the employer, have been
exhausted.

Unconstitutional

An unconstitutional strike is one which takes place in breach of the agreed procedure. Employers are just as likely to act in breach of procedures as are trade unions, and it follows that a 'strike' in such circumstances may be perfectly constitutional. In such a situation the workers may perceive themselves to have been locked out. This is one of the weaknesses of regarding all stoppages as strikes.

'The Right to Strike'

It follows from the above that the classifications referred to in respect of strikes can be applied to other forms of industrial action such as working to rule, overtime bans and so on. There is no right in the United Kingdom to take part in such action and therefore no 'right to strike'. Going on strike is fair reason for dismissal and so is any other industrial action which could be deemed to breach the contract. The 1999 Employment Relations Act introduced some protection from dismissal during and immediately after official industrial action. The law in the United Kingdom, in respect of industrial action, tends to revolve around the right to organise it – immunities to the organisers – rather than the right to take part in it.

Rights to organise industrial action have never been expressed as such in UK law; they have always been expressed as immunities from liabilities which would have arisen if the actions had not been done in contemplation or furtherance of a trade dispute. For example, persuading somebody to break a contract, which organising industrial action often amounts to, would normally lead to the possibility of being sued for loss arising from such action. Immunity removes the possibility of being sued. Before the introduction of the labour laws under the Conservative Governments of the 1980s and 1990s, the definition of a trade dispute was a wide one; trade union funds were immune from civil actions in tort. Picketing – attending at or near a person's place of work, or anywhere else other than that person's home, to peacefully persuade that person to take place in industrial action – was allowed.

In the period referred to, laws were amended to narrow the definition of a trade dispute and to limit the immunities in respect of organisation of industrial action. The immunity previously granted to union funds was removed. Picketing outside a place of work other than one's own (secondary picketing), taking action against an employer not directly concerned (secondary industrial action), and official action without a ballot, notice of a ballot, and confined to defined constituencies, all lost their immunity. The closed shop was effectively rendered unlawful, along with action taken to force employers to use contractors which recognised or employed union members.

All of the above activities raise civil liabilities; they are not in themselves criminal matters. However, an injunction might be sought to prevent or stop any of these, and failure to observe such is contempt of court incurring the possibility of fines or the sequestration and freezing of assets. The law is framed in such a way that unions rather than individuals are predominantly liable.

Where such action takes place without union support, the right of the employer to selectively dismiss participants was also introduced. This would also apply to those who organise such action if they are in the employment of the employer affected. Such control of unofficial action, along with the requirement on the union to repudiate it, is designed to put pressure on workers acting independently whilst avoiding the martyrdom which might follow from legal sanctions.

The above gives something of the flavour of changes which have taken place in the 1980s and 1990s. These were reinforced by the willingness of the police to play a more interventionist role in industrial disputes. This was particularly demonstrated during the miners' strike of 1984–5. To some extent this can be related back to the use of flying pickets – an accumulation of pickets from all over the country outside places of work – associated with the miners' strike of 1972. During that strike the police responded to the dangers of mass picketing by closing Saltley coke depot. Since then the police have worked to prevent such gatherings, and thus a repeat of Saltley, by taking measures to hinder the arrival of pickets, often by stopping and dispersing them before arriving at their target. This was first observed under a Labour Government during the Grunwick dispute of 1976, and repeated during the 1980s at the *Stockport Messenger*, during the miners' strike of 1984–5 and during the Wapping dispute involving *The Times*.

An express purpose of the legislation was to reduce the incidence of industrial action. As suggested above, the only measure we have of this relates to stoppages and by implication strikes. The relevant data suggests a reduction in such activity since the legislation was introduced. However, there were other factors at play, and any assessment of the impact of legislation needs to assess all of the causes of strikes.

Stoppage Patterns in the United Kingdom

In the United Kingdom stoppages of work in relation to industrial disputes are included in the statistics if they are concerned with terms and conditions of employment; last at least one day; include 10 or more workers or result in an aggregate of days lost which is greater than 100. The workers included are those directly or indirectly involved at the place of work where the stoppage takes place. People laid off, and days lost, elsewhere are not included. These statistics allow for the compilation of three indicators of strike activity: the total number of working days lost, the number of strikes (stoppages) and the number of workers taking part. The methods used in collecting the data are generally acknowledged to contain weaknesses, but there is sufficient consistency to allow meaning to be given to trends.

General Trends

The long-term trend in strike patterns in the United Kingdom to the mid-1970s showed an increase in the number of strikes combined with a decrease in the number of days lost. This is illustrated in Figures 10.1 and 10.2. Table 10.1 brings this data up to date, covering the past 20 years. During this latter period, all indicators have shown a downward trend, particularly if we adjust for individual strikes, or sequences, which distort the trends. For example, if we take days lost per year per thousand workers, the figures show an average of 157 for 1960–9; 569 for 1970–9 and 332 for 1980–9. The latter two periods could suggest a rising trend from the 1960s, but beginning to fall again. If we had chosen 1979–89, which would include the so-called winter of discontent of 1978–9 and the miners' strike of 1984–5, this trend would have

FIGURE 10.1 *Industrial stoppages, 1893—1976, UK*

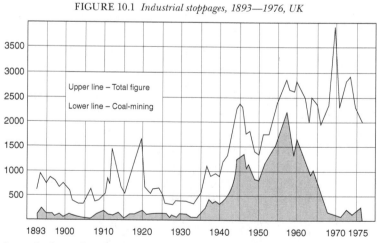

Source: *Employment Gazette*, various.

FIGURE 10.2 *Working days lost from industrial stoppings, 1893—1976, UK*

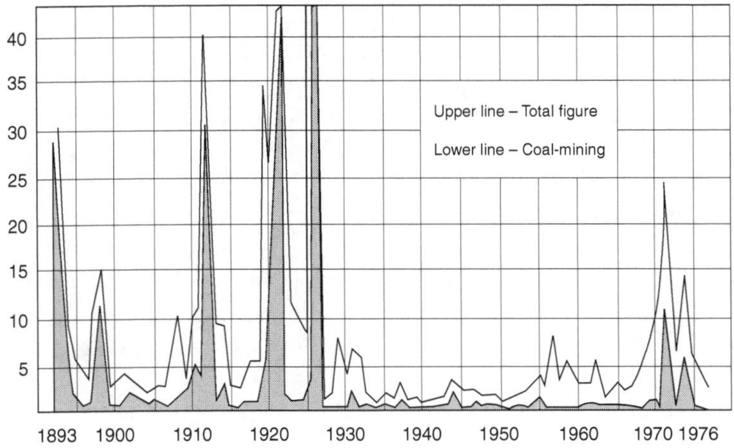

Upper line – Total figure

Lower line – Coal-mining

Source: Employment Gazette, various.

TABLE 10.1 *Number of stoppages and working days lost (United Kingdom)*

Year	Working days lost (000s)	Working days lost per 1,000 employees[1]	Workers involved (000s)	Stoppages[2]	Stoppages involving the loss of 100 000 working days or more
1987	3546	155	887	1,016	3
1988	3702	157	790	781	8
1989	4128	172	727	701	6
1990	1903	78	298	630	3
1991	761	32	176	369	1
1992	528	23	148	253	–
1993	649	28	385	211	2
1994	278	12	107	205	–
1995	415	18	174	235	–
1996	1303	55	364	244	2
1997	235	10	130	216	–
1998	282	11	93	166	–
1999	242	10	141	205	–
2000	499	20	183	212	1
2001	525	20	180	194	1
2002	1323	51	943	146	2
2003	499	19	151	133	–
2004	905	34	293	130	3
2005	157	6	93	116	–
2006	755	28	713	158	1

Notes:
1 Based on the (September 2006) estimates of employee jobs.
2 Stoppages in progress during year.

indicated a remarkable increase. It is also clear that 1989 was unusual. With a rate of 50 days lost per year per worker in the 1990s, the suggestion would be a dramatic fall in that decade, rather than a 20-year trend of decline. The best interpretation is that there had been a 20-year decline in strike action, however measured. In the year 2005, however measured, strike activity in the United Kingdom was at an all time low.

As far as the distribution of strike activity between sectors is concerned, the most notable change has been in the increase in strike activity in the service sector, along with that sector accounting for a greater proportion of such activity during this period. This could be explained by the relative growth of that sector, compared with other sectors, and the impact of restructuring on public employment and the finance sector.

With regard to the length of strikes there is contradictory evidence. According to Edwards (1995: 440), 'strikes lasting no more than a day continued at a relatively steady level'. This reflects data projected over the period 1971–93. According to Millward *et al.* (1992: 283), 'the most dramatic fall was in the incidence of very short strikes'. This reflects data for 1986–90. Both are agreed that there was a decline in longer strikes.

In Chapter 3, explanations of union membership and density were given in terms of sectoral growth and decline, the decline of industries traditionally unionised, a change in the gender and ethnic distribution of the labour force and so on. All of these changes could be similarly related to the level of strike activity: the decline in both may be caused by the same factors. Similarly, whether or not the decline in both is secular or cyclical can be argued either way.

Causes of Strikes

There is no general theory of what causes strikes to happen when and where they do. Why they happen at all is a matter of contention. On the latter point, those who take a unitarist view would tend to emphasise failures of communication and the incidence of troublemakers and agitators. Those who take a pluralist view emphasise the effects of change, whether it be the introduction of new technology, the effects of competition or the impact of the trade cycle. From a conflict point of view, strikes are a symptom of the relationship between capital and labour, which depends upon exploitation. This relationship will vary in form and content at any point in time and over time in ways which do not allow precise predictions to be made. However, the essential ingredient of production for profit and the consequent exploitation will remain and guarantee worker resistance in a variety of forms.

Perhaps the major significance of these perspectives is that those who hold them have different views about how to control strike activity. Punitive labour law and 'proper' management would certainly fit the unitarist view. The Donovan emphasis on institutional arrangements designed to minimise conflict and maximise output would certainly fit pluralism. In the conflict model the relationship between capital and labour is based on antagonisms, with the employer using all means available to control the labour force, and at different times different strategies will predominate. In periods when the labour force is strong, recognition and granting bargaining arrangements might be a way of incorporating the labour force into capitalist objectives. Resistance will be predominantly unofficial, and reflected in tactical, numerous, small, targeted strikes. Periods of transition – when shifts in the balance of power take place – might result in large confrontational set pieces, until a new balance adjusts the relationship.

Numerous attempts have been made to explain strike variations over time, from occupation to occupation, from industry to industry, and between countries. Time periods, jobs, industries and countries have been classified as more or less strike prone. Before the advent of football hooliganism, going on strike used to be referred to as the 'British disease'. Explanations of country variations range from political trade-offs – governments exchanging political concessions with the working class – to Protestant emphases on individualism (fewer strikes), Catholic emphases on collectivism (more strikes) and Buddhist emphases on harmony (see Poole, 1986). The propensities of the labour force in a particular industry or industries to strike may be explained in terms of groups of isolated workers living in close communities and working in arduous environments, such as dockworkers and miners, or in terms of monotony and boredom, such as car workers on continuous-flow production lines. Such explanations do not survive international or inter-temporal comparisons.

The comparative figures in Table 10.2 show that the United Kingdom has tended to occupy a middle-of-the-league position over time in the OECD country league table for strike activity. It would be foolish to try and draw any particular conclusions from such statistics about the impact of strike activity on economic performance or about society in general. This is a point that has been well understood for a long time – as the following exchange indicates – but one which is often obscured:

> The Chairman: I think you stated the other day, Mr Taylor, that up until last year you did not know of any strikes where scientific management had been introduced during the time since it has been introduced.
> Mr Taylor: Yes, for 30 years.

TABLE 10.2 Labour disputes: working days not worked per 1000 employees[1] in all industries and services

	1996	1997	1998	1999	2000	2001	2002	2003	2004	2005	Average[2] 1996–2000	Average[2] 2001–05	Average[2] 1996–2005	Percentage change 1996–2000 to 2001–05
United Kingdom	55	10	11	10	20	20	51	19	34	6	21	26	23	24
Austria	0	6	0	0	1	0	3	398	0	0	1	80	41	7900
Belgium	48	13	28	8	8	69ᴿ	—	—	—	—	21	—	—	—
Denmark	32	42	1317	38	51	24	79	23	31	21	296	36	165	-88
Finland	11	56	70	10	126	30	36	42	21	322	56	91	74	63
France	57	42	51	64	114	82	—	10ᴿ	9ᴿ	—	66	34	53	-48
Germany	3	2	1	2	0	1	10	5	2	1	2	4	3	100
Ireland	110	69	32	168	72	82	15	26	14	17	91	30	57	-67
Italy	137	84	40	62	59	67	311	124	44	56	76	120	99	58
Luxembourg	2	0	0	0	5	0	0	0	0	0	1	0	1	-100
Netherlands	1	2	5	11	1	6	35	2	9	6	4	12	8	200
Portugal	17	25	28	19	11	11	29	15	12	7	20	15	17	-25
Spain	165	182	121	132	296	152	379	59	306	62	182	189	186	4
Sweden	17	7	0	22	0	3	0	164	4	0	9	34	22	278
EU14 average[3]	53	37	53	36	60	43ᴿ	109	44ᴿ	49ᴿ	25	48	53	50	10
Cyprus					—	—	—	—	35	—	—	—	—	—
Estonia					—	—	—	—	0	0	—	—	—	—
Latvia					0	0	3	0	0	0	7	1	0	-86
Lithuania					7	2	0	0	0	1	—	—	—	—

Malta					—	—	—	—	11	0	—	—	9	—
Hungary					46	2	0	1	6	0	—	2	2	—
Poland					7	0	0	1	0	0	—	0	1	—
Slovakia					0	0	0	0	0	0	—	—	—	—
EU22 average[3]					—	—	—	—	43[R]	16	—	—	—	—
Iceland	0	292	557	0	368	1571	0	0	1052	0	245	552	401	125
Norway	286	4	141	3	239	0	72	0	68	5	134	29	80	-78
Switzerland	2	0	7	1	1	6	6	2	11[R]	0	2	5	4	150
Turkey	30	19	29	23	35	28	4	14	8[R]	15	27	14	20	-48
Australia	131	77	72	89	61	51	33	54	45[R]	28	85	42	62	-51
Canada	280	296	196	190	125	162	218	122	226	280	215	202	208	-6
Japan	1	2	2	2	1	1	0	0	0[R]	—	1	0	1	-100
New Zealand	51	18	9	12	8	37	23	13	4	18	19	18	19	-5
United States	42	38	42	16	161	9	32	8	8	10	61	13	36	-79
OECD average[4]	51	41	46	29	86	27[R]	47	33[R]	31[R]	29	51	33	42	-35

The Chairman: Isn't it also true that peaceful relations almost invariably exist between master and slave, that no strikes occur?
(F.W. Taylor's testimony before the Special House Committee, 25 January 1912)

Following from the above, it is not surprising that there is a theoretical model of strike variation over time that is linked to the trade cycle. It is argued that in periods of recession workers are weak and less willing to go on strike, while in a period of boom they are more confident and assertive. The sustained period of full employment from 1945 to 1970 is often seen in this model, in the United Kingdom, as an explanation of the large strike wave of 1968–74. The model has been criticised on the grounds that workers might have more reason to defend themselves in a recession, and employers find it more difficult to concede, but having more reason to defend oneself is quite different from being able to; making concessions leads to greater demands.

Commenting on this general model, Ferner and Hyman (1994: 263) tell us that 'Evidence that economic conditions have had a clear and uniform effect on strike activity is...very limited.' However, they do not dismiss it, suggesting that the effects of unemployment 'are mediated by industrial relations and political institutions'. Later in the same essay they do tell us that defensive strikes in the public sector may be to do with 'resistance against job loss, work intensification, or declining relative pay...a response to the delicate process of sharing the costs of recession and economic restructuring', and they also refer to 'more aggressive action by groups with a more secure and advantaged labour market situation' (p. 276). Large set-piece strikes – the miners' strike of 1984–5 being a good example – fit the transitional phase of defensiveness; the 1972 and 1974 miners' strikes fit a transitional phase of aggressiveness. Both could be linked to market changes, but nobody would suggest that such an explanation would fit all details. Examining economic change seems to be a good starting point in explaining strike patterns. It is a model of explanation which tells us little about the possible roles of immediate events, actors or inherent relationships but does place a useful emphasis on the importance of shifting power bases.

In the United Kingdom the downward trend in industrial action, however measured, does tend to be explained in terms of the impact of labour law and economic circumstances. The precise role of the law is difficult to interpret. The miners in the United Kingdom were on strike for a year in 1984–5 and acted in breach of a whole range of laws. The reader is probably best left to make a judgement as to the relative importance of economic pressures and the law.

At a very explicit level, the reasons given for taking strike action have been classified (Knowles, 1952). Official statistics do incorporate information which can be used to allocate reasons under these headings:

1. **Basic issues** – over wages and hours of work.
2. **Solidarity issues** – recognition, the closed shop or disputes between unions.
3. **Frictional issue**s – disputes over discipline, redundancy, working arrangements.

The statistics depend upon stated reasons as a basis for such a classification. These may not be the actual reasons and there is some difficulty in disentangling one reason from another. However, the statistics suggest some variation over time in the preponderance of one or other of these classifications as stated reasons. This is reflected in Figure 10.3 – the peak periods being described as periods of wage militancy, tending to occur when trade union and worker organisation are strong.

Reference was made to Reid (2004) in Chapter 3 and his view of the importance of the trade cycle. On page 422 he suggests that trade unions are currently in '…a period of major recovery in their strength…' –

FIGURE 10.3 *Percentage of all strikes conducted over wage and wage-related issues in the UK, 1893—1980*

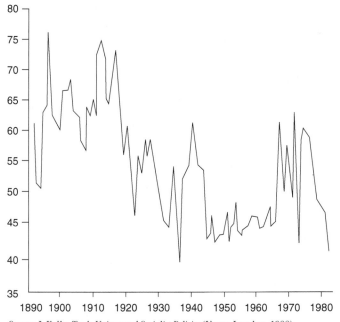

Source: J. Kelly, *Trade Unions and Socialist Policies* (Verso, London, 1988).

linked to economic growth since 1995. This may be optimistic. He does not predict an increase in industrial action but hopes to see trade union efforts more constructively channelled.

The Cost of Strikes

Strikes are generally seen as being detrimental to the economy as a whole. The difficulty with this kind of proposition is that there is also a view that strikes might bring issues to a head and generate beneficial change. This view is partly rooted in the notion that conflict is not always dysfunctional and might be a powerful catalyst for progress. Strikes are an inevitable and necessary consequence of this conflict.

If we examine the miners' strike of 1984–5, it is possible to describe it as having had a devastating effect on production, the balance of payments and so on by examining the economic costs at the time. On the other hand, it might be described as a watershed in management–trade union relationships, weakening the trade union movement's use of monopoly bargaining power which helped to secure long-term gains in productivity and competitiveness. It could also be described as a victory of competitive and individualistic values over cooperative and collective values. Workers who lost money in the strike, and ultimately their jobs, might see themselves as having set down a costly marker which would discourage such confrontations in future. It may also be seen as a symbol of trade union militancy of a heroic kind which provides a reference point for future generations, in the way that earlier generations used the 1930s as a measure of capitalist excesses.

Often it is pointed out that in individual disputes, even where the strikers win, they lose pay in excess of foreseeable future gains. This kind of analysis fails to take account of the potential effect of such action on the future behaviour of the employer. Sometimes losses of output – and pay – are made up by increased production and overtime after the strike. There are also occasions when employers provoke strikes to deplete stocks or conduct maintenance work.

What follows from the above is that strikes, industrial action and conflict, are complex phenomena whether we are concerned with their trends, comparisons, costs, dynamics or causes. This in fact is the rather bland conclusion reached in the literature. However, from a perspective point of view it is possible to reach conclusions, although these are likely to be contradictory. All parties seemed to draw some comfort from the miners' strike of 1984–5.

In a text of this type this is an inevitably brief comment on industrial conflict and is focused mainly on strikes. However the text in general has referred to the conflictual elements within the field of labour relations and the different perspectives on these. The pervasiveness of strikes makes any suggestion that they are irrational responses simplistic. Similarly, from a conflict perspective, the word 'disease', as in 'British disease', could easily be replaced by the word 'healthiness'. If the nature of the employment relationship and work in general is perceived as oppressive for most workers, then any sign of resistance must be seen as healthy from such a point of view.

Conclusion and Further Reading

The literature in this area has produced some useful conceptualisations which allow for logical discussion of related issues but has produced little theoretical content in the sense of working hypotheses of sound predictive value. Economic variables seem to offer most in terms of determining factors, albeit at a highly generalised level.

Kessler and Bayliss (1995: ch. 11) provide additional empirical evidence and a good account of the UK law in this field. Knowles (1952) remains a classic for the serious reader and Hyman (1989) is essential reading.

11

Pay

In Chapter 2, 'The Market for Labour', there was considerable discussion of how pay is determined and why pay differences emerge. Economists have notions of net advantages based on the proposition that work implies disutility – some level of dissatisfaction arising from the constraints placed on our freedom by having to go to work and by having to expend effort. In addition, when we are at work we may have to perform tedious, monotonous or dangerous tasks. There is also the belief that someone benefits from what we do and that we ought to benefit in return.

People generally need to work – whether at home or in a factory, office or hospital – to survive. It is expected that work will bring some kind of return related to the skills we bring to bear, skills which in themselves may cost both effort and money to develop. The net-advantages approach of the economist suggests that in a perfectly free market if we added together all the costs of going to work, including acquiring skills, the effort and boredom of work, risk and discontent, and then did the same with all the benefits, pay, job satisfaction and meeting people, then everybody, whether in work or out of work, would accrue exactly the same net advantages – the difference between costs and benefits. Higher monetary rewards are simply a consequence of harder work or investment in skills or some other disutility such as risk or boredom.

We do not live in such a perfectly competitive world and the idea that one could be created is perfect nonsense. That does not mean that there is not competition for both jobs and rewards. The nature of the labour market was discussed in Chapter 2. Here we are concerned with the nature of the reward package at the level of the enterprise and the way that this might be used to secure such objectives as recruitment, retention and motivation. We are also concerned with the way in which the workforce seeks to affect the reward package in search of compensation for the nuisances associated with having to work.

For the purpose of analysis the examination of the reward or remuneration package will be confined to the more tangible returns, such as pay for hours worked, or quantity produced, and other monetary benefits, such as pensions and expenses. The composition of such a package does tell us something about the means available to motivate or control the workforce at the employer's disposal. This does not mean that less tangible benefits such as work environment, participation and so on are not important. It is simply that the relationship between the employer and employees or the organised workforce is dominated by the more tangible rewards and possible penalties.

The importance of competition in the marketplace is not questioned here. What is questioned is the notion that it works in accordance with neoclassical models or that it can be made to work smoothly. Monopoly conditions can protect employers from market forces. However, a useful neoclassical assumption – useful because it has some predictive value – is that employers try to maximise their profits. (A similar assumption is built into conflict models.) It follows from this that employers will try to minimise the cost of labour while maximising the return from it and will replace labour with machinery when it is profitable to do so. The fact that companies go out of business in expanding markets illustrates the possibility that employers in some cases ignore competitive pressures and suffer the consequences, are not alert to the impact of technological development, lose in the race to develop new technologies, or are undercut by lower labour costs in other economies.

Productivity

To understand the relationship between costs and returns, an understanding of the concept of productivity is vital. If we take labour as a factor of production, then, other things being equal, its productivity is identified by the ratio of output to labour input: output/labour. For example, if 10 persons produce a total output of 100, output per person (average output) is 10. Where another person's is added and total output goes to 110, average output remains the same: 10. If total output had risen to 121, then average output would be 11 – an increase of 10 per cent. Average output is a measure of productivity. In the above example it would be possible to say that productivity had risen by 10 per cent. Taking measures of output and input in this way – for example tonnes per man shift, as used in the coal industry – is a physical measure of productivity.

The employer will be interested in the physical measure but probably more interested in a financial measure. All of the above could have been expressed in pounds sterling instead of physical units. Units of labour could be multiplied by the cost of employing them, and units of output could be multiplied by their market price. This would give a monetary relationship. If the input of labour, the cost of labour and the units of output all remain the same but the market price of the units of output rises, then the employer will be better off. It follows that changes in the price of the product – which might have nothing to do with the employer – can affect the monetary ratio. Variations in the cost of labour will also affect this.

When oil prices rose in the early 1970s, it was possible for the coal industry to increase its prices in response to a shift in demand. Labour in the coal industry took advantage of this by striking for large pay increases. The significance of the market cannot be overplayed. It also affects the notion of a wage–effort relationship. On a day-by-day basis the employer will be trying to link pay to the effort of the labour force in an attempt to secure a relationship such that higher pay generates commensurate increases in output. The value of output will be subject to the vagaries of the market. Other things being equal, if output can be increased at a faster rate than costs, then it is possible for the employer to increase profits or reduce prices for competitive reasons. If sales increase at a faster rate than price falls, profits may also be increased.

It further follows from the above that employers might incur additional costs if suppliers increase prices. This could be responded to by trying to reduce wage costs. Attempts to link pay to profitability rather than productivity reflect these problems. Similarly, if oil prices increase, this could reduce the living standards of workers. At the same time, employers' costs may be rising and attempts to compensate employees for their fall in living standards create a double burden on the employer. What options are available for dealing with pay?

Added Value

Perhaps the best way into understanding the options open to an employer and the role of payment systems is via the concept of added value. A firm can be conceived of as having an income which is determined by the total value of its sales revenue plus any other sources of income, such as interest on loans. If we deduct from this the cost of bought-in materials and services, such as raw materials, electricity, gas, hire charges and so on, we have left what is called 'added value' – or, the income of the firm. This income can then be distributed in a variety of ways (see Figure 11.1). Labour could be allocated more or less of the income, as also could the purchase of new machinery or plant, and less or more could be distributed to the shareholders.

This model of the firm's income makes no mention of profit – it is unnecessary to do so because all of the income is accounted for by describing who gets it. However, the model is important because it generates certain insights into some notions of reward systems. For example, what can profit sharing possibly mean? Does it mean allocating some of the dividend section to labour? What does employee shareholding mean? Does it mean allocating shares to labour instead of pay, and, if so, where does the money saved go? It could, of course go on investment – the purchase of plant and machinery. This would then generate a future reward in terms of dividends to labour. The same result could be achieved by

FIGURE 11.1 (a) *Trading results*

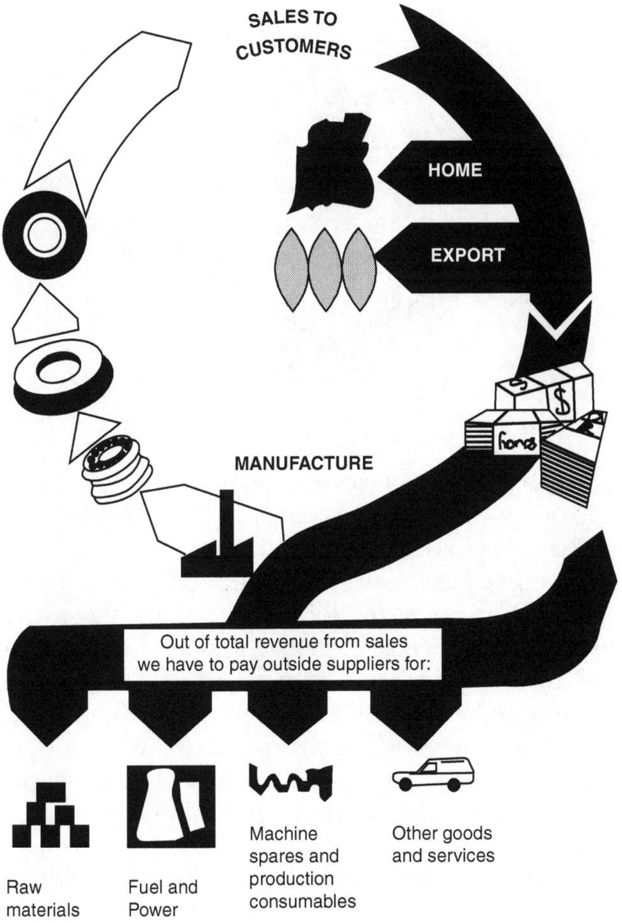
SALES TO
CUSTOMERS
HOME
EXPORT
MANUFACTURE
Out of total revenue from sales
we have to pay outside suppliers for:
Raw
materials
Fuel and
Power
Machine
spares and
production
consumables
Other goods
and services

FIGURE 11.1 (b) *Added value*

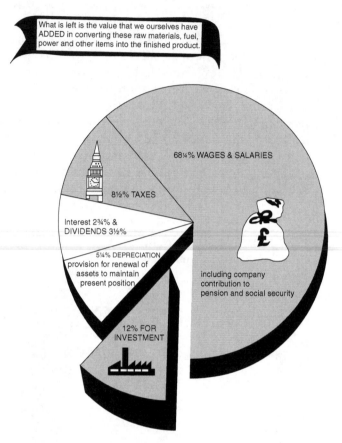

widening the wages and salaries section at some future date, unless, of course, employees who leave the company also receive dividends.

Another way of rewarding labour linked to the total performance of the company might be to guarantee into the future a fixed proportion of value added to go on wages and salaries – the bigger the 'cake', the bigger this section or slice. Profit sharing is always a difficult approach because of the varying accountancy concepts of profit. Securing employee commitment on the basis of shareholding is difficult because of varying practices on dividend distribution and the different types of shares. Only in very rare cases are employee shares accompanied by voting rights – there are limits to employee involvement, whatever the rhetoric. In addition, an employee who commits income to shares in his or her own company is saving in such a way that if the company fails then both savings and income are lost.

Suffice to say that there is a long history of attempts to link added value to pay as a means of securing the longer-term commitment and motivation of employees. Where individual effort is difficult to disentangle from group effort, such schemes seem to have had their attractions. Difficulties relate to the size, scale and complexity of the organisation and the levels to which such concepts can be disaggregated. A drive in industry has been to devolve budgets and establish cost centres with some scope for generating savings or surpluses. Often these contain allocations of budgets and costs, designed to generate pressures on employees rather than to reflect any realistic devolvement of decision making, combined with a continuous shifting of 'goalposts' – especially in the public sector.

Time Payments and Performance Payments

It is assumed that the sensible employer expects some return to be generated from whatever is allocated to pay. Many areas of work are not amenable to a detailed study of the input of effort by employees. Effort is not easily defined, let alone measured, and many attempted definitions do not correlate with output and even fewer with the value of output. Most employees in the United Kingdom, probably around three-quarters of the total, are paid according to time spent at work, with no attempt being made to link it directly to performance. This is a wonderfully simple method of payment, based on the assumption that a combination of supervision, discipline, individual self-respect, peer group pressure and a sensible concern for the future of one's employment might be sufficient to motivate the employee. It also recognises that many of the alternatives available generate more problems than they were designed to solve.

Time payments can require supervision to be effective. There will always be a feeling that there ought to be a more direct method of linking pay to indicators of effort, however remote from it, which will generate optimum performance from individual to individual, however difficult it is to measure performance, even if this results in a different pay package for each individual. In fact, given that all people differ, the competitive ideal would be a different pay and performance package for each worker.

There are many relationships which can be established between pure time-linked and pure performance-linked pay. Underpinning time payments, there might be a study of work requiring certain levels of output or achievement over time. Measured-day-work systems set work-study-based output levels, and if targets are approximately achieved then a fixed level of pay is secured. These could be increased or reduced in some cases if targets were more than or less than achieved over certain time periods, such as monthly or quarterly. Fixed levels of pay operate within the time periods. Such systems are applicable where units of output are easily measurable. (Measuring output is not the same as measuring effort; it is only a proxy for it.) Where output is less easily measured, performance appraisal systems may be used. In office work, levels of attendance, quality of work, getting on with colleagues, dressing smartly and so on may be taken into account. Reference is made to both quantitative and qualitative indicators of performance. In all these cases, it will generally be a proportion of pay that is allocated to performance, with say 80 per cent being time based and 20 per cent performance based.

Perhaps the closest relationship occurs in piece-rate systems, where pay is by the piece or unit of output. For a potter it might be pay per cup made or decorated; for a seller of encyclopaedias it might be number sold. Even with these systems there will be a base rate of pay beyond which the performance payments begin. Payments might then vary directly with output; at a slower rate than output; at a faster rate than output; they may be subject to a cut-off and so on. No doubt the reader can discover all the possible relationships available. That such variations exist owes more to the persuasive power of consultants and to management's everlasting desire to find a substitute for managing, than it does to identifiable and measurable results.

There are other problems, although clearly connected. Work study is often carried out in such a way that too little or too much time is allowed for rest or break periods. Workers studied usually learn to conspire to make their work look more complicated and arduous than it really is. Essentially work study as related to payment systems is about estimating the length of time a task should take and assessing the degree of effort involved in achieving that time. For example, tasks are broken down into cycles and elements, each cycle being made up of so many elements. If the task is screwing the top on a bottle then one element might be pick up bottle, another pick up top, another screw on top, another put down bottle – the whole being a cycle. After workers are timed performing this cycle a recorded time is established as an average. This is then adjusted according to a rating based on an assessment of the speed and intensity with which the observed workers operated. If normal walking speed is 3 miles per hour, this will be the time allocated for walking, even if the operative walks at 4 miles per hour. Walking at 4 miles per hour will be rewarded appropriately. All the times then have to be adjusted to allow for relaxation, natural breaks, interruptions to the flow of materials and so on. Ultimately, work study then determines the amount of time allowed for the job cycle.

With so many variables, work study is an imprecise art. Times allowed are often described as tight or loose; changes in materials, job layout and so on may all affect the system over a period of time. On this basis, tasks may be allocated times and the operative may be rewarded for saving time which will then be used to generate additional units of output.

The payments which are actually made for work done will be related to the whole of the above. This may well result in different workers being rewarded differently in circumstances where they all feel that they are doing the same or similar work. Subjective elements will work their way into whichever method of assessing performance is used. Perceived anomalies can lead to dissatisfaction and to leapfrogging wage claims. Skilled negotiators will manipulate the situation, and workers given loose times will conspire to ensure that these are not made obvious. The term 'rate buster' is used to describe the worker who secures earnings so large that they alert management, who then try to establish a new rate for effort. All of the above is complicated by the fact that pay has to be negotiated as a factor separate from the setting of targets.

Performance-Related Pay

A feature of the recent management climate appears to have been the belief that targets which are meaningful can be established in all types of occupations and be used as a basis for generating additional productivity. The systems referred to above which relate pay to units of output have been traditionally associated with manual work. Management has been seeking ways of creating performance targets for all types of workers including the most senior staff. For an account of such developments, and a classification of the variety of approaches on offer, see Kessler (1994). Here we will confine ourselves to some general observations.

It is relatively easy to list a spectrum of pay systems ranging from time-based to time-plus-bonus, based on individual or group performance measures, supplemented by work study or appraisal systems, and list the weaknesses of each. Pure time requires supervision and might be weak on motivation; other systems require complex methods of measurement and create anomalies and insecurities. All, whether based on quantitative measures (units of output, targets such as size of waiting list for a hospital trust) or on qualitative measures (demeanour, attitudes) involve subjective elements of assessment or relatively arbitrary definitions. They also generate bureaucratic inputs in terms of measurement and interview systems.

Superficially, the idea that workers should be rewarded according to performance is attractive. It accords with more generally, if not universally, held views about what is fair. The problem with such an idea lies in the practice and the difficulties associated with identifying meaningful measures of performance. Measures of performance – performance indicators – can have effects on the work itself which are usually unintended. It is possible to identify certain tendencies, as follows:

1. **People pursue the indicators and not what the indicators are supposed to measure** If for a hospital ward the bed occupancy rate is an indicator of performance then an improvement in the indicator might be achieved by keeping patients in beds for longer periods. Management might try to counter this possibility by adding bed turnover rate as an indicator. Switching people from bed to bed may be used to maintain both indicators. To counter this, length of stay may be introduced. This could lead to increases in discharges and readmissions and so on, ad *infinitum.*
2. **Performance indicators increase at an exponential rate** This is explained in (1) above.
3. **Targets are always achieved** Where targets are selected and set as objectives these will be achieved at the expense of those aspects of the job not included.
4. **Performance payments tend towards equality** Given the subjective element in performance measurement, employees who are rated low will tend to feel discriminated against. This will be especially the case where a team is involved. For example, executive directors of NHS trusts were partly paid according to performance. Differential payments are expected, but inevitably cause discontent and can affect the concept of a team, which a board generally is. Many trusts have removed such payments at director level, because of the problems, and are now busy introducing them at lower levels, in spite of these problems.

Another difficulty with contracts of employment which emphasise the relationship between pay and performance is that they place emphasis on the effort–pay bargain. This emphasis on the notion of a purely instrumental relationship between the worker and work will tend to weaken loyalty to the organisation. For most workers this might not create any problems for the organisation. However, with professional and managerial staff this could be of some consequence; it is precisely among such staff that greater attempts are being made to impose such relationships.

What is being suggested is that the claims often made for performance-related pay as a motivator, or to retain effective staff, are not obviously implied in the model. In practice, schemes do not survive for very long. However, they may achieve other objectives. Such schemes can be used to focus on the individual, rather than the collective, and be used to undermine union influence. They may be used to induce a competitive and market-oriented attitude – particularly in the public sector.

In practice, organisations may not be making choices according to some absolute logic which links a particular pay scheme to clearly defined productivity and profit outcomes. At any particular point in time organisations have to take account of their own individual histories and current circumstances, market conditions and new technologies. Management systems of any type will be manipulated by the parties in pursuit of conflicting objectives, and pay systems are no exception. Any pay system will deteriorate over time in terms of the objectives set by management, and attempts will be made to secure a new order by further changes, which at the time of their introduction will be rationalised as ultimate solutions to the pay–effort bargain. It is not surprising that there is a cycle of pronounced panaceas in which methods attempted in the past are resuscitated, rephrased according to current linguistic devices, and introduced as a solution to current problems. All that can be said with any degree of certainty is that a performance-related pay scheme, where introduced, will be as short-lived as the time it takes those affected to learn to manipulate it.

This section has discussed pay systems in general terms. It was noted that in practice such systems tended to be based on time, with a performance bonus added in some cases. This does not mean that the time element will be identical for all categories of employee within an organisation, regardless of the type of work done. Even where pay is purely time-based, it will vary between groups. Within each group there will be a standard payment based on the number of hours spent at work. What determines the differences between groups?

Job Evaluation

If we think back to the net-advantages approach to the allocation of wages, there is a notion within it that some tasks at work require greater experience or training and carry greater or lesser degrees of responsibility, are more strenuous, boring or what have you than others. It follows from this, and from observation, that workers expect reward structures to reflect some or all of these variations in what is referred to as job content. Job evaluation is a technique which has been developed in an attempt to rationalise hierarchies of pay in a way which incorporates the need to reflect such variables and to establish pay relationships intended to create stability between the differently paid groups. An expression used to characterise a prerequisite for a 'successful' job evaluation scheme is that the outcome should be 'felt-fair' – that those who are affected by it should feel that the pay differences are actually justified by the criteria incorporated.

According to Millward *et al.* (1992: 268), between 1984 and 1990 'The proportion of work places with any job evaluation rose from 21 to 26 per cent, suggesting an increase in overall coverage.' They also note an increase in the use of what are called analytical schemes. Of these types of schemes, the most widely used is points rating. Equal value legislation basically requires analytical schemes and *points rating* is the most widely used of such schemes. We will examine this particular type of scheme to highlight the general principles involved in job evaluation – for a good introduction and explanation of the various schemes available see ACAS (1990).

Job evaluation begins with detailed job descriptions, which are designed to identify exactly what a particular job entails on a day-by-day basis. Jobs may range from routine manual or clerical activities performed under close supervision to jobs which are varied, require decisions to be made by the job holder and carry degrees of responsibility. They may also require varying degrees of physical and mental effort and may be performed in environments which are more or less exposed to danger or the physical elements. Job descriptions will be designed to identify what are generally regarded as factors which are worthy of some element of reward.

Such factors will usually be defined in advance of the job descriptions to facilitate their incorporation and identification. A typical selection of factors is the following:

1. skill, which would include such subfactors as experience, training and educational qualifications required;
2. responsibility, which could include such subfactors as responsibility for supervision (perhaps measured in terms of numbers of people supervised), responsibility for decisions with financial implications (e.g. can spend up to £x or make decisions with £x consequences), responsibility for materials and so on;
3. physical effort;
4. mental effort;
5. working conditions.

Jobs will be analysed according to the extent that the factors are required and awarded points. For example, the maximum score for responsibility might be 100 points, and each job will be given a score on that factor. Routine jobs will score low and the more complex jobs will score higher. In the first instance, what are seen as jobs typical of the total range of jobs, usually called benchmark jobs, will be subjected to this process and a job hierarchy will emerge based on the range of scores. This will then be tested against all the other jobs represented in the benchmarks. The scores achieved by all the individual jobs could be plotted on a scatter graph as illustrated in Figure 11.2. The vertical axis shows current pay rates (before the implementation of the job evaluation) and the horizontal axis shows scores achieved as a result of the job evaluation.

The distribution of jobs which emerges in Figure 11.2, given the axes, is roughly equivalent to what one would expect such an exercise to produce. The steps shown in this figure identify clusters of jobs which have achieved similar scores. These clusters are usually used to provide a basis for selecting the appropriate number of grades against which pay rates will be established. Notionally, every single job could have a separate pay rate. Pay grades attempt to simplify the pay structure and make it more stable. Those jobs which do not fit the clusters in any obvious way illustrate that these jobs appear to have been underpaid or overpaid by the existing pay structure. These are the anomalies which will have led to the need for a job evaluation. In the new pay structure, the underpaid jobs could be moved up to fall into the cluster associated with the new job evaluation scores. Those above the clusters related to their job evaluation scores – the overpaid jobs – could have their pay held constant until they are caught up by general pay increases or they

FIGURE 11.2 *Scores plotted on scattergraph*

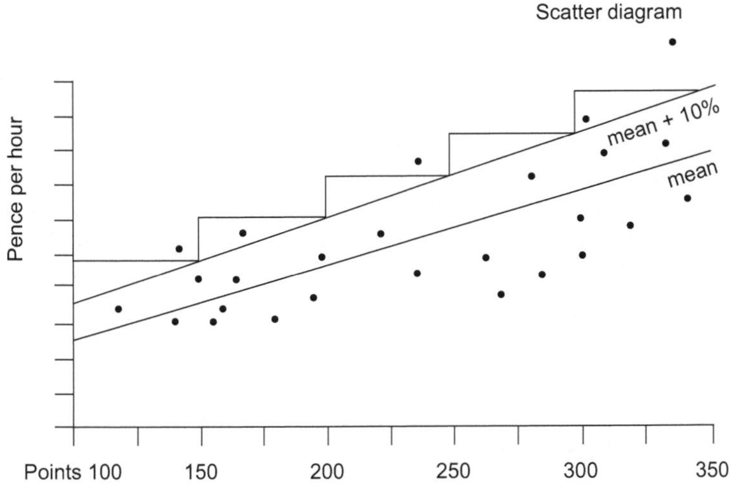

could be bought out by lump-sum payments. Jobs which fall well out-side the trend of clusters are often referred to as 'red circle' jobs – this follows from the convention of drawing a red circle around them on the scatter graph. Where a job is held at a rate above its job evaluation score pending general pay increases, it is described as a 'red circle' rate, and this description can then be used to explain its anomalous position pending absorption.

If the purpose of the evaluation is to produce an accepted hierarchy of pay and prevent fragmented bargaining around perceived anomal-ies, then those affected must believe that the established hierarchy is in some way fair. An implication of this is that those affected must under-stand the nature of the scheme, which can usually be achieved only by some degree of participation. Workers need to play their part in creat-ing job descriptions, determining the factors, agreeing the weighting of factors (e.g. responsibility might be scored out of 100, working condi-tions out of 40), allocating the scores, agreeing the gradings and so on. To be effective, job evaluation usually requires some representative structure, which usually implies union recognition. According to Millward *et al.* (1992: 269), 'The introduction of job evaluation there-fore seems to be associated with, although not confined to, workplaces with well-established trade unions.' This implication, combined with the decline in trade union membership, has led to some attack on job evaluation, which is generally rationalised in terms of its bureaucratic nature and the inflexibility implied in relating rewards to job content. Where job evaluation exists, seeking flexibility can result in appeals against existing grades on the grounds of changes in job content.

It is inevitable that where job evaluation does exist there will be some mechanism for appeal by job holders in respect of grades originally allocated and in the light of job changes. Appeal panels usually require joint membership of workers and managers if the scheme is to retain legitimacy. Essentially job evaluation entails a rationale which can be referred to when workers want to know why they get paid what they do compared with others. It is not an abstract, ultimately scientific place-ment of jobs, but a treaty based on criteria deemed to have been accept-able to the parties at the time. It is a structured and systematic approach to determining differentials which has to be seen as acceptable to those affected. Not surprisingly, changes in market conditions, relative scar-city of skills, obsolescence of skills, new technology and other changes will work towards the need for regular review of pay structures based on job evaluation.

Although participation has been mentioned as important to secure a workable scheme, it does not follow that trade unions will always want to participate. Generally they will wish to do so, but there has been some history of resistance. Such resistance usually represented some fear that they may be seen to have been party to the introduction of a scheme which, if it works out badly, might create negotiating problems. Such a situation could undermine the credibility of trade union representatives.

The NHS introduced a clinical grading structure in 1988 and in 1998 was still hearing appeals which were trying to determine the appropriate grade for staff on 1 April 1988. Such delays are hardly conducive to generating confidence in job evaluation. Part of the problem was that the general grievance procedure was used for dealing with such appeals rather than creating a specialised procedure. This could have been an oversight. The outcomes of the scheme were interesting, because they did tell us something about job evaluation. An examination of the distribution of grades – the system is nationally based – showed that within such groups as the midwives, higher grades were generally achieved in high-employment areas than in low-employment ones. This suggests that although nominally identically applied, the criteria can be influenced by local supply and demand conditions. It also shows that such schemes can be flexible enough to incorporate local market conditions, even with identical criteria, when applied on a national basis. However, if the national application is designed to suggest national standards of training and care, then this suggestion will increasingly be undermined by regional variations in grade distributions.

What does emerge is that economic considerations automatically influence the valuation of factors. If a requirement for a post is a graduate level qualification, the weight of this relative to other factors will decline, other things being equal, if the supply of graduates increases. Becoming a graduate may be as difficult as it ever was, but the relative value of such a qualification can decline, and this will be reflected in job evaluations.

Brown and Walsh (1994: 447) say 'The high tide of job evaluation is probably past.' This they attribute to some of the points already mentioned – flexibility, for example – but also, the growing tendency to link pay to the careers and knowledge of individual employees. An additional possibility is that in a period of relatively high unemployment, job security becomes a far greater issue than differentials. Management finds it easier to deal with individuals when trade unions are weak and easier to control leapfrogging pay claims. Perhaps the extreme of individualised contracts lies in the concept of the 'cafeteria' approach, particularly as applied to managers. They may be allowed to choose a package to a given cost to the employer which could include pay, a choice of car, a pension, BUPA contributions, and school fees for children, in exchange for a given number of hours of work per year, performance objectives and tenure. The reader is left to imagine the range of possibilities, the bureaucratic consequences, the effects on loyalty and supervision and the possibilities for conflict emerging from the variety of concoctions available to the uninhibited entrepreneurial mind.

Since 1997, job evaluation has been implemented on a large scale in the public sector – new schemes in the NHS and local government, for example, with attempts to extend such schemes within the education sector and the Fire and Rescue Service. In the NHS, all employees apart from doctors and senior managers have been included in a job evaluation scheme under the heading of *Agenda for Change*. The dangers of equal value cases being brought against employers was one rationalisation for this. Another was the need to increase flexibility between jobs. The scheme itself is quite elaborate. With fifteen factors, numerous levels within each factor, eight job bands, equivalent to grade groupings, up to 93 different jobs and with thresholds within grades to be crossed on the basis of performance assessment and skills acquisition, trusts were faced with a massive implementation problem. Pressures were also created to implement the scheme quickly and on the basis of a soft concept of partnership with the trade unions. Given the NHS was expanding at its fastest rate ever, with job shortages in every category of employment, not surprisingly the costs were far in excess of those predicted, thus contributing to the trust deficits and shedding of labour which developed rapidly throughout 2006. At the same time, the NHS attempted productivity deals with doctors and GPs – both pushed through quickly for political reasons – resulting in the highest paid doctors and GPs in the world, also adding to deficits and job losses. Not surprisingly *Agenda for Change* uncovered equal value cases.

What the above shows is the importance of context. For the NHS the context in the first decade of the second millennium was closer to the 1960s than the 1980s in terms of trade union power. Its negotiators were schooled in 1980s/1990s business school literature. Its top leadership programme has nothing to say about trade unions, power, negotiating theory, and pay in an industry with at least 16 powerful unions per trust.

Arguments Used in Pay Bargaining

What follows from the whole of the above is that certain arguments will be used in pay bargaining. The following briefly summarises these.

Productivity

Workers tend to argue that increases in productivity should be rewarded by increases in pay. The employer may have an interest in generating additional productivity, and it has been illustrated above that employers have a tendency to argue that pay should be linked to productivity for precisely this purpose. It was suggested above that employers are more likely to be interested in the value of output rather than its precise quantity and thus more interested in financial indicators such as profitability. They will also be interested in the source of productivity increases, which could be new capital.

Profitability

This is a difficult concept to pin down in any meaningful way in any organisation. Attempts to link pay to profitability, however desirable to the parties in principle, are fraught with difficulties in practice. This is illustrated by the value-added concept. Also, company accounts give a historical record and may not be any guide to the future. Whatever the weaknesses of the various measures of these performance indicators, discussed earlier, they are increasingly insisted upon by employers as the major factors to be considered in pay determination. It is useful to remind ourselves of Enron – a top performer and Harvard Business School's company of the year in the year before its exposure and collapse.

Cost of Living

The cost-of-living argument has been widely used for a long period of time. From 1945 until the late 1970s in particular there was an expectation by workers that they would get better off each year. The cost-of-living index tells people not only what the rate of inflation is but also the minimum per cent pay increase required to maintain living standards. It is still widely quoted in negotiations.

Market theorists emphasise ability to pay as the most logical basis for determining pay increases – the cost-of-living argument is seen as essentially irrelevant. If the cost of living rises because of, for example, an increase in oil prices imposed by oil suppliers then the cost-of-living argument could impose a double burden on employers. Their costs will be directly affected by the oil price changes; they will receive wage demands which ask them to compensate their workforce for the decline in living standards. Increases in import prices should have detrimental effects – at least in the short run. The counter argument is that cost-of-living increases might distort the market but often maintain differentials which are seen as fair and thus avoid conflict. If the vagaries of the marketplace have immediate but random impacts in terms of productivity and profitability, then market responses may simply reinforce instabilities and fluctuations. The market cannot be ignored – the question is how to deal with it. Institutional arrangements should exist which allow some mitigation of market forces in the short run, while allowing for planned adjustments to longer-term structural changes.

Comparability/Relativities

This is an argument to the effect that similar posts in other organisations are being paid more. Union negotiators will try to persuade employers that they need to match other organisations on pay and conditions if they are to retain an adequate labour force.

Differentials

As suggested above, arguments about differentials – differences in pay between different groups in the same organisation – underpin the idea of job evaluation. Workers often ask for pay increases on the basis of what has happened to other groups within the organisation. It has traditionally been seen as a basis for leapfrogging pay claims, although, as suggested earlier, it, like all arguments for pay increases, loses its effectiveness in periods of high unemployment and under the pressures of external competition.

Incomes Policies

Government ministers constantly exhort bargainers to moderate their demands and offers in the field of pay. Pay increases are seen as a cost increase which cause prices to be higher than they would otherwise be. This is not to say that pay increases are the sole cause of inflation, but they are an important factor. The government is always concerned that UK prices should not rise faster than those of competitors, because this affects our capacity to sell abroad and thus our balance of payments.

In the past, the government has attempted to address this problem through policies designed to directly control wages. These have usually depended upon some tripartite arrangement between the government, the TUC and the CBI, through which agreement has been sought to regulate wage increases in accordance with some idea of what the nation can afford to pay, usually linked to the growth rate of the economy. This might for example be 3 per cent, possibly allowed as a general increase, with additional amounts in special cases as rewards for exceptionally high productivity increases. Flat-rate increases might be introduced to offer more benefit to the lower paid. Policies can be based on exhortation, agreement or statutory force. All have been tried.

There are so many forces at play that administering such policies is always immensely difficult. Powerful groups will fight to retain differentials; the low paid will fight to erode differentials. Norms will be circumvented by such things as promotions, hidden bonuses and so on. Policing incomes policies is a major problem. The evidence, both abroad and in the United Kingdom, is that such policies can be quite effective in stabilising prices and promoting economic growth. They depend upon a degree of consensus between capital and labour. In the United Kingdom, no major party has entered an election with an incomes policy as part of the manifesto – such policies have been fallen back upon.

Incomes policies do have implications for labour relations. They not only require unions to exist, they give them a more central role in the economy. Pluralism is the perspective which supports the idea of incomes policies; they have no part in a unitarist or conflict approach. A possible economic strategy to create greater employment is to increase public expenditure in combination with an incomes policy. To be fully effective for the United Kingdom, it probably needs to be Europe-wide, and to contain some control over imports of goods into the European Union, as well as exports of capital from it. None of this is in accordance with thinking about the European Union as a bastion of free market economics. Varying interest rates in response to the pressures of low-wage-cost competition, with the aim of everything being adjusted by flexible exchange rates, has been seen to be, and will continue to be, a source of increasing unemployment and falling living standards. Since the previous edition of this book we have had high economic growth rates, to some extent fuelled by the growth of China and Russia, and war and invasions. Pressure on wages has been to a large extent contained by high immigration rates of labour from the expanded European Union.

Pay has been dealt with at this point in the text because the author believes that this issue is the central one in the field of industrial relations. Everything else is linked to, and revolves around, its determination. Control of pay is the battleground for which the parties marshal their forces and the outcomes of the subsequent battles have an impact on our economic and social systems.

12

The New Industrial Relations

This chapter title was used with some reservations in the two previous editions of this book. In the first edition this was linked to concepts of 'Japanisation' which carried over into the second edition – reflecting the views of recent publications. In both cases the theme of the chapter was that there was not a great deal happening in the field that was really new. This contradiction was reflected in recent literature. For example, Geary (1995: 392) tells us 'It must be concluded, therefore, that the current managerial means of labour regulation do not constitute a fundamental departure from past practice.' This comment is based on a review of evidence relating to work practices across a range of organisations. Such a view can be contrasted with that of Millward (1994: 117):

> The transformation that has taken place in Britain's industrial relations since 1979 is now so much part of the conventional wisdom that further analysis of it may seem unnecessary...So radical has been the change since 1979 that industrial relations scholars have appeared to many people to be an endangered species, rather like the institutions that many of them study.

No doubt these statements can be reconciled by distinguishing between 'labour regulation', 'industrial relations' and a definition of 'past practice' which begins a lot earlier than pre-1979. However, they do communicate different images of the world – one which emphasises continuity and one which emphasises change. That continuity and change characterise historical development is the kind of comment which further allows for reconciliation of these apparently different perspectives.

The view taken in the earlier editions was that many of the then current management practices were those one would associate with a shift in the balance of power between capital and labour. As Millward states in the same reference, management has 'regained the right to manage'. His choice of the word 'regained' suggests a return to a state of affairs that perhaps previously existed and one which favours management. The purpose of this chapter is to review some of the practices of management in recent years by examining some of the rhetoric behind the various labels of practice referred to above and to look at some of the developments associated with the European Union, and to conclude with some description of international trade union and employer organisation.

The Japanese Model

Millward (1994) identifies three main variants of 'the new industrial relations'. The first of these he describes as the 'Japanese model', the core elements of which are said to be: recognition of a single trade union with sole bargaining rights; pendulum arbitration as a basis for enforcing a 'no-strike' agreement; access by all employees to a consultation forum; 'single-status' employment conditions; freedom of management to organise work. It is designated as Japanese on the basis that it characterised the system introduced by Toshiba Consumer Products in their Plymouth factory in 1981. Price and Price (1994: 543) offer a similar, relatively restricted, definition of Japanisation:

> The single-union 'no-strike' deals at firms like Nissan, Toshiba and Hitachi have received wide media attention, but in practice the more influential changes have probably been those abolishing status distinctions such as separate canteens, car parks, and different types of clothing, and the introduction of quality circles and other group-based methods of involving the workers in the quality of production.

Geary (1995) summarises research findings comparing the practices of Japanese companies in the United Kingdom with those of UK-owned companies, and those of other foreign-owned companies in the United Kingdom. Here the approach to Japanisation is essentially how different are the practices of Japanese-owned companies to those of other companies in the United Kingdom. The answer seems to be that they are not very different when their total behaviour is examined. However, he does make the point that

> While the direct effect of Japanese employment practices would appear to be limited, it seems clear that it has had a noticeable indirect effect by arming British employers with a powerful vocabulary with which to justify their actions...attacks on union demarcations and the quest for greater flexibility are old concerns, but when cloaked in the language of HRM and with the need to compete with the Japanese, they are given added legitimacy and impetus. (p. 388)

The range of practices considered by Geary in relation to the term Japanisation is wider than that of Millward. Oliver and Wilkinson (1992) extend the concept much further in their book *The Japanization of British Industry*. They consider total quality control, just-in-time, continuous improvement, accounting methodology, hierarchy – in fact, virtually the whole gamut of industrial practice and identify a Japanese orientation in all of these areas. In other words, there is not a set of practices which is applied in Japanese companies and not elsewhere, but a Japanese approach to the various aspects of management. These they describe in chapter 2 of their book, which is based on practice in Japan.

Nevertheless, Oliver and Wilkinson do identify a core theme:

> Although many manufacturing practices are currently being labelled as 'Japanese', one theme that runs through most of these practices is the central significance of quality, and the control of processes in order to achieve this. (p. 20)
>
> The control of quality is a responsibility of every individual employee and should be built in at every stage of the production process – there is no need for quality inspectors at the end of the production line, or a quality control department which acted as a 'policeman to production'. (p. 21)

Reference is made to the influence of American quality control experts on Japanese thinking, such as Juran, Deming and Feigenbaum, who were clearly not prophets in their own land. Lyddon (1996, p. 90) quotes a British engineer, Woollard, writing in 1925:

> The ideal of continuous flow must be present from the design and raw material stages up to and even beyond the sales stage ... unless the product of the factory maintains a certain ... quality, the 'flow' of orders ceases and continuous production becomes impossible.

What Lyddon demonstrates is that Woollard enunciated many of the principles associated with efficient flow production, whether these are linked to notions of TQM, of JIT, of Japanisation or what have you. Clearly much of what was seen as central to so-called Japanese production methods was well known by the production engineers of the longer-established economies. A possible conclusion is that these practices do not stand as the 'best' in their own right but that they require a workforce not capable of resisting their implementation. This could be why Deming and colleagues first implemented such practices in Japan in the immediate aftermath of the Second World War.

Coffey (2007) writes about the myth of Japanese efficiency and a fictionalisation of history in accounts of lean production methods.

A Case Study

One way of identifying the ingredients of the approach to the management of the workforce implied in all of the above is to outline the content of a description of the implementation of change in an actual company. Although the report is dated it does touch on themes associated with the recent history of employment relations using the rhetoric of the time. The company was a relatively small one – 300 employees at the time and approximately 300 now, having reduced staff in 1998 to approximately 200.

IRS (1996) contains an article titled *Organisational Change in Bonas Machine Company*. It is suggested (p. 5) that the programme of change was motivated by competitive threats to the business and by internal problems. The first stage of implementation is described as *changing company culture*. In 1992, an analysis was carried out which identified 'strong leadership' but a lack of employee development. 'Workers carried out specialised jobs within a bureaucratic and hierarchical structure. The relationship between management and the recognised union, the AEEU, was hostile. Consequently, employee relations were poor.'

To begin the change in culture, seminars for the workforce were introduced which explained the nature of the product life cycle, highlighting the threat from a major competitor, which had developed a technology similar to the one which gave Bonas some short-run competitive advantage. There were also seminars on 'the Japanese way' (p. 6), showing how Japanese companies operated and how they had performed better than European equivalents. An examination of the local economy was used to illustrate the decline of traditional industries and skills and the need for greater flexibility in the organisation. Shop stewards and managers were given joint training in such things as negotiating skills and teamworking, with the emphasis on working to a 'common purpose'.

The next stage was to introduce 'improvement workshops', which focused on problem-solving techniques and training in these, with some introduction to *kaizen* (see below). 'Several senior and middle managers left the company, unable to adapt to the new ways of working' (p. 7). Once it was perceived that the need for change was clearly understood, it was then felt necessary to introduce strategic objectives. 'In 1993 the company evolved what it calls a "stunning vision"... The vision was for Bonas "to be a world class organisation by 1999".' This general strategy was backed up with a list of specific targets, covering over a hundred processes and activities, with deadlines for achievement. These were fed into individual targets through monthly performance reviews which required individual employees to identify the extent to which they were contributing to the achievement of the overall corporate objectives. Reference is made to the introduction of 'visual management' – 'employing banners, graphs and tables throughout the factory'. What are described as 'radar charts' were also introduced, divided into two parts – 'delighting our customer' and 'securing the future'. Within these charts monthly targets were set – for example, by October 1996, 80 per cent of all employees would be involved in *kaizen*.

Kaizen is described as a 'Japanese word…meaning improving on goodness'. This is the term associated with the idea of 'continuous improvement' and seen, in the company, as 'one of the most important reasons for Japan's economic success' (p. 9). Everybody is expected to continuously seek out ways of improving what they do. To facilitate this process, training was given in such things as 'work study, ergonomics, standard procedure writing, health and safety and management skills, as well as development of the skills of logic and reasoning'. Structures were introduced to allow for improvements which needed some planning and co-ordination of others to 'immediately implemented changes'. Management was trained to be more responsive to employee initiatives and to offer praise, encouragement and guidance – to facilitate rather than to direct.

The company also introduced team working, described as 'cellular manufacturing'. Team leaders were carefully selected using role play and psychometric testing, and once appointed they were trained to NVQ level three. This took place in 1992, and in 1994 all employees had to apply for a job in a team. According to IRS (p. 9) 'Workers lay out their own cell, set their work standards, decide production levels and solve their problems.' Within the team there would be a shared philosophy.

All of the above is very much encapsulated in what the company's literature describes as 'Bonas Machine Company's "philosophy of work" – seven behaviour standards'. These include 'sharing the vision': staff are expected to actively participate in achieving the shared vision of becoming world class by 1999; 'total flexibility': change has to be regarded as normal; 'team working': the shared philosophy is 'delighting the customer'; 'lifetime education': training and development are normal and continuing processes and employees are encouraged to demand training; 'supplier–customer relationship': achieving targets and quality levels and thus delighting the customer; 'self-management': team members set standards and work to maintain continuous improvement.

Achievement of targets in terms of the seven behaviour standards was assessed as part of an appraisal system which affected salary progression. Each individual has a SWOT analysis twice a year examining strengths, weaknesses, opportunities and threats as part of the review.

JIT and TQM

JIT was referred to in the case study. Essentially JIT is about 'eliminating waste', although it has often been associated specifically with minimising the holding of stocks, and, in exaggerated cases, holding zero stocks. Economists would talk about optimising stocks. However, waste could refer to waiting time, breakdowns and so on. This concept is often treated as unproblematic. 'Eliminating waste' could be seen as a tautology: it all depends upon the definition of waste. One person's waiting time is another person's rest period. JIT may well improve productivity at the expense of work intensity.

Ideally, with JIT, bought-in materials arrive at the point of production exactly as required, without the need to have such parts in stock. The supplier delivers on time. The product is then collected immediately by the customer. If this process imposes costs on the supplier, these costs will remain in the value chain and will ultimately affect the price to the consumer. It is important that the main producer, or purchaser, in the process co-ordinates the flow of supplies. The rhetoric of the theorists, or propagandists, in this area is that there should be a collaborative relationship with the suppliers. This, in many cases, involves rigorous inspection of the production process of the suppliers and the imposition of cost constraints on them by the purchasers. The relatively new internal market in the NHS, which separates purchasers from suppliers, facilitates this process and creates a situation where the purchasers are able to exercise considerable control over the management of suppliers, in this case trusts.

Where suppliers are in competition, their survival can become dependent upon large monopsonistic purchasers. ('Monopsony' is the term used by economists to describe a situation where there is a single purchaser – monopoly relates to the single or large seller.) The threat is always that they can shift to another supplier, and in global markets such suppliers may employ highly exploited labour, including children. In the past, with labour shortages, vertical integration, the buying up of suppliers by purchasers, was used to guarantee supplies. In current markets, contracting out production can take place, with purchasing power acting as a constraint on the newly 'independent' suppliers.

If the flow of production is to be maintained in an increasingly JIT environment, then quality has to be maintained throughout the production process – 'getting it right first time' is a popular slogan within the rhetoric. TQM and JIT are inextricably interlinked. Employees are expected to control their own quality at every stage and information technology facilitates this. There is no final inspection process. Following from this is the need for a 'committed' and 'loyal' workforce, 'empowered' to make decisions. The model expounded is a unitarist one, with no place for industrial action or conflict. 'Quality' is a byword of the organisation.

Flexibility

This term is usually associated with the use of labour. JIT could be linked to flexibility of the purchase of parts and materials. Subcontracting of services could be seen as a way of reducing stocks of labour. The same is true of overtime working. Peripheral and core labour forces have been discussed earlier, along with functional flexibility – each worker performing a range of tasks, having been trained to be 'multi-skilled'. Pay and benefits flexibility have already been referred to. Flexibility in hours may include annualised hours, a target number of hours to be worked in a year according to seasonal and fluctuating demands for production, with each hour being worked at the same rate of pay regardless of when worked. Job sharing and the increased use of part-time and temporary workers fit the flexibility model.

Flexibility is a word with positive connotations – people prefer to declare themselves flexible rather than inflexible. In practice, it can lead to increased work intensity, job insecurity, loss of employment rights and low pay. It creates new categories of labour, which has implications for collective bargaining and trade union organisation.

Perspectives on Japanisation

From a unitarist point of view all of the above is about improving performance. As Milo Minderbinder would say, 'everybody benefits' (Heller, 1962). The peripheral workers benefit from the 'trickle down effect' of higher productivity, absolutely if not relatively. Jobs are retained which would be lost but for the increased competitiveness which follows. For the pluralist, all of this is dependent upon short-run forces related to the labour market, and if tighter labour markets emerge much of the stability provided by organised labour will be absent. The weakening of trade unions removes channels of communications at the macro level, which might be necessary if governments are to deal with re-emergent inflationary levels and if UK labour is to be influential in EU developments.

The approach also places too much emphasis on managerial practices as a factor in Japanese economic performance. It ignores the role of the Japanese Government in economic planning, the provision of long-term investment finance, the educational system and guaranteed home markets via the use of protectionism. It also exaggerated the so-called success of the Japanese economy – as recent years have shown.

From a conflict perspective, the above is linked to a *crisis of capitalism*, leading to an increased exploitation of the labour force. Trade unions are being undermined to secure not just a more flexible labour force, but a weaker, more malleable one. Historically the productivity of American labour was used as an excuse for introducing Taylorism and associated techniques; the German 'economic miracle' was a managerial rallying point in the 1960s and 1970s; and Japan was being used for the same purposes. The techniques are independent of Japan; they just represent longstanding control mechanisms which need to be rationalised slightly differently at different points in history. What we have is not post-Taylorism, but a Taylorism supplemented by information technology and a pervasive rhetoric concocted by the newly established business schools. Workers are now so cowed that they do their own work study under the guise of continuous improvement.

More recently the quality movement rhetoric has been translated into what is referred to as the Six Sigma quality programme. Jack Welch, former CEO of General Electric, makes the following observation in his autobiography:

> For years as colleagues, neither of us had been fans of the quality movement. We both thought that the earlier quality programs were too heavy on slogans and light on results....In the early 1990s we flirted with a Deming program in our aircraft engine business. I didn't buy it as a company wide initiative because I thought it was too theoretical. (2003: 328).

Nevertheless, Welch recognised that quality had become an issue in respect of the company performance. A close colleague had '...become fervent about six sigma...He said for most companies the average was 35,000 defects per million operations. Getting to a Six Sigma quality level means that you have fewer than *3.4 defects* per million operations in a manufacturing or service process.' As Welch observes 'That's 99.99966 percent of perfection.' (p. 328). To get the message across they brought in '...a former Motorola manager who was running the Six Sigma Academy in Scotsdale, Arizona. If there is a Six Sigma zealot, Harry's the guy.'

Six Sigma programmes appear to contain some of the usual suspects – Value Stream Mapping, Lean Processing, Total Process Maintenance, for example. However, there is an emphasis on understanding statistical techniques – Analysis of Variance, Cause and Effect Analysis, Hypothesis Testing and Correlation and Regression analysis, for example. Lean Processing is, of course, about eliminating waste. The bywords of Six Sigma, and Lean Six Sigma, apparently a higher form of the art, are define, measure, analyse, improve and control.

It may well be that Senior Management need to develop an evangelical culture in order to persuade themselves to engage in the meticulous day-to-day management of the enterprise and such an approach may achieve what the corporate mind perceives to be 'results'. The Six Sigma approach appears to be a more muscular form of the quality movement – there are yellow belt, green belt, black belt and even master black belt practitioners of the art. Master black belt practitioners no doubt qualify to be gurus. Given that GE is the main provider of medical equipment to UK Hospital Trusts with PFI developments there is no doubt that Six Sigma missionaries will clarify and expand their message based on widespread American experience of integrating new technologies into healthcare settings.

Whatever the perspective the reader brings, one has to be a little sceptical about managers who have 'stunning visions' of stunning banality and enter into messianic mode when propagating their approaches to management. As James Thurber once said, 'the onset of utter meaninglessness is imminent'. This is not an insignificant point. A common discussion, in the author's experience, amongst those battered by the outpourings of the quality movement, is 'Do they really believe what they say?' Do they really believe, for example, that world-class excellence is a stunning vision? The answer to this question would appear to be either yes or no, with either answer being equally worrying. The same is true of many of their claims. In fact the rhetoric of management in the United Kingdom has now become a source of satire across its broadcasting and publishing media in general.

HRM

Millward (1994) identifies HRM as one of the three forms of the new industrial relations. He tells us the following about HRM:

> To some this offered the prospect of avoiding unions by kindness. Although variously used, often with evangelistic overtones, the term generally encompassed the following elements: managerial policies designed to engender employee commitment to managerial goals, employee flexibility in terms of the work or jobs performed, a general emphasis on quality in both outputs and processes, and finally, an integration of management's personnel (or 'human resource') policies with its strategic business planning. (p. 3)

Put like this, HRM could be seen to be another term for TQM, JIT, WCM and the package described in the case study above. Probably the more logical way to describe the package, and Millward's list, is as current management practices. In the academic field, regardless of the convoluted debate on what HRM really is, it does seem to have become a term which simply replaces personnel management to describe areas of activity which organisations inevitably become involved in.

Traditionally the study of personnel management dealt with three main areas of activity: employee resourcing, employee development and industrial relations. HRM texts have generally renamed two of these: 'human resourcing' recognises that in an increasingly flexible world not all human resources used will be employees, while industrial relations has been replaced by 'employee relations', which emphasises the individual and moves away from the collective implications of the earlier term. All of the practices described can easily be slotted into these three categories and can be analysed accordingly.

For example, if currently in the resourcing process there is more emphasis on flexibility, the use of psychometric testing and so on, this can be described and explained. Similarly, so can a more unitarist approach, individualism, performance-related pay and so on. Using HRM as synonymous with TQM seems pointless. Changing the title of personnel management to HRM might seem equally pointless, but this is what has really happened.

The rhetoric of cultural change has been used to accompany techniques to increase productivity in companies which may have encountered strong opposition from the labour force in recent decades. It has also been used to rationalise privatisation and internal markets. Lean production is associated with work reorganisation of the type that Taylor would have been delighted to deliver: total examination of the work process, including the rigorous application of work study techniques; pay related to performance and productivity; shedding of workers and managers, aided by information technology; securing the collaboration of the workforce, often inspired by fear and insecurity; increased work intensity for those who remain in work; legislation designed to weaken autonomous organisations of workers; and the dilution of employment rights. This characterisation is at least as plausible as that of commitment, empowerment, loyalty, open communications and involvement.

Employee Participation

Employee participation is an expression which has been given a wide variety of meanings. Unitarist ideology can place an emphasis on the functional benefits of employee participation which may be seen as an adjunct to efficient management. Within this perspective communicating with employees through 'visual management', team briefings, getting them to play a part in quality circles and such things as advisory boards, would be seen as participation. The current emphasis is on individual participation, as representatives of sections of the whole workforce, rather than through autonomous representative organisations, such as trade unions.

From a pluralist point of view, collective bargaining is seen as a form of participation. Negotiation implies some influence on the decision-making process, which is not necessarily the case with the approach referred to under unitarism. Some theorists have identified trade unions as forming an opposition – though a permanent one – in the parliamentary sense. As mentioned earlier, the Donovan Commission (1968) suggested that collective bargaining 'Properly conducted...is the most effective means of giving workers the right to representation in decisions affecting their working lives, a right which is or should be the prerogative of every worker in a democratic society.'

From a conflict point of view, workers use their collective strength to inhibit the power of the employer. In the early days of trade unions, many expressed within their rulebooks the overthrow of the capitalist system as an objective. A consequence of the achievement of such an objective would be the ownership and control of the means of production by, and in the interests of, the working class. Workers' control is a necessary precondition for democracy at the workplace, and in society as a whole. Concepts of participation range, therefore, from merely providing workers or employees with information to full control of the economy by the working class, with enterprises directed by elected representatives of their workforces.

Another way of expressing this range is to suggest that there are unitarist approaches based on managerial ideas of efficiency, pluralist approaches emphasising joint decision making and conflict notions of revolution. Although it is possible to argue that unitarist approaches based on such activities as advisory boards and quality circles have had something of a resurgence, a major part of the debate in the United Kingdom over the last 20 years or so has revolved around institutional devices based on European experience and generally linked to the idea of appointing workers to boards of directors.

In 1975 the EC issued a Draft Directive on the Harmonisation of Company Law, usually referred to as the Draft Fifth Directive. This contained provision for worker participation. A model much promulgated at the time was one based on the system in Germany, where companies had a two-tier board system – a day-to-day management board overseen by a supervisory board with some power to veto decisions of the management board. Workers were represented on the supervisory board. In the United Kingdom a committee of inquiry into industrial democracy was set up in 1975 which reported in 1977 – the Bullock Report. It proposed a one-tier system solely based on union representation on the board rather than worker or employee representation – in other words, worker members would be chosen via union nominations and elections. Boards would consist of equal numbers of managers and workers, with a small number of independent members – this became known as the $2x + 1y$ formula.

An experiment following the Bullock model was attempted in the Post Office, but did not last very long. Workers had been appointed to the board of the nationalised British Steel Corporation as early as 1965. The experiment did not generate a great deal of enthusiasm among the unions taking part – worker directors tended to become alienated from the workers they represented and it was soon discovered that not all decisions were openly made at formal board meetings.

Unions in the United Kingdom were generally ambivalent about such schemes, believing that they could lead to incorporation of representatives and difficulties in challenging decisions to which they had notionally become a party to making. Attempts to base representation on models such as the German one of general employee representation were often seen as methods of bypassing established negotiating structures and thus undermining union influence and organisation. Hugh Scanlon, a trade union leader at the time, expressed the view that the trade unions did not have to 'plead the Fifth Directive' to secure a say in decision making at the level of the enterprise. He believed that union bargaining power could be used to challenge any type of board decision if unions were so inclined.

If the unions were ambivalent, the employers were not – they objected to the whole idea of such representation, and, in the United Kingdom, they generally still do. Throughout the 1980s, they were supported by the Government, which was equally hostile to collective bargaining. The European Works Council (EWC) Directive of 1994 was opposed by the UK Government, which was allowed to opt out from its provisions. Trade unions in the United Kingdom have supported this development, recognising that whatever the mechanism for representation, the European experience is that trade unions end up playing a prominent role in the process. Also, given the weaknesses of trade unions in the present economic climate, it seems to be further recognised that anything which might give legislative support to worker representation might ultimately give a greater degree of legitimacy to trade unions.

The requirements of the Directive are such that many UK-based companies are covered on the mainland of Europe, and EWCs without representation from the parental operations of EU-based companies would lack credibility. This has led a large number of UK-based companies to allow such representation. An EWC is expected to have the right to meet with the central management of the company at least once a year and to be provided with information and consultation on the general financial situation of the company, its structure, investment plans, employment trends, cutbacks, closures and so on. There are complexities surrounding the implementation of the Directive which space does not allow to be explored here. As with all consultation and information provisions, whether in statute or collective agreements, what they mean in practice is often hard to determine in advance. The impressions emanating from the parties seem to be that for companies such arrangements are a nuisance, for unions they do not offer much on the surface, but they do at least provide an opportunity for members to meet colleagues from abroad and develop their own agenda. Where EWCs are established, it is provided for that they should consist of between 3 and 30 members, with representatives from relevant states, appointed by employee representatives, or the total workforce, according to national provision.

No doubt the progress of EWCs will be monitored enthusiastically by academics, and we will learn from this exactly what their potential is. Under the Social Action Programme, and European Court decisions, the European Union has affected individual rights to consultation, provided equality of opportunity and introduced significant health and safety regulations, along with collective rights. Not surprisingly, trade unions in the United Kingdom have responded by being supportive of EU development. Beneath this level of response – seeking warmth in a cold climate – is the recognition that the European Union is essentially free market oriented and is unlikely to deliver to unions benefits which are strongly opposed by the government. The role of trade unions in the United Kingdom is more likely to be affected by the inability of UK industry to compete without government intervention than it is by EU developments, although the two are clearly linked.

Following the implementation of the EWC Directive, the United Kingdom was one of three countries – the others being Ireland and Spain – perceived to have what was referred to as a 'representation gap.' This was based on the fact that other member states were seen to have provisions for consultation at national level, whilst the three referred to did not. National systems were seen to provide a platform to more effective EWC operation.

In April 2005, the Information and Consultation of Employees Regulations came into force covering Great Britain (Northern Ireland is covered, but by a separate piece of legislation). These regulations were a response to EC Directive No. 2002/14 which established a general framework for informing and consulting employees in the European Community. In the United Kingdom the acronym relating to this is NICER – National Information and Consultation of Employees Regulations. The EWC regulations are referred to as TICER –

Transnational Information and Consultation of Employees Regulations. In the first instance NICER applied to businesses with 150 or more employees – to be extended by April 2008 to those employing more than 50. It has been estimated that once fully implemented 3 per cent of businesses and 75 per cent of employees in the United Kingdom will be covered.

There are various mechanisms which are available to establish an agreement covering information provision and consultation arrangements. These do not need to be discussed here in any detail. The net effect is that employees may themselves trigger such agreements, trade unions are more likely to do so, and may dominate representation, and employees may, with the required support challenge such arrangements. Once established there will need to be agreement on consultation methods and the nature of the information to be provided. There are recommended methods of consultation and types of information. Two employers' organisations – one in the print industry and one in the paper industry – have recently negotiated partnership agreements at national level which contain model agreements for member businesses.

There are many large businesses operating at national level. For such businesses the consultation forum will need to operate at national level – examples would be Ford UK, Tesco, Virgin Rail, British Airways and so on. These will need to link such forums to the national one, developing local constituencies. In the public sector there are complications. Each NHS Trust, each school, each fire authority appears to qualify as a separate undertaking. How these will be treated remains to be seen.

All the points made above relating to worker consultation – trade union ambivalence, employer resentment, what does it all really mean – apply to the discussion of works councils in this respect. At the time of writing there was no sign of great activity. However this is likely to change over time. Business problems, trade union rivalries, and company-sponsored schemes are likely to generate reactions.

International Labour Relations

Capital has always organised itself on both a national and international basis. World production is dominated by multinational corporations. These factors have generated responses from both labour and national governments, and these responses are reflected in international trading arrangements and institutions. At the levels of both the United Nations and the European Union, for example, there has been concern with, and attempts to control, the influence of multinational corporations across national frontiers. Corporations with plants situated in a number of countries may use their internal markets to affect profit levels and taxation, depending upon tax levels or even trade union militancy.

For example, a plant in Germany supplying parts to a plant in the United Kingdom has to decide upon the price to be charged – a process known as transfer pricing. The price charged could affect the relative profits declared at each of the two plants. Tax levels might influence such decisions, and governments and trade unions will be interested in this. Different labour laws and practices might affect overall costs and thus attract investment from other countries if these work to lower costs. Fewer restrictions on hours of work, employing children, lax health and safety laws and such measures are now often referred to as 'social dumping'. Naturally, governments will try to unite to establish common practices – the European Union talks about creating a level playing field on which competition can take place. International trade union organisations develop codes of practice in such areas and negotiate with governments.

The International Labour Organisation (ILO)

The ILO was founded in 1919 as part of the First World War settlement. Originally part of the League of Nations, it continued after the Second World War as part of the United Nations. The Annual International Labour Conference consists of four delegates from each member state, made up of two government representatives, an employer representative and a worker representative. At the conference, conventions and recommendations are adopted with regard to labour and employment matters and submitted to member states. A governing body is elected by the ILO's electoral college, and places on it are allocated in proportion to the distribution of delegates outlined above.

The governing body supervises the work of the International Labour Office, which is based in Geneva. The ILO is responsible for conducting research, carrying out investigations and developing technical cooperation, and has a publications division. It also fosters training of workers, and their representatives, particularly in developing countries. Currently the ILO is a major provider of data on international and comparative labour relations. Conventions and recommendations from the ILO are a major source of labour law.

Member states are not bound to accept the conventions and recommendations of the ILO. These are expected to have some moral force, although key ones are often surrounded by possible qualifications to them in national laws. For example, the obligation to encourage collective bargaining is qualified by the expressions 'only where necessary' and 'by measures appropriate to national conditions'. This is inevitable given the nature of the United Nations and its coverage.

In 1989 the Committee of Experts of the ILO criticised UK labour law on several grounds, including the following:

1. the ban on trade union membership at GCHQ (since lifted);
2. the prevention of trade unions from disciplining members in breach of decisions on industrial action;
3. preventing unions from indemnifying officials against fines arising from industrial action;
4. restrictions on industrial action were seen to be too great;
5. the right of an employer to dismiss solely on the grounds of taking part in industrial action;
6. the removal of negotiating rights from teachers at national level.

In December 2006 the influence of the ILO was reflected in a statement from the President of the World Bank when he announced that the Bank had taken the decision that all infrastructure projects funded by it would be required to fully respect all core labour standards laid down by the ILO.

Employers' Organisations

Given the multinational nature of capital, formal organisations of employers are less necessary than those for labour. Nevertheless, they do exist. The International Organisation of Employers (IOE), founded in 1920, operates on a global level. Its objectives include the promotion of private enterprise along with the more specific interests of employers. It gives advice to members and provides internationally based research. At the United Nations and ILO it acts as a pressure group pursuing member interests.

Traditionally, it opposed membership of employers from the so-called communist states, but, given the collapse of the traditional regimes in these states, its membership now includes most of these. In 2006, it claimed to represent 143 national employers' organisations in 138 countries. The IOE has traditionally advocated market-based solutions to economic problems in these countries, but did manage a joint declaration with the ICFTU (see below) on a social action programme which included the need for free and independent trade unions. In 2006, in a speech in Moscow, its President outlined its approach to nation states' economic problems – 'stabilisation, liberalisation and privatisation.'

Trade Union Organisations

International links between trade unions are difficult to establish in ways which allow them to seriously confront the power and mobility of multinational capital. Apart from different structures and degrees of organisation of unions within individual countries, unions, unlike employers, have a history of substantial ideological differences. These are often reflected in the fact that many countries have more than one trade union centre or TUC equivalent, often based on political and religious differences. This led to competing confederations at all levels.

There is a long history of cooperation at an international level between unions on a craft or trade basis – secretariats for some emerged in the late 19th century. However, at the level of the world confederation of trade union centres, the history is more recent. Until recently there were three such main bodies – the ICFTU, the World Federation of Trade Unions (WFTU) and the World Confederation of Labour (WCL). Figure 12.1 illustrates something of the history of these organisations, the Red Trade Union International (RTUI) representing a division on political grounds which occurred in the 1920s. British communists tried to persuade the Russians not to establish a new confederation, but failed. Between 1945 and 1949 there was a brief period of unity but eventually the cold war divided the unions again. Some communist unions, especially in France and Spain, joined the WFTU, but it was mainly based on communist-bloc state-run unions from Eastern Europe, plus similarly run unions from countries such as Cuba, Vietnam and Iraq.

Perhaps the major rivalry between the ICFTU and the WFTU manifested itself in the less economically developed parts of the world such as the African and Asian continents and Latin American and Caribbean countries. Both to a large extent were reinforcing the imperialist objectives of the blocs they represented. The WFTU survived the changes of 1989, but lost some of its affiliates to the ICFTU, including union centres from Poland, Bulgaria, Romania, Czechoslovakia and the German Democratic Republic (GDR). Its largest affiliate, the Russian-based All-Union Central Council of Trade Unions (AUCCTU), reformed itself and became the General Confederation of Trade Unions (GCTU) in 1992. In 2006, it claimed to represent 75 million members through the affiliation of national trade union centres from the Commonwealth of Independent States. The GCTU is now seen as a regional centre; it is not affiliated to an international body, and has its headquarters in Moscow. The membership of the WFTU has continued to decline at a considerable rate – a fact acknowledged at its fifteenth, four-yearly, World Congress held in Havana in 2005. It does not provide data on the scale of its membership or decline. It describes itself as 'Class Oriented – Uniting – Democratic – Modern – Independent'.

FIGURE 12.1 *History of the international trade union movement*

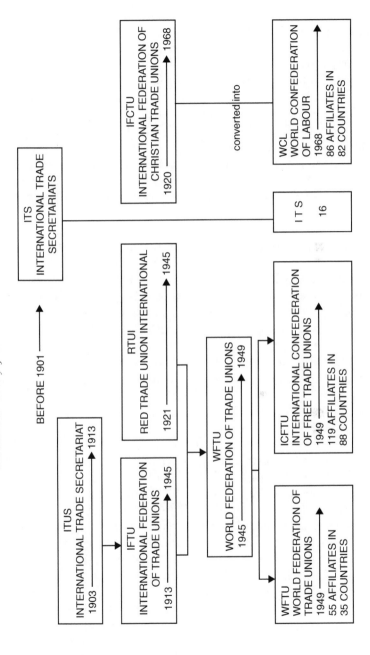

The ICFTU provided information and research, workers' education and so on. It, with the support of the WFTU and WCL, reached agreement on pressing for the social clause to be included in the General Agreement on Tariffs and Trade (GATT; see above). Figure 12.2 illustrates something of the ICFTU structure. Its European regional organisation was replaced by the ETUC. Many of the International Trade Secretariats (ITS) affiliated to the ICFTU predated it and acted autonomously. These grew out of trade and industry organisations, and included such bodies as the International Metalworkers' Federation (IMF), the International Chemical Workers' Federation (ICF) and similar bodies representing textile workers, printworkers, mineworkers, food and media workers. Occasionally they have provided a platform for dealing with internationally based disputes but are mainly forums for research, the exchange of information and the identification of problems.

In October 2006, the ICFTU and the WCL were dissolved and joined together to become the International Trade Union Confederation (ITUC). It represents 166 million trade unionists in 156 countries and territories. Within this, it has 42 national trade union centres affiliated from 27 countries in Central and Eastern Europe and the Commonwealth of Independent States. In 2006, it declared its priorities to be the improvement of international labour standards; tackling the multinationals; developing trade union rights; tackling equality, women, race and migrant issues; improving trade union organisation and recruitment.

Also, at the end of 2006, the International Trade Secretariats re-named themselves as 'global unions, and formed a council of global unions'.

Europe

The international organisation described above is very much replicated at the European level. The ETUC represented, in 2006, 60 million workers from 36 countries, through 81 member organisations. It had 12 European industry federations. Traditionally WFTU unions were prohibited membership, whilst WCL unions were accepted. Since 1990, communist-led unions, such as the Italian-based Confederazione Italiana Sindacati Lavoratori (CISL), have been admitted, and the French Conféderation Générale du Travail (CGT) is on the verge of entry at the time of writing. National centres from countries such as Malta, Cyprus and Turkey are affiliated. In 1990, the ETUC established the European Trade Union Forum (ETUF) as a basis for the assimilation of former communist bloc unions. This also broadened its focus beyond acting almost exclusively as an EU pressure group.

In spite of the growth potential emerging from the influx of new unions, the ETUC has been weakened by the decline in power of its

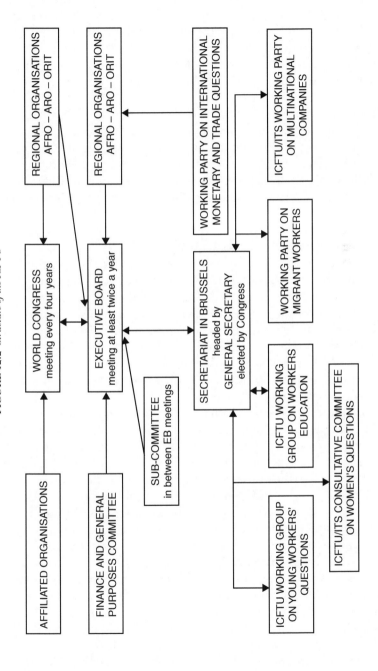

FIGURE 12.2 *Structure of the ICFTU*

established membership throughout its traditional bases. As a pressure group it has been outweighed by the efforts of Union des Confédérations de l'Industrie et des Employeurs d'Europe (UNICE), the organisation of European employers, which was formed specifically to deal with the European Union. In 2006, UNICE had 39 members from 33 countries including Central and Eastern Europe. There is also an organisation of European public-sector employers, the European Centre of Public Enterprises (CEEP).

EU institutions had provided through the European Union's Economic and Social Committee (ECOSOC) a forum for the meeting of capital and labour, diluted by other groups such as those representative of consumers and environmentalists. To some extent it provided a platform for the launch of Social Europe in the late 1980s but did not survive in influence the decline of social partnerships in member states. The Committee of Regions, established under Maastricht, and designed to bypass member states by dealing directly with regions, is now the emerging forum for the social partners.

The ETUC has industry-based committees such as the European Metalworkers' Federation (EMF), and other parallels to the ITS referred to above. To some extent these have been seen as the basis for establishing European-wide collective bargaining. This has been reflected in the establishment of internationally based workers' councils related to single multinational companies. These include Thompson Grand Public, Airbus Industrie, Bull and latterly Volkswagen. No doubt these developments will be fostered by the statutory requirements for EWCs referred to above.

In spite of international alliances of labour, the history is one of competition rather than collaboration. EWCs can as easily create strains between national unions as they can create understanding, particularly when they are asked to offer views on company strategies which might involve closures in some countries and not in others. Competition for jobs creates divisions within and between unions, and this process is reflected internationally. Employers in multinational companies can use their united control of plants across countries to foster this competition – they have in the past, and no doubt will continue to do so in the future.

Capital is already using its mobility to take advantage of the recently released supply of labour in Eastern Europe – now intensified by the increased accession to EU membership. For the foreseeable future, labour is facing a labour market which will weaken its capacity to organise. The major limiting factor could be the potential social, and consequent political, problems arising from the frustration of the expectations of labour in the western European countries, and the United States. As suggested earlier in the text, varying interest rates is no substitute for

detailed economic policy, which includes taxation, government spending, and the identification and rectification of obvious defects in the
working of the market.

From a unitarist point of view, what we have seen in recent years is a
move to the compelling logic of the free-market competitive system on
a world-wide basis. Pluralists see the former communist bloc societies as
now recognising the existence of divergent interests and accepting the
need to accommodate these through political opposition parties and
the emergence of free trade unions. A conflict perspective may see what
is happening as the extension of the power and influence of capitalism,
having been well served by so-called 'communism,' to provoke and
accommodate restructuring to embrace emerging consumerism in
these areas, and to create a reserve of labour.

Each perspective can be said to explain everything, and therefore
nothing. This is not the view of the author of this book. The perspectives model has been brought to bear to suggest that our organisation
and understanding of facts will be influenced by the political views
(perspectives) we bring to bear on them, as much as, if not more than,
we will be influenced by the limited theoretical propositions derived
from the inadequate techniques of social scientists.

13

The Old and the New

Reference has been made earlier in the text to continuity and change. The field of industrial relations is equally characterised by continuity and change. For example, there are strong pockets of traditional collective bargaining relationships in both the public sector and the private sector. These pockets are characterised by high union density and some prevalence of the issues that characterised earlier periods of industrial relations. Policy makers, unions and employers have to take account of this area of industrial relations and the problems which exist there. How problems and issues manifest themselves often relates to economic context. For example, in the public sector, we have experienced massive growth in the NHS which has a very high union density with the membership located in a multiplicity of unions. This has led to attempts at forms of productivity bargaining which have resulted in very high pay increases without the required productivity and produced considerable deficits in Hospital Trust finances. In the private sector the National Union of Rail, Maritime and Transport Workers (RMT), which organises rail workers, is the fastest growing union in the country and maintains a high union density. Recently privatised in conditions which led to cost reductions seriously affecting the safety of staff and passengers and the pay and terms and conditions of its employees, the industry is expanding at a rate which has allowed the union to claw back a lot of the concessions it made during the privatisation process. The RMT has secured considerable improvements in pay funded by relatively easily secured pay increases, using traditional industrial action and threats of such action.

It could be argued that the fire dispute of 2002–3 was perhaps something of a throwback to the period of the 1960s–70s, although the position of the FBU was perhaps more precarious than that of its counterparts in health and rail. There was no measurable growth in the demand for the service and no clear labour shortages. The same could be said of the position of workers at British Airways who in 2005 became involved in the dispute at Gate Gourmet, who acted as caterers to British Airways and which led to secondary industrial action costing British Airways large sums of money. At the time, British Airways was a comparatively successful airline but unlike the UK Fire and Rescue Service it was facing considerable competition from other airlines and challenges to its advantageous position at Heathrow. At the time of writing, a ballot of British Airways cabin staff was taking place to validate an agreement following industrial action in early 2007.

In the UK manufacturing and processing sector there are still highly unionised but threatened areas of activity – threatened by competition from China and Eastern Europe.

Each of the above scenarios requires different techniques of management that need to be linked to traditional industrial relations skills – often in short supply. The NHS is probably the best example of an organisation suffering from a failure to understand traditional industrial relations. Strong trade unions have managed to secure large pay increases on the back of what would have been described as, in the 1960s and 1970s, 'phoney productivity deals'. A lack of skill was demonstrated at both national and local level. Easily achieved targets which could be readily detached from any meaningful concept of productivity were negotiated at national level and then predictably detached at local level. Whilst these negotiations were taking place, leadership programmes organised by the NHS taught nothing about trade unions, negotiating theory and techniques, pay determination and pay structures. There was, of course, a notion of partnership with the trade unions which would lead to mutually beneficial progress. However, this was essentially a 'soft partnership' concept based on expressions and aspirations of goodwill by employers and unions, cosily translated into notions of 'win-win', which are rendered meaningless by the politics of implementation. There is often the view that pay determination relates to securing a technical solution, when in fact pay determination is an intensely political process in which the parties focus their use of power to secure an outcome to suit themselves.

Routes to Partnership

Partnership is a concept that neatly bridges the old and the new. It could be compared with the growth of productivity bargaining in the earlier period. It could be linked to notions of modernisation. It is a term that is now widely used. It can be given a long history and varying degrees of complexity both inside and outside the employment relationship. Here the focus is on the employment relationship and it is linked to Walton and McKersie's concept of the integrative bargaining subprocess based on attempts at joint problem solving. At one extreme of the literature, what partnership denotes is unitarism, collaboration by, and manipulation of, the workers to their detriment. At the other extreme it denotes a transformation of the employment relationship into shared decision making with empowerment and commitment of the workforce and new and successful ways of working together. At a more mundane level it typifies the kind of compromise reached by employers and trade unions faced with strong competitive pressures. The UK debate in the labour relations literature mainly revolves around these alternative perspectives and is often ideological in content rather than empirical and generally neglects the process.

The American literature is more focused on context, process and content. What are the circumstances leading the parties to move in the direction of partnership? What do they actually do when they attempt to move in this direction? What tends to emerge from the process? Both here and in the United States, there have been longer-term changes in the economic context that have weakened the power of trade unions. The decline in trade union membership began earlier in the United States and has progressed further. In both cases, the economics of recession and globalised competition were key factors and in both cases were reinforced by political and legislative forces. This is the longer-term context for trade unions, and for many the present situation is precarious. However, the United States still has pockets of strong trade unionism in important sectors of the economy.

Ironically, partnership development requires the presence of a trade union with some strength. A typical scenario is that the employer or employers face a crisis, the union understands the consequences of sheer adversarialism and the parties agree to look jointly and openly at all the options. There could, of course, be other scenarios – opening a new factory, privatisation or even so-called modernisation programmes. The idea is that the parties work together to try to secure a better future for the enterprise with working practices becoming more flexible and workers benefiting from greater job security and a share of any gains. This fits very closely the concept of productivity bargaining as put forward in the 1960s and 1970s – although the threats to trade union survival in that environment were probably underestimated by trade unions. However, the language is different, with an emphasis on partnership rather than bargaining. Essentially in the Walton and McKersie literature partnership is cooperation at enterprise level with commitment at the place of work.

The process will be very much affected by the perceptions brought to the situation which gives rise to some discussion of partnership. A union might disbelieve management's version of events and the state of the enterprise. Management might believe that the requirement for change is so great it cannot really waste time engaging the union. In the process, management might underestimate the union's capacity to resist change. In analysing change, Walton *et al.* (2000) suggest that change should be seen through a negotiating lens. They recognise that other perspectives are important in the management of change but believe that the negotiating perspective provides important and salutary insights.

In their text they identify three strategic change options linked to negotiating tactics – forcing, fostering and escape. Forcing change would mean attempting to overcome opposition by simply insisting on change and being willing to resist opposition to the proposed changes. This approach brings into alignment, according to the authors, three tactical processes:

1. distributive bargaining;
2. the heightening of intergroup tension, either intentionally or unintentionally;
3. the promotion of solidarity in one's own organization and divisions in the other organization.

Walton et al. (2000)

This process obviously involves risks that the authors describe as following from 'acts of commission'. Conflict could escalate out of control in a forcing process. Failure or defeat could also follow with disunity arising in one's own organisation, leaving behind a possible legacy of continued distrust. In the UK fire dispute of 2002–3, it could be argued that the FBU initiated the forcing process. This followed an inquiry in 2000 which had been used to prevent the escalation of a dispute over modernisation – in fact an employer's attempt to force change that could have resulted in all out strike action to coincide with the millennium. However, once the union decided to break the formula method of determining pay by asking for a 40 per cent pay increase and responding to the employers' rejection of this by setting strike dates, it was inevitable that there would be counter-forcing and escalation. It was also inevitable that 'modernisation' of the fire service was firmly on the agenda. Ultimately the perception of failure by the FBU membership led to a change in their leadership.

Fostering, according to the authors, also requires the alignment of three tactical processes:

1. integrative bargaining;
2. the enhancement of intergroup trust;
3. the promotion of internal consensus in both parties.

Walton et al. (2000)

Inevitably there are risks associated with this strategy and these are described as being the consequence of 'errors of omission'. These include such things as insufficient work on relationships, inadequate understanding of, or work on, the substantive issues and failure to generate sufficient internal consensus. The approach of the NHS Plan emphasised partnership as a necessary approach to the implementation of a modernisation programme. It was also backed up by massive expenditure increases, increases in job numbers and job improvement programmes. The outcome has been referred to above. Increased expenditures did not generate productivity increases and a great deal of the money went into pay. Partnership became a way of delaying agreement on pay and change.

At the time of writing the Royal Colleges of Nursing and Midwifery are threatening industrial action, along with UNISON and Amicus, whilst the medical profession is expressing discontent and withdrawing cooperation. The above model helps to explain this. The partnership relationship with the unions was a 'soft' one – and there was clearly a misalignment of the unions' approaches to collective bargaining and that of the Department of Health. The Department had not done the substantive work required to properly understand the nature of productivity bargaining and had failed to take account of the context within which such bargaining was taking place. Trusts were set short deadlines within which to bring all consultants on to their new contracts and to implement Agenda for Change for other staff, meaning that at the places of work there was no real time to work on either substantive or relational issues. Having run up deficits, there has been a cutting back of the workforce to levels which still far exceed those which existed at the start of the process – turning a fostering process combined with expansion into a situation where there is widespread employee discontent.

The way in which the above is expressed suggests that fostering and forcing initiatives may come from both the unions and the employers. In fact, in the literature on trade union membership recruitment a distinction is made between union organising campaigns forcing recognition and securing new members and using partnership agreements for the same purpose. Which of these is most effective is unlikely to be a matter of free choice – context is important. Williams and Adam-Smith (2006) tell us 'Kelly (2004) observes that union organizing campaigns resulting in new recognition agreements have been more effective than partnership in extending unionization.' It may of course be that partnership is simply a method of preserving unionisation where the alternative is being forced into derecognition. For the union there may be little choice in a globally competitive environment. The focus here, as suggested at the beginning, is on those areas where there is still relatively strong trade unionism able to prevent change by imposing substantial costs on the employer whilst recognising that change is inevitable and possibly necessary. Unions in the UK Print and Paper industries recognised the dangers of increased competition from Eastern Europe and China and took the initiative in securing partnership agreements – uniquely on an industry-wide basis – with the industry Employers' Associations. These initiatives were provided with supporting funding from the Department of Trade and Industry.

The third strategic option – escape – from an employer's point of view could simply mean escape from the union. This would include such things as removing jobs of union members by subcontracting work out, closing down and moving to greenfield sites, replacing union with non-union labour, derecognition and so on. There is also the possibility of transferring work abroad to lower paid non-unionised locations. All of these options have been widely used in recent decades. In the public sector this could, of course, involve the use of private sector provision. If consultants will not use scanners outside of working hours, make private sector equipment available. Private Finance Initiative (PFI) funded hospitals may have a fully privately funded and managed hospital built on site which would provide a readily available alternative for providing services where internal staff were perhaps demanding higher pay for additional work. The escape option is not one that trade unions can easily secure. Interestingly, the Government likes to refer to PFIs as Public Private Partnerships (PPP). They certainly do not work like that. They are often used to introduce a competitive threat in situations where they can take up easy options in the market leaving the public provider to do the more costly elements of the provision.

In relation to the above strategic options the Walton *et al.* model concludes by identifying seven of what they call realities:

1. *'Change management is a negotiated process and not a directed one.'* This conceptualisation is an important antidote to the notion that change can be driven through by the 'right' style of leadership adhering to a clearly identified and structured plan. There will be opposition which can create resistance and which therefore may force adjustment to the process and its objectives. This 'reality' is supplemented by the second one.

2. *'Change agent influence is an essential, yet highly contingent resource.'* This suggests that leadership is important but how it manifests itself in terms of quality of influence depends very much on how the process unfolds and upon the influence of events.

3. *'Change efforts are shaped as much by considerations of feasibility as by considerations of desirability.'* The strategy chosen by management will

depend very much on their perceptions of the distribution of power. In effect, nobody really wishes to negotiate – they simply wish to get their way. If forcing is seen to be straightforward feasible, then it has attractions. Fostering is the alternative where forcing is seen to have unacceptable risks and potentially unsustainable costs.

4. *'Outcomes are often unanticipated and unwelcome, not merely disappointing.'* Many strategies assume that there might be a shortfall in terms of achievement. The assumption that they might produce an outcome worse than the situation they start from is rarely considered. On the other hand it is possible that an outcome emerges which is far superior to the one originally planned. The American Health Company, Kaiser Permanente, began by attempting a downsizing programme using a forcing strategy. The unions resisted so effectively that negotiations took place leading to a strategy based on fostering and partnership resulting in considerable productivity gains and expansion.

5. *'Contexts are dynamic, not a set of "givens".'* This has certainly proved to be the case with the NHS. There is now a clear strategy from the Department of Health of trying to claw back concessions made during the expansion period. Public sector expenditure is now coming under pressure as a result of the Treasury inflation targets being exceeded.

6. *'Resistance to change is often active and rational, not merely passive and emotional.'* This is basically saying that resistance to change often has a logic which needs to be identified and may well require an employer to accommodate some of a union's concerns.

7. *'Change scenarios are marked by pivotal events and other dynamics that render plans obsolete.'* This is a clear statement of what constitutes the difference between a negotiating approach to change and notions that there is some way of developing a clear plan that can be sequentially implemented. The reactions of those affected are not easily predicted. Similarly, changes in context can have an impact. For example, 9/11 had a considerable effect, worldwide, on the airline industry.

In practice, both unions and employers use a combination of forcing and fostering, although one or the other approach will predominate. Fostering could be used for divide-and-rule purposes during the forcing process. The model above distinguishes between top down fostering – via the union leaders – and bottom up fostering via the union members. Top down could create suspicions amongst union members – perhaps the members viewing the union as collaborating at their expense. Union leaders could see bottom up as a manipulation of their members, undermining the union leadership role. Williams and Adam-Smith (2006: 194) quote Wills in respect of a partnership agreement with Barclays:

> According to one union member: How it seems to be working is that the union hierarchy go and have their meeting and discussions with the bank, negotiate whatever and they come back to me as a union member and say 'this is what's been offered to you, this is the option, how do you feel about it?' I don't think we're actually consulted when it comes down to making any sort of hard-and-fast decisions as to what our contracts are going to look like.

The research seems to indicate that partnership agreement is more likely to be achieved by a sequence of forcing followed by fostering.

Basically in this model what are referred to as partnership agreements by the parties to them can be characterised as having evolved within some sort of fostering or forcing relationship or both. Whether the outcome is beneficial in any absolute way, it is not possible to determine. It might be possible to judge them in terms of whether or not there is expansion in output and profitability or in terms of job security, but even these are difficult criteria to measure and demonstrate to be outcomes actually determined by the process. What the above model does is give examples of behaviours in the partnership arena – the parties characterising the arena as a partnership one. The authors do express their personal beliefs, and perhaps this is the only way that judgements can be made. 'We believe that a change in the social contract is required... We also believe that society will be healthier if labor and management move toward commitment and cooperation while preserving the integrity and strength of their respective institutions.'

Partnership Principles

The TUC Partnership Institute has laid down what it considers to be the principles of partnership. These are

1. a shared commitment to the success of the enterprise;
2. recognition of legitimate interests;
3. commitment to employment security – making employees employable;
4. focus on the quality of working life;
5. transparency;
6. added value/win-win.

The unions committed believe that such an approach will reinforce collective bargaining and will give the unions a strategic influence in the company.

Partnership requires strong independent trade unions. They also believe that such an approach meets the aspirations of members. It also reflects the view that adversarialism will not deliver. They also believe that partnership agreements benefit employers because they help to meet competitive pressures by motivating the workforce, improving industrial relations and generating a more flexible workforce.

The partnership agreements reached in the Printing Industry and the Paper Industry could be described as partnership agreements between the unions and the employers at national level. Both employers' associations contain member companies and plants where there is no trade union recognition. Many plants where they have recognition have unions and management that rely on traditional adversarialism. For those parts of the union and industry the national agreement can only be seen as an educational device designed to initiate and rationalise a new approach. Reaching such an agreement at national level was seen by the parties to be a major achievement. However, its success will only be measured on the ground – at plant level.

The change at national level represented a major rebalancing of the relationships between the employers and unions. Cutcher-Gershenfeld's (2003) characterisation of traditional bargaining behaviours matched the historical relationship between the parties:

> Develop target and resistance positions in advance.
> Overstate opening positions.
> Commit to these positions early and publicly.
> Channel communications through a spokesperson.
> Give as little as possible for what you get.
> Always keep the other side off balance.
> Mobilize support from constituents.
> Divide and conquer the other side.
> An agreement reluctantly accepted is a sign of success.

In the negotiating theory literature, this traditional approach is predominantly characterised by 'position based bargaining'.

Cutcher-Gershenfeld distinguishes the above from interest-based bargaining (IBB) behaviours. These comprise:

> Assess all stakeholders' interests in advance.
> Convert positional demands from constituents into interests.
> Use subcommittees and task forces for joint data collection and analysis.
> Frame issues based on interests – avoid positional statements.
> Encourage open exchange of information and joint problem solving.
> Generate as many options as possible on each issue.
> Take on the constraints of your counterparts.
> Ensure constituents are educated and knowledgeable on the issues.
> Anticipate contract administration – troubleshoot agreements.
> An agreement enthusiastically ratified by all parties is a sign of success.

IBB is really about identifying clearly what the issue is that a position is being taken on. In the fire service negotiations reference was often made to the firefighters' unwillingness to work overtime. This was defended by the union on the basis that they thought overtime was family unfriendly. Everybody knew that firefighters often had additional jobs – driving taxis, cleaning windows, decorating and so on. At the same time, their pay was determined annually on the basis of an external pay relationship. Each year their *earnings* were brought into line with the upper quartile of skilled manual workers earnings. Overtime increased the earnings of firefighters and therefore reduced the value of their annual increase. The real interest was that overtime was worth nothing or could only increase some firefighters earnings at the expense of other firefighters. The debate should have centred on the value of the formula.

An obvious difficulty here could be linked to intra-organisational bargaining – how do you shift from position to interest without being accused of 'selling colleagues down the river'? In other words, any suggestion by a colleague on the union side that examining overtime as an issue in itself and then examining the formula could be seen as suggesting a concession to the management position.

In terms of process, the Print Industry negotiations, through which the first of the two agreements was negotiated, were interesting. The parties decided to appoint an independent Chair to the negotiations. His role was to chair the meetings of a steering committee, the union side led by its General Secretary, the employers' side led by its Chief Executive Officer, with a dozen or so members to each side. At the first meeting, joint working parties were established to deal with a selection of issues – for example learning and skills, health and safety, dignity and diversity at work and so on. ACAS set up a series of meetings of employees and union representatives in various regions of the country to produce research on their attitudes to current industrial relations in the industry on a focus group basis. The Chair was not given a role beyond moving through agenda items and ensuring the smooth progress of negotiations.

Determining the agenda for the second meeting was not difficult – reports from the working parties and progress on the ACAS research were obvious items. It was suggested that the director of the TUC Partnership Institute could give a talk. The following meeting was presented with a talk outlining the TUC principles of partnership, as listed above. At national level, the unions and employers already had working groups on the various issues to be dealt with by the negotiations and they simply took over the places on the working parties. Inevitably they were simply reporting back on entrenched positions.

Similarly, the ACAS findings reflected traditional adversarial attitudes. The agenda for the next meeting was a replica of the previous meeting's agenda.

Eventually the General Secretary of the union raised the issue of lack of progress with the Chair. This gave the Chair the opportunity to influence the process. Two teams of four people, one from each side, took over from the steering committee, with an agreement to report back to the steering committee. There was sufficient trust between the two sides to open up the negotiations to an interest-based approach and they had the strength to report back on progress to their principles securing support as they did so. The Independent Chair was able to play a more involved role by opening up positional exchanges to statements of interest.

The agreement reached was significantly different from the national agreement that it replaced. There were substantive changes made in sick pay schemes – employers were prepared to recommend an increase in exchange for systematic absence control using the Bradford Points System, which allows for a review of benefits when absenteeism takes on a high points profile. Similar deals were done on other issues. In other words, union cooperation would be provided in specific ways in exchange for improved benefits to allow the deal to be sold to employers at local level. Monitoring of all aspects of the agreement has been built into its various provisions and this should help in the future to judge the extent to which the parties value the various outcomes.

An objective of the parties was to modernise the agreement and give it a more attractive format. This involved moving to a more modern use of language, reflecting the changed structure of the industry and using more neutral language. It also meant digitalising it and introducing a Code of Practice with sections matching those of the agreement. What became very clear was the extensive range of modern employment law, affecting virtually every aspect of the agreement. The language was also changed to reflect this and the Code of Practice has electronic addresses which direct the reader to legislation, commentaries on the legislation, codes of practice, ACAS guidance, the Information Commissioner where there are codes of practice covering a whole range of privacy issues, including video surveillance, covert monitoring and so on. Privacy considerations are all dealt with by the Information Commission Codes and this removed the need to do other than simply refer to the Codes. An advantage of all of this is that small firms are able to see that requirements on their behaviour are not simply reflecting the idiosyncrasies of the employers' organisation.

The Code of Practice also gives advice on the implementation of the agreement, explaining the options available. There are also case studies showing achievements in such things as absence control and its beneficial effects and providing the opportunity of demonstrating the use of the Bradford Points System in practice. There is also a case study on the benefits of a company's continued commitment to training and development across all its operations.

The agreement contains its own definition of partnership. It first of all consists of an understanding by both employers and employees that they have common interests and that they need to work together to understand these. It also acknowledges that each of the parties has legitimate separate interests that each party seeks to persuade the other to satisfy so far as they are able to do so. What it does say is that the parties agree that in pursuit of their common and separate interests, the respective parties should maintain the highest professional standards, and the highest levels of trust and respect, in their relationships with each other.

Earlier in this chapter reference was made to a 'soft' partnership relationship. This refers to the kind of situation in which the relationship is established on a sort of 'sweetness and light' basis. Partnership is clearly better than mutually destructive adversarialism and therefore this is obviously the approach to adopt. Everything is translated into possible win–win outcomes and the way forward is simple. It was notable that in the Print Industry negotiations where there was failure to agree the parties tended to accuse each other of not really being committed to partnership. In such circumstances, and there is evidence of this in the NHS, a situation can emerge where disagreement produces inertia. The parties take up the position that no progress can be achieved until agreement on the issue is reached. In practice, this becomes a device where one or other of the parties actually uses the relationship to hold up change or to avoid a particular tactical or strategic development.

IBB is not a substitute for adversarialism. It is about making sure that the issues are clearly on the table and that their substance is discussed openly without being obscured by historical positions or euphemisms and with the objective of trying to identify mutually beneficial outcomes. Where this is not possible then it may be necessary to make a decision to fail to agree and move on – to recognise and respect separate interests and to respond professionally. Partnership is not about being nice to each other – it is a business-oriented activity. It is possible to think in terms of an 'adversarial partnership'.

The agreement identified what the parties deemed to be common interests. These included achieving significant improvements in company profitability; providing companies with the flexibility they need to respond to fluctuations in customer demand; providing employees with a safe, secure and satisfying working environment; ensuring that employees' contributions to the company are properly recognised; providing employees with information and consulting them about decisions that impact upon them; providing employees with the training and retraining necessary for them to perform their jobs efficiently and safely and to cope with changes to their duties and responsibilities; and ensuring that managers and employees adopt a culture of joint responsibility.

The agreement is designed to influence what happens in member companies. Case studies were referred to above as having been included to demonstrate what might be considered to be best practice. The agreement also contains model agreements for the use of temporary labour, dignity at work, information and consultation and so on. Both parties will ultimately judge the agreement in terms of the extent to which it helps them to retain members of their organisation. The logic is obvious – a more profitable industry will help both parties to do this. The purpose of the agreement is to try to make it more profitable in order to guarantee mutual survival and expansion. Of course it might not do this.

The literature on partnership provides us with a number of truisms. It requires a strong trade union – this does not affect the numerous workers who are not affected by trade unions. It is widely asserted that they do not improve job security and that they are often tied to a management agenda and are therefore often the result of a management initiative reflecting the general weakness of trade unions. All of this is true. Nevertheless, it is equally true that it is inevitable that trade unions might well perceive that through the process referred to above they might well help to buttress the company and therefore employment and hopefully membership. What was clear in the Print Industry process, and that in the Paper Industry, was that highly sophisticated trade unionists and employer representatives saw value in the process and, if nothing else, they had reviewed the relationship between them and learned to better understand that relationship whilst at the same time believing that they really had set in motion something worthwhile and mutually beneficial. Given that the fundamental relationship between the parties is unlikely to change significantly in the foreseeable future from one with conflictual elements demanding negotiation and compromise, it is not surprising that they will experiment with possible variants on the nature of that relationship.

In terms of possibilities and context, the NHS is probably currently ripe for establishing a partnership process. Both trade unions and employers have been disappointed by the outcomes of recent change management processes. The Government is also unhappy at its failure to secure the political capital they expected to emerge from the large investment in the health care system. A partnership approach may emerge after a period of forcing as employers try to claw back concessions, especially on pay. After a period of contraction and privatisation, the RMT are not likely to compromise their position whilst the industry is expanding. The leadership has been ideologically influenced by its recent history and would not be inclined towards the partnership route at this stage. An outcome of the fire dispute was the loss of the leadership election by the General Secretary, with the Assistant General Secretaryship being similarly replaced. Theoretically, a tendency towards partnership arrangements would be the employers' approach, but this is likely, in the short run, to be thwarted on ideological grounds at national level. However, the decentralisation of some key bargaining issues following the strike could produce local partnership developments.

Conclusion

HRM literature underplays the importance of organised labour, collective bargaining and all that goes with these – especially the need to deal with conflict. The neglect of these issues has had serious effects in the UK public sector. There will continue to be a need to understand the nature of these issues and the importance of context.

Bibliography

ACAS (1983) *Collective Bargaining in Britain: Its Extent and Level* (London: HMSO).

ACAS (1987) *Discipline at Work* (London: ACAS).

ACAS (1989) *The ACAS Role in Conciliation, Arbitration and Mediation* (London: ACAS).

ACAS (1990) *Job Evaluation: An Introduction* (London: ACAS).

ACAS (1996) *Annual Report* (London: ACAS).

ACAS (2004a) Code of Practice 1 *Disciplinary and Grievance Procedures* (London: ACAS).

ACAS (2004b) *Discipline and Grievances at Work Handbook* (London: ACAS).

ACAS Annual Report 2003–04 (2005) (London: The Stationery Office).

ACAS Annual Report 2005–06 (2007) (London: The Stationery Office).

Anderman, S.D. (1993) *Labour Law* (London: Butterworth).

Bain, G.S. and Elsheikh, F. (1976) *Union Growth and the Business Cycle* (Oxford: Blackwell).

Biskind, P. (2001) *Seeing is Beliving* (Bloomsbury).

Booth, A.L. (1995) *The Economics of the Trade Union* (Cambridge University Press).

Braverman, H. (1974) *Labor and Monopoly Capital* (New York: Monthly Review Press).

Brown, W. and Walsh, J. (1994) 'Managing Pay in Britain', in Sisson (1994).

Brown, W., Marginson, P. and Walsh, J. (1995) 'Management: Pay Determination and Collective bargaining' in Edwards (1995).

Burchill, F. (1995) 'Professional Unions in the National Health Service', *Review of Employment Topics*, Vol. 3, no. 1.

Burchill, F. (1999) 'Walton and McKersie: A behavioral theory of labor negotiations,' *Historical Studies in Industrial Relations*, Vol. 8, Autumn 1999, pp. 137–68.

Burchill, F. (2000a) 'The pay review body system: A comment and a consequence,' *Historical Studies in Industrial Relations*, Vol. 10, Autumn 2000, pp.141–57.

Burchill, F. (2000b) 'The road to partnership? Forcing change in the UK further education sector', *Employee Relations*, Vol. 23. no. 2, pp. 146–63.

Burchill, F. (2000c) *Inquiry into the Machinery for Determining Firefighters' Conditions of Service,* Cm 4699, (London: The Stationery Office). Burchill, F (2004) 'The UK fire service dispute 2002–2003', *Employee Relations*, Vol. 26, no. 4, pp. 404–21.

Burchill, F. and Casey, A. (1996) *Human Resource Management: The NHS – A Case Study* (London: Macmillan).

Caines, E. (1992) 'Stop Money with Menaces', *The Guardian*, 2 July 1993.

Cairnes, J.E. (1874) *Some Leading Principles of Political Economy Newly Explained* (New York: Harper).

Cutcher-Gershenfeld, J. (2003) 'How Process Matters: A Five-Phase Model for Examining Interest-Based Bargainining', in Kochan and Lipsky (2003).

Donovan, Lord (1968) 'Royal Commission on Trade Unions and Employers' Associations 1965–1968', *Report*, Cmnd. 3623 (London: HMSO).

Edwards, P. (ed.) (1995) *Industrial Relations: Theory and Practice in Britain* (Oxford: Blackwell).

Ferner, A. and Hyman, R. (1992) *Industrial Relations in the New Europe* (Oxford: Blackwell).

Ferner, A. and Hyman, R. (1994) *New Frontiers in European Industrial Relations* (Oxford: Blackwell).

Fredman, S. and Morris, G. (1989) 'The State as employer: Setting a new example', *Personnel Management*, August, pp. 25–29.

Galbraith, J.K. (1967) *The New Industrial State* (Harmondsworth: Penguin).

Geary, J.F. (1995) 'Work Practices: The Structure of Work', in Edwards (1995).

Heller, J. (1962) *Catch 22* (London: Jonathan Cape).

Hobsbawm, E. (1994) *The Age of Extremes* (London: Michael Joseph).

House of Commons (1993–4) Employment Committee. Third Report, *The Future of Trade Unions, Volume 1: Report and Proceedings of the Committee* (London: HMSO).

Hutton, W. (1995) *The State We're In* (London: Jonathan Cape).

Hyman, R. (1987) 'Strategy or structure: Capital, labour and control', *Work, Employment and Society*, Vol. 1, no. 1, pp. 25–55.

Hyman, R. (1989) *Strikes* (London: Fontana).

IRS Employment Review (1994) *Employers' Associations; Membership; Services; Activities*, no. 552, pp. 4–13.

IRS Employment Review (1995) *Discipline at Work – The Practice*, no. 591, pp. 4–11.

IRS Employment Review (1996) *Organisational Change in Bonas Machine Company*, no. 610, pp. 5–10.

Kelly, J. and Heery, E. (1994) *Working for the Union* (Cambridge: Cambridge University Press).

Kersley B., Alpin C., Forth J., Bryson A., Bewley H., Dix, G. and Oxenbridge, S. (2006) *Inside the Workplace: Findings from the 2004 Workplace Employment Relations Survey* (London: Routledge).

Kessler, I. (1994) 'Performance Pay', in Sisson (1994).

Kessler, S. and Bayliss, F. (1995) *Contemporary British Industrial Relations* (Basingstoke: Macmillan).

Knowles, K.G.J.C. (1952) *Strikes – A Study of Industrial Conflict* (Oxford: Blackwell).

Kochan, T.A. and Lipsky, D.B. (eds) (2003) *Negotiations and Change* (Ithaca, NY: Cornell University Press).

Kochan, T.A., Katz, H. and McKersie, R.B. (1986) *The Transformation of American Industrial Relations* (New York: Basic Books).

Lipsey, R.G. and Chrystal, A.C. (1995) *Positive Economics* (Oxford: Oxford University Press).

Lowry, P. (1990) *Employment Disputes and the Third Party* (Basingstoke: Macmillan).

Lyddon, D. (1996) 'The myth of mass production and the mass production of myth', *Historical Studies in Industrial Relations*, Vol. 1, no. 1, pp. 77–105.

McCarthy, W.E.J. (1976) *Making Whitley Work: A Review of the NHS Whitley Council System* (London: HMSO).

McIlroy, J. (1995) *Trade Unions in Britain Today* (Manchester: Manchester University Press).

Marchington, M., Wilkinson, M., Ackers, P. and Goodman, J. (1993) 'The influence of managerial relations on waves of employee involvement', *British Journal of Industrial Relations*, Vol. 31, no. 4, pp. 553–76.

Millward, N. (1994) *The New Industrial Relations* (London: Policy Studies Institute.

Millward, N., Stevens, M., Smart, D. and Hawes, W.R. (1992) *Workplace Industrial Relations in Transition* (Aldershot: Dartmouth).

Milner, S. (1995) 'The coverage of collective pay-setting institutions in Britain, 1895–1990', *British Journal of Industrial Relations*, Vol. 33, no. 1, pp. 69–92.

Oliver, N. and Wilkinson, B. (1992) *The Japanisation of British Industry: New Developments in the 1990s* (Oxford: Blackwell).

Organisation for Economic Co-operation and Development (OECD) (1993) *The Level and Coverage of Collective Bargaining: A Cross-national Study of Patterns and Trends* (OECD: Paris).

Ormerod, P. (1994) *The Death of Economics* (London: Faber).

Poole, M. (1986) *Industrial Relations: Origins and Patterns of National Diversity* (London: Routledge and Kegan Paul).

Price, L. and Price, R. (1994) 'Change and Continuity in the Status Divide', in Sisson (1994).

Purcell, J. and Ahlstrand, B. (1994) *Human Resource Management in the Multi-Divisional Company* (Oxford: Oxford University Press).

Reid, A.J. (2005) *United We Stand* (London: Penguin).

Salamon, M. (1992) *Industrial Relations* (Hemel Hempstead: Prentice-Hall).

Samuelson, P.A. (1958) *Economics* (New York: McGraw-Hill).

Seifert, R. and Sibley, T. (2005) *United They Stood* (London: Lawrence and Wishart).

Sisson, K. (ed.) (1994) *Personnel Management: A Comprehensive Guide to Theory and Practice in Great Britain* (Oxford: Blackwell).

Storey, J. (1992) *Developments in the Management of Human Resources* (Oxford: Blackwell).

Storey, J. and Sisson, K. (1993) *Managing Human Resources and Industrial Relations* (Buckingham: Open University Press).

Trades Union Congress (TUC) (1995) *Your Voice at Work: TUC Proposals for Rights to Representation at Work* (London: Trades Union Congress).

Treble, J.G. (1986) 'How new is final offer arbitration?', *Industrial Relations*, Vol. 25, no.1, pp. 92–4.

Turner, H.A. (1962) *Trade Union Growth, Structure and Policy: A Comparative Study of the Cotton Unions* (London: Allen & Unwin).

Undy, R., Ellis, V., McCarthy, W.E.J. and Halmos A.M. (1981) *Change in Trade Unions* (London: Hutchinson).

Waddington, J. and Whitston, C. (1995) 'Trade Unions: Growth, Structure and Policy', in Edwards (1995).

Walton, R.E. and McKersie, R.B. (1965) *A Behavioral Theory of Labor Negotiations* (New York: McGraw-Hill).

Walton, R.E., Cutcher-Gershenfeld, J., and McKersie, R.B., (2000) *Strategic Negotiations* (Ithaca, NY: Cornell University Press).

Webb, S. and Webb, B. (1902) *The History of Trade Unionism* (London: Webb and Webb; first published 1894).

Webb, S. and Webb, B. (1920) [1897] *Industrial Democracy* (London: Longmans Green).

Welch, Jack (2003) *Straight From the Gut* (London: Headline Book Publishing).

Williams, S. and Adam-Smith, D. (2006) *Contemporary Employment Relations: A Critical Introduction.* (Oxford: Oxford University Press).

Winchester, D. and Bach, S. (1995) 'The State: The Public Sector', in Edwards (1995).

Index

Introductory Note

References such as '178–9' indicate (not necessarily continuous) discussion of a topic across a range of pages, whilst '7t1.1' indicates a reference to Table 1.1 on page 7 and '134f10.1' a reference to Figure 10.1 on page 134. Wherever possible in the case of topics with many references, these have either been divided into sub-topics or the most significant discussions of the topic are indicated by page numbers in bold.